All Believers Are Brothers

All Believers
Are Brothers

———◆———

Written and Edited by
Roland Gammon

DOUBLEDAY & COMPANY, INC.
GARDEN CITY, NEW YORK
1969

Grateful thanks are extended to the following publishers for permission to use material from their books:

American Tract Society for material from "World Record Holder" by Kipchoge Keino.

John Day Company for material from *For Spacious Skies* by Pearl S. Buck, copyright 1966 by the Pearl S. Buck Foundation, Inc.

E. P. Dutton for the chapter on Mrs. Franklin D. Roosevelt from the book *Faith Is a Star*, written and edited by Roland Gammon. Copyright, ©, 1963 by Southern Baptist Convention Radio & Television Commission Co., Inc., and used by permission of E. P. Dutton & Co., Inc.; for material from the book *Conversations with Casals* by J. Ma. Corredor. Copyright, ©, 1956 by E. P. Dutton & Co., Inc. Dutton Paperback Edition. Reprinted by permission of the publishers.

Harper & Row, Publishers, Incorporated, for material from *Man in the Modern World* by Julian Huxley and from *Stride Toward Freedom* by Martin Luther King, Jr.

Holt, Rinehart and Winston, Inc., for material from *Out of My Life and Thought* by Albert Schweitzer. Translated by C. T. Campion. Copyright 1933, 1949, © 1961 by Holt, Rinehart and Winston, Inc. Reprinted by permission of Holt, Rinehart and Winston, Inc.

Alfred A. Knopf, Inc., for material from *Markings* by Dag Hammarskjold, copyright © 1964 by Alfred A. Knopf, Inc., and Faber and Faber, Ltd.

Little, Brown & Co., for material from *With Love* by Maurice Chevalier, as told to Eileen and Robert Mason Pollock.

The Viking Press, Inc., for material from *My Lord, What a Morning* by Marian Anderson.

To my dear Dad
CHARLES C. GAMMON
Dean of Maine Druggists
and
A gentleman who is great
because he is greatly good.

Contents

Introduction

In an age of unfaith and the antihero, there are few things more difficult than to become a hero. As American novelist Nathaniel Hawthorne observed, "A hero cannot be a hero unless in a heroic world." And yet nothing is more sorely sought by millions of all classes and creeds today than a heroism that can remake our unheroic world, that can match power with poetry and doubt with belief, that can infuse the temper of the times and the march of materialism with an idealism of spirit which alone provides purpose, vision and love. Because both individuals and nations need moral ideals fully as much as money, machines, and the awesome output of America's horn of plenty, all of us yearn for "those brave translunar things" which the first poets knew. Consciously or unconsciously, the majority of men must keep before them what William Butler Yeats called "images of magnificence," inspiring at once a larger-than-life greatness and opening again the universal gateways to faith, truth, and beauty.

That revival of heroic vision is the sole purpose of this book. When five years ago I completed a book on outstanding Americans and their religious beliefs, *Faith Is a Star,* I knew that a sequel on world leaders was inevitable; indeed, I began the research and reporting, travel and interviews preparatory to writing the sequel even before the American study was published. A title for this new volume, *All Believers Are Brothers,* I had long held in mind, taken as it is from the Holy Koran and implying as it does that exalted men and women everywhere meet in the common light of deeper religious truth. If to believe is to pray and to pray is to know, then I conclude that the devotees of modern man's great living religions—Hindu, Buddhist, Moslem, Jewish, Christian, Baha'i, and their flowering "New Thought" offshoots—all finally attain the same mountaintop of spiritual experience where the same stars of faith emerge and shine. "Truth is one," sang the Vedic master, "but sages call it by various names."

So, on the premise that all life is a divine summons and that certain world citizens—the heroes, champions, sages, statesmen, yeasayers, "parfit knights" of old—embody this vision best, I set to work. Some I interviewed were the universe-makers, the international il- luminati, the acclaimed movers and shakers of the earth; some were the humbler believers and gentler doers—the mothers, mis- sionaries, teachers, artists, doctors, scholars, scientists—whose con- cern for the future and love for their fellow man enhance human hope and happiness wherever their lives reach. For them, heroic living means little or nothing except as it is humanized to include charity, sacrifice, even failure and death. For them, whether over- coming personal travail or taking up arms against the world's sea of troubles, their strength and force in life comes from a faith in things unseen. Always strong convictions preceded strong actions; always true greatness included a reverence for mankind and a regard for religion.

"We draw new life," William James asserted, "from the heroic example." I felt this more deeply than ever when I interviewed serene-smiling U Thant in his thirty-eighth-floor U.N. office or watched white-maned Dr. Schweitzer feed his fawns in the Lam- baréné jungles or listened to Eleanor Roosevelt read her favorite scriptural passage, the thirteenth chapter of First Corinthians, to a Sunday-school class at the American Church in Paris. I felt this same life-lifting spirit whether talking to Marian Anderson after one of her Easter Sunday concerts at Carnegie Hall or with sprightly "rainbow artist" Marc Chagall at his white-walled villa overlooking the Mediterranean or with bearded Koran-quoting Sir Zafrulla Khan at the World Court or with ruddy-cheeked Dwight D. Eisenhower who at the Waldorf-Astoria tossed aside his *Herald Tribune*, jumped to his feet to greet me, and with hardly a question being asked, proceeded to talk for an hour about personal re- ligious experience from his Abilene boyhood through the agonizing hours of D day to the presidential years in the White House.

Although over the years the writing of *All Believers Are Brothers* has been an arduous and expensive project, the over-all experience has been an enriching one. The reason, of course, is that I walked with kings and commoners who shared a God-transfiguring faith and whose lives reflected those hidden sources of strength which only the devout know. My adventurous journeys were frequent and far-flung—to Europe, North Africa, the Middle East, Pakistan, India, China, Nepal, a scatter of U.S. states; and yet, conveniently and amusingly enough, many eventful interviews took place right in New York's celebrated Vanity Fair, the Waldorf-Astoria, where I saw such statesmen as Pearson of Canada, Humphrey of the United States and Radhakrishnan of India, such scholars as Bertrand Russell, Robert Oppenheimer and Sir Julian Huxley, such visiting royalty as the Shah of Iran, King Mahendra of Nepal and Emperor Haile Selassie of Ethiopia. Without cavil or contradiction, New York is the Serendip of Cities, drawing sooner or later to its tall-towered island the geniuses, goddesses and Meistersingers of the New Age!

The New Age . . . Yes! and the men and women featured in this book are its star-clad way-showers. For, truly this is mankind's most challenging time of change and the epoch when, for the first time, the human race is becoming unified into one self-conscious cultural body. Thus, amid such terrors of transition as war, revolution, racial revolt, mass poverty, mass movement, mass communications, the collapse of empires and the creation of scores of nation-states—above all the first bold thrusts of mankind out among the stars—new heroes must emerge; new universal men, new unifying teachers, new apostles of excellence now must lead us. As philosopher-painter Earl Hubbard points out, "This is the first age of mankind, and for the first time in history we now have the capacity to lift the majority of men high enough to ignite a sense of goodness." And, in a more strictly religious reference, England's Brother Mandus stresses "the signs and wonders which today represent the dawn of a new age . . . and the most significant fact that this is nothing less than a Divine Awakening in which the whole world is involved." Obviously, in such a fundamentally explosive time when the flame shadow of the Infinite breaks in upon us, only those intellectual freeholders and spiritual sun-treaders whose home is the moral universe within and the starry universe without are fit to keep our rendezvous with destiny.

Thus, each one of us who would resist the apathy, the ignorance, the unbridled violence, godless grasping and senseless slamming and banging of the most perilous epoch in history, must take a stand for excellence—and for personal responsibility as each one understands it. In all our seeking and serving, in our daily work, worship and, yes, even in our frantic funfests and affluent party-going, we must preserve the integrity of solitude and live in public as in private what Alfred North Whitehead calls "the habitual vision of greatness." And here in blessed America, where God slowly, yet surely, seems to be building the New Jerusalem, the task is perhaps most dangerous and difficult of all. For, only in a democracy can each citizen become his own taskmaster and only in a democracy can each citizen insist upon the excellence in thought, word and deed which ensures a superior society; and again, only in a love-lighted democracy that eventually must embrace the earth, can each of us become the sensitive fighter who knows and insists that heroic man is his own star, who experiences the Holy within the finite in his daily existence and who ever pleads for wholeness in life and reverence for all that lives, for the union of men and women and the unity of nations, for spirit in matter, past in present, peace on earth, beauty in ordinary things, the dead remembered, nature cherished, God revered by His evolving creation. Herein is the heart of the matter, for in the end, as philosopher José Martí has written, "mountains culminate in peaks and nations in great men."

> *Since what we choose is what we are,*
> *And what we love we yet shall be;*
> *The goal may ever shine afar,*
> *The will to win it makes us free.*

ROLAND GAMMON
New York, N.Y.
Winter, 1969

All Believers Are Brothers

Dwight D. Eisenhower

There is nothing wrong with America that the faith, love of freedom, intelligence and energy of her citizens cannot cure.

Dwight D. Eisenhower served for eight years as the thirty-fourth President of the United States. When he retired in 1961 he was seventy years old and had completed fifty years of service to his country. In that half-century of action and accomplishment, General Eisenhower rose from West Point cadet to staff officer under General MacArthur in the Philippines to chief of the War Department's Plans Division at the outbreak of World War II. Since 1911, an extraordinary combination of rare religious faith and extensive military training had prepared "Ike" Eisenhower for the momentous assignments which followed.

In 1942 Eisenhower commanded the Allied forces which routed Field Marshal Rommel's dreaded Afrika Korps. In 1943 he was commander-in-chief of the Allied Expeditionary Force which conquered Sicily and eliminated Italy as an Axis power. In 1944 he was appointed by President Roosevelt as supreme commander of the American, British and French forces which assaulted fortress Europe, and from June, 1944, to the war's end in May, 1945, he directed the massive land, sea and air armadas which destroyed Hitler's war machine. During this critical time he was made General of the Army.

Following the war "Ike" served successively as Army chief of staff, president of Columbia University and President of the United States. His presidential achievements included ending the Korean "police action," launching of America's space and nuclear submarine programs, checking the nation's upward price spiral, the extension of Social Security coverage to an additional ten million people and the admittance of Alaska and Hawaii to statehood. Until his recent death, the former President was active in Republican politics and numerous civic and charitable causes. His son, John, now serves as U. S. Ambassador to Belgium.

Crusade for Peace

Of the many instances when religious faith has sustained me in life, the first came when I was a teen-ager, and marked a turning point in my life. I had fallen, skinned my left knee and, when a painful infection later became so bad that I fell ill with a high fever, my parents discovered my swollen and discolored leg. Old Dr. Conklin, the family physician, eventually advised amputation to save my life.

When the horror of this prospect swept over me, I raised from the bed to shout, "Not me! I won't allow it! I'd rather die!" Later I made my older brother Edgar promise not to let the doctor cut off my leg no matter what happened, and he literally stood guard duty outside my bedroom during every call of the doctor at our home. Though I was desperately ill for two weeks, my parents respected my own decision. At the same time they, both deeply religious, included in their daily prayers petitions for my recovery, never doubting that the Almighty would hear them. In two weeks I was out of bed and able to walk. To me, this demonstration of their faith was a lesson I never forgot.

In crises during World War II, I turned to God when there was no one else to help. Two occasions involved our paratroopers. One night during the invasion of Sicily an armada of American aircraft was reported off course because of unexpectedly high winds and there was imminent danger that thousands of our sky troops would be dropped into the sea. I remember praying, "O God, they are in thy Almighty Hand." Incredibly enough, the lead plane later regained its bearings and the drop was at least partly successful.

On the eve of the massive D-day assault on Europe, the soul-racking problem arose as to whether to send two American airborne divisions against the Nazi-fortified Cherbourg peninsula. British Air Chief Leigh-Mallory advised against what he termed "this futile slaughter," and yet it seemed that to cancel the airborne attack would endanger the whole critical invasion of Utah Beach. I could only go to my tent to review every step of our elaborate planning and to ask God's guidance in making the right decision. I finally decided that the aerial attack would go as planned, and the paratroopers accomplished their dangerous mission with casualties far below those predicted by the experts.

When in peacetime it became my high honor to serve the nation as President, I opened my first inaugural with a short prayer I had written that morning: "Give us, we pray O God, the power to discern clearly right from wrong and allow all our actions to be governed thereby and by the laws of the land. Especially we pray that our concern shall be for all the people regardless of station, race or calling." During the ensuing eight years I never opened a Cabinet meeting without a minute of silent prayer.

A lifetime of soldiering and public service confirms my conviction that nobody can go through six years of war and two terms of the Presidency without faith. And although I have seldom displayed or discussed my religious philosophy with anyone, a deep Bible-centered faith has colored my life since childhood. Devout parents, who loved the Bible as dearly as life itself, made sure of that. Indeed, before I was eighteen, I had read through the entire Bible and discussed it, chapter by chapter, with my mother.

I believe that faith in God and the Judaeo-Christian ethic inspired the Founding Fathers of the United States. These remarkable men— Washington, Jefferson, Madison, Hamilton, Franklin, John Adams, John Hancock and Patrick Henry, to name a few of them—were men of deep religious conviction and in the New World they were trying to establish an entirely new form of government. We are a religious nation today because in the Declaration of Independence they stated their full reliance on "the laws of nature and nature's God" and because they published before the world these self-evident truths: "that all men are created equal, that they are endowed by their Creator with certain unalienable Rights; that among these are Life, Liberty and the pursuit of Happiness. . . ."

In contrast with this concept of the sacredness of life, modern atheistic dictatorships treat men as nothing more than animals or educated mules. How many materialistic psychologists and smart-alec professors sneer that men invented God in a childish search for security; yet, I have noticed that men in the foxholes or at the moment of death turn to some higher Power for comfort and courage. Thus it is that I believe there is nothing wrong with America today that the love of freedom, intelligence, energy and religious faith of her citizens cannot cure.

David Ben-Gurion

The sole greatness which awaits us, one inherent in our character, is greatness of spirit.

David Ben-Gurion, father of his country and prime minister of Israel for fifteen years, ranks in the Jewish pantheon with such immortals as Moses, Maimonides, David and King Solomon. Now eighty-two and living in semiretirement in a desert communal village, the venerable philosopher-statesman still seeks "truth," reads and writes during half his waking hours, counsels his countrymen with a prophet's fire. For, Ben-Gurion after fifty years as the resourceful leader of modern Zionism, still pioneers to secure and strengthen the homeland he helped establish.

Born into a religious family in Plonsk, Poland, in 1886, Ben-Gurion received a traditional Jewish education, became active as a youth in the Zionist labor movement. Before he was twenty-one, he had settled in Palestine and put into practice his belief that Zionism means a return to the soil of Zion, to till it and defend it. After helping organize the Jewish Legion in World War I, he returned to the Holy Land as a member of the Allied armies. During the postwar years, he was among the founders of the General Federation of Jewish Labor and the Israel labor party.

From 1935 to 1948, the stocky, shock-haired patriot served as chairman of the Jewish Agency Executive and so guided the long tumultuous struggle for Israel's independence. On May 14, 1948, as prime minister and minister of defense, he proclaimed the establishment of the Jewish state "to be known as Israel." Since that hour, in peace and war, he has proved a modern Ezra in the tasks of state building and the in-gathering of his dispersed people.

World-famous as a reader and quoter of the Bible, David Ben-Gurion also is a student of Hinduism, Buddhism and Greek philosophy. His published works, which have been printed in Hebrew, Yiddish, English and German, include *The Vision and the Road, The Sinai Campaign* and *The Rebirth and Destiny of Israel.* Both a man of action and a man of thought, he has received awards, titles and honorary degrees from half a dozen universities. Mr. Ben-Gurion is married and has three children; a son, Amos, is inspector general of the Israel Police Force.

The Supremacy of the Spirit

Exactly twenty years after my birth near Warsaw to Zionist missionary parents, I stood on the deck of a decrepit cargo ship in Jaffa harbor peering for the first time through morning mists at the opalescent coast of Palestine. The time was October, 1906, and my first excited glimpses of the Holy Land of my ancestors produced an unforgettable exaltation within me. Although the air smelled of charity and bakshish, my arrival in our ancient homeland fused forever in my life the prophetic faith of the Torah and the Zionist zeal of my father and mother. In that hour, adolescent dream became challenging reality.

My tall, bow-tied father, Reb Avigdor Green, already was a leader of the Lovers of Zion in Russian-occupied Poland. The Zionist movement was being born, the first European pioneers were going to work the land in Palestine, the first colonies—Ekron, Gedera, Petah Tikva, Rishon le Zion, Zikhron Jacob—had been established there through the philanthropy of Baron Edmond de Rothschild; so, it was with my father's blessing that I had embarked from Odessa, sailed with peasant refugees and their above-deck livestock across the Black Sea, watched the spires and crosses of the Orthodox Byzantine cities give way to the Moslem minarets of the Bosporus until at last we emerged into the open waters of the Mediterranean. Now, heart pounding, I went ashore and walked to the nearest moshava or village with scores of other eastern European adventurers.

That night, my first night on homeland soil, is forever engraved on my heart with the exultation of achievement. I lay awake—who could sleep through his first night in the Land? The spirit of my childhood and my dreams had triumphed and was joyous! I was in the Land of Israel, in a Jewish village there, and its name was Petah Tikva—Gate of Hope! Far from Plonsk, in a place exotic yet familiar in my dreams, I felt I had come home.

The howling of jackals in the vineyard, the braying of donkeys in the stables, the croaking of frogs in the ponds, the scent of blossoming acacia, the murmur of the distant sea, the darkening shadows of the groves, the enchantment of the stars in the deep blue—everything intoxicated me. I was rapturously happy—yet all was strange and bewildering, as though I were errant in a legendary kingdom. Could it be?

I stretched out my hand, and what I touched was solid. My soul was in tumult, one emotion drowned my very being: lo, I am in the Land of Israel! And the Land of Israel was here, wherever I turned or trod. . . . I trod its earth, above my head were skies and stars I had never seen before. . . . All night long I sat and communed with my new heaven. . . .

This Bible-inspired exaltation—and the biblical truth and tradition that made it possible—set the moral tone of my life from that day forward. Although there were many Jews of my acquaintance who believed that the Messiah would come to free Israel, I believed in the prophets of the Old Testament, the Hebrew heritage of law and virtue and the possibility of a national renaissance to re-establish them. As my father had taught me: "Each man his own Messiah, and each Messiah a Messiah of the Jewish people."

Today, with sixty years of turbulent times behind me and Israel's statehood restored, I still am one of those who believe wholeheartedly in the prophecy of Isaiah: "I, the Lord, have called thee in righteousness, and have taken hold of thy hand, and kept thee, and set thee for a covenant of the people, for a light of the nations" (42:6). That is not the only prophecy of his in which I believe. Isaiah said: "I will bring thy seed from the East, and gather thee from the West; I will say to the North, 'Give up'; and to the South: 'Keep not back, bring My sons from far, and My daughters from the end of the earth'" (43:5–6). And he also said: "And it shall come to pass in the end of days, that the mountain of the Lord's house shall be established as the top of the mountains, and shall be exalted above the hills; and all nations shall flow unto it. And they shall beat their swords into ploughshares, and their spears into pruning-hooks; nation shall not lift up sword against nation, neither shall they learn war any more" (2:2–4). One of these prophecies has already begun to be realized in our days, and in the first two decades of the resuscitation of the Jewish state in our ancient homeland we have brought in nearly two million Jews from over a hundred countries, from east and west, north and south.

Every people has a share in the heritage of the human race, just as every man, without distinction of race, religion or birthplace, is equal in rights and duties, and of equal worth. And just as there are divinely-blessed personalities, who by their intellect have enriched the human treasury with art, literature and science, so there are peoples of special greatness who have left an exceptional imprint on human culture. The Jewish people in days gone by was privileged to be one of the three ancient peoples that bequeathed immortal values to humankind, and, in large measure, fashioned the pattern of many peoples in all parts of the earth. The three peoples were Israel, Greece and India; all three in their religion and philosophy have greatly influenced my own thinking.

The renascence of Israel in our day has not been merely political and material in character. Israel cannot endure without strength and power, but we still hold fast to the faith that has accompanied our people for thousands of years, faith in the supremacy of the spirit. Not the spirit opposed to matter and divorced from it—the duality of matter and spirit was foreign to Jewish outlook in biblical times, as it is foreign to the science of our present. We believed, and still believe, in the supremacy of the spirit that pervades matter and rules it. On this faith is founded the historic mission and destiny of the state of Israel.

And the supremacy of the spirit implies not only the supremacy of science and intelligence, but also that of conscience and of morality, of which the authentic and practical expression in our lives is halutziut, the quality of pioneering and personal dedication to man's mission in life. The return of Israel to its land in our time is without parallel in history. We are receiving the fragments of a people scattered throughout the world, to rebuild the ruins of a small and poor country surrounded by enemies, and to establish a model society constructed upon a basis of liberty, equality, cooperation and love of our fellow men.

In my own life I have tried to preserve and deepen that quality of pioneering and personal dedication. In late 1953 at age sixty-seven, for example, I resigned as Israel's prime minister in order to move to Sde Boker in the Negev Desert. Israel was not leaderless, the fate of the nation did not depend on who was prime minister and, after a decade of tumult and travail in Jerusalem, I wanted to work and worship as the prophets of old in a remote desert kibbutz. In a farewell broadcast to the nation I quoted the prophet Habakkuk: "Righteous man lives by his faith. He will not preach to others, will not act the saint by calling on others to live justly, will not look for fault in his neighbor, but he will practice his faith in his daily life. He will live it."

During my fourteen months in the desert as laborer, writer and sheepherder, I deepened my reverence for work, understood the importance of an orange grove or a sugar field, saw more clearly that there was too much crowding, too much empty talk, too much chasing after comfort and wealth in our cities. To my mind, the surroundings most worthy of human beings are natural surroundings. The more a man is able to remove himself from the artificial life of modern civilization and stand face to face with wild and primary nature as it was fashioned by the Creator—and in this sense the desert is ideal—the more he is able to get at the truth of existence and of his mission on earth.

It was no accident that the Torah was given in the desert and that Israel's greatest teacher, Moses, led his people into the wilderness.

Born of the spirit, one of the marvels of our generation has been the victory of the Israel defense forces; but it was not by its weapons or its numbers that the young Israel army withstood the onslaughts of the enemy hosts. Its secret weapon was the high moral quality of our youth. The upbuilding of the country, too, the hundreds of villages that sprang up as if overnight in every corner of the land, the discovery of water in a desert left arid and barren since the dawn of Creation, the hundreds of thousands of immigrants assembled in the homeland within a brief space of time—all these things were not done by means of technology and finance alone. A decisive factor was also the power of that same tenacious spirit that inspires our people. The Jews of Yemen and Babylon were speeded to Israel by modern aircraft. But the real driving force was the messianic vision they had preserved in their hearts from the moment they went into exile, over 2500 years ago. Had it not been for that spirit they would not have clung to their Jewishness, they would never have returned to Israel.

The longing and yearning for a Jewish state were alive in the Jewish people all the years and generations since our second Temple was destroyed. What produced the miracle in our day? What converted the prayer, the yearning and the longing of the heart into the reality of national independence? It was the will to pioneer action that was awakened in the hearts of the lonely few, who went forth eighty years ago from behind the walls of the Old City of Jerusalem and from the distant exile of Hungary. They came together to establish the first Jewish village of our time. They were followed by scores and then by hundreds, and then by thousands and hundreds of thousands. It was they who made the miracle.

The establishment of the third state of Israel in our time has opened a new era. At its establishment, the state comprised some 650,000 Jews. It still comprises less than two million Jews today. We have yet to consummate the process of rebuilding. And while engaged in our national regeneration we must always remember the messianic vision of redemption that preserved us for thousands of years. That vision foresaw not only the complete redemption of the Jewish people, but of all humanity. For there can be no whole and lasting redemption of one people without the redemption of all nations. And we shall discharge the great and difficult task that is laid upon us only if we are true to the great vision of the Latter Days which Israel's prophets foresaw and which will surely come to pass. The vision will be realized in all its fullness if, side by side with all our practical efforts, we also cling tightly to spiritual values: the achievements of science, the ethics of the prophets, and pioneering that fulfills.

Helen Keller

I trust, and nothing disturbs that trust. I recognize the beneficence of the power which we all worship as supreme —Order, Fate, Great Spirit, Nature, God.

Miss Helen Keller, in Mark Twain's seasoned judgment, was one of the two greatest women who ever lived. His other heroine, Joan of Arc, lived five hundred years ago and led the inspired army that freed France, yet both women possessed a limitless faith which enabled them to surmount the most poignant personal anguish. For her brief, brave life and martyrdom at the stake, the Maid of Orleans was eventually made a saint; for millions of human beings today, Helen Keller was a living flesh-and-blood saint until her recent death.

Less than two years after she was born in Tuscumbia, Alabama, Helen Keller was stricken with a brain disease that left her blind, deaf and eventually mute. The extraordinary series of events which enabled her to escape her personal prison of soundless darkness was climaxed when she met the American inventor, Alexander Graham Bell. It was Dr. Bell, a lifelong friend of the deaf and dumb, who introduced her to Anne Sullivan—"the miracle worker" who for the next fifty years was to become Miss Keller's constant companion and teacher. Of dedicated Anne Sullivan, who knew something of blindness because of her own poor vision, Helen Keller was later to write: "The most important day in all my life is the one on which my teacher came to me."

Gradually, with loving patience and amazing skills, the "teacher" brought her young pupil step by step through the hand-tapping manual alphabet, the use of Braille, the mastery of her first words, sentences, and short articles. Eventually, in addition to her use of hand communications and Braille machines, Miss Keller also learned to speak —so that later she could travel, lecture and especially console those like herself who were blind and deaf. And, while never losing that common touch, she became world-famous and walked with kings; five U. S. Presidents—Wilson, Coolidge, Roosevelt, Eisenhower and Kennedy —entertained her in the White House.

During her 88-year lifetime, a grateful humanity, especially the blind of a hundred nations, honored her as "the world's first lady of courage." A graduate of Radcliffe College, she received honorary degrees from such far-flung universities as Harvard, Temple, Glasgow, Berlin, and Delhi, India. After the American Foundation for the Blind opened its offices in 1921, she joined that organization and until her death acted as a counselor on national and international relations. Among her many books are *Out of the Dark, The World I Live In, Let Us Have Faith, The Story of My Life* and *Peace at Eventide.*

In the Garden of the Lord

A simple childlike faith in a Divine Friend solves all the problems that come to us by land or sea. Faith teaches us to use our talents to the fullest extent, however slight they may be. Faith is a responsibility for us as well as a privilege.

Faith does not oblige us to be unusually endowed, but receptive. To say others may have it, but we cannot, is wanton self-limitation. To be alert for whatever surprises may glow within us is to have at our command a zest for living which outweighs all material possessions. Continents sink; empires disintegrate; but faith and the universe of heroic minds abide forever.

Religion is the fruit of faith, and to ask for religion without faith is to ask for the flower without the seed. Many world religions have spread inspiring hope upon earth, but one faith has been their tree just as good will is the one root of all truly beneficent activities.

Faith has such might because next to love it is the force most inherent in one's own awareness. It directs to the light when darkness prevails; it supplies incentive to action and converts ideas into realities. It fires the imagination, and this is essential, for one must envision the higher life and behave as if it were a fact before it can unfold. But though faith belongs to the future, its energy irradiates the present, just as the green leaf pigment—the delicate link between the sun and life—permeates the vegetable world.

Faith, like philosophy, endows me with a unity I miss in the chaos of material experience devoid of sight and hearing. But like everyone else I have eyes in my soul. Through faith I create the world I gaze upon; I make my own day and night, tint the clouds with iridescent fires, and behold! a midnight is strewn with other stars. It is faith which lights us into sustaining realities beyond those perceived by the physical senses.

Faith transmutes circumstance, time, condition and mood into vitality. This is why Christ's teaching was momentously effective nineteen centuries ago and still is so today among those who truly respond to it. Then we wake to see with new eyes and hear with new ears the beauty and harmony of God's real world.

I am blind and have never seen a rainbow, but I have been told of its beauty. I know that its beauty is always broken and incomplete. Never does it stretch across the heavens in full perfection. So it is with all things as we know them here below. Life itself is as imperfect and broken for every one of us as the span of the rainbow. Not until we have taken the step from life into Eternity shall we understand the meaning of Browning's words: "On the earth the broken arcs; in the heaven, a perfect round."

The most important question is not the sort of environment we have but the kind of thoughts we think every day, the kind of ideals we are following; in a word, the kind of men and women we really are. . . . Join the great company of those who make the barren places of life fruitful with kindness.

The joy of surmounting obstacles which once seemed unremovable, and pushing the frontier of accomplishment further—what joy is there like unto it? Keep your face to the sunshine and you cannot see the shadow.

The reason, I am sure, why God permitted me to lose both sight and hearing seems clear now—that through me He might cleave a rock unbroken before and let quickening streams flow through other lives desolate as my own once was. I believe that life is given to us so we may glow in love, and I believe that God is in me as the sun is in the color and fragrance of a flower—the Light in my darkness, the Voice in my silence.

It would be wonderful to find myself free from even a small part of my physical limitations . . . to walk around town alone . . . to come and go without a word to anyone . . . to read the newspapers without waiting, and pick out a pretty handkerchief or a becoming hat in the shops.

I trust, and nothing that happens disturbs my trust. I recognize

the beneficence of the Power which we all worship as supreme—
Order, Fate, the Great Spirit, Nature, God. I recognize this power
in the sun that makes all things grow and keeps life afoot. I make a
friend of this indefinable force, and straightway feel glad, brave, and
ready for any lot heaven may decree for me. This is my religion of
optimism.

The conflict between the artistic impulse and the calculating
scientific tendency in modern times repels me—a future civilization
is likely to be hard, practical, monotonous. I feel fortunate indeed
that it has been possible for me to be a barbarian, to enjoy sculpture,
poetry, happy make-believe in bleak corners of my limitations. It
seems to me more urgent than ever to foster in the present young
generation a spiritual philosophy and imagination that shall keep the
morning dew in their souls when an age arrives that knows not the
muses.

I believe that we can live on earth according to the teachings of
Jesus, and that the greatest happiness will come to the world when
man obeys His commandment that "ye love one another." For three
things I thank God every day of my life—that He has vouchsafed
my knowledge of His works, deep thanks that He has set in my
darkness the lamp of faith, deep, deepest thanks that I have another
life to look forward to—a life joyous with light and flowers and
heavenly song.

Perhaps a little verse I wrote years ago will suggest to you how I
feel about life:

> They took away what should have been my eyes,
> (But I remembered Milton's Paradise).
> They took away what should have been my ears,
> (Beethoven came and wiped away my tears).
> They took away what should have been my tongue,
> (But I talked with God when I was young).
> He would not let them take away my soul—
> Possessing that, I still possess the whole.

Julian S. Huxley

*Our business in the world today is seen to be the im-
position of the best and most enduring of our human
standards upon ourselves and our planet. The enjoyment
of beauty and interest, the achievement of goodness and
efficiency, the enhancement of life and its variety—these
are the harvest which our human uniqueness should be
called upon to yield.*

Sir Julian Huxley of London, scientific scion of the traditionally
intellectual British family, is one of the world's foremost biologists,
humanists and philosophical authors. Grandson of the courageous
Thomas H. Huxley, the anthropologist and essayist who became famous as "Darwin's bulldog," and brother of the late great Aldous Huxley,
novelist, philosopher and mystic, Sir Julian bestrides the contemporary scene as not only a noted scientist but also an apostle of twentieth-
century humanism which sees mankind as the newly-appointed manag-
ing director "of the big business of evolution" and "the human species
now on the threshold of a new experience as different from ours
as ours is from that of Pekin man."

Born in England in 1887 and educated at Eton and Oxford,
young Huxley began to attract academic attention from the time he
won the University's Newdegate Prize for Poetry in 1908, and took
First Class Honors in Zoology in the subsequent year. His teaching
and lecturing career has taken him from Oxford to London University
to McGill University in Montreal to Rice Institute in Texas. His
many public service achievements include becoming an officer of
such commissions as United Kingdom National Parks, Higbee Education
in West Africa and the Scientific and Cultural History of Mankind.
In 1956 he received the Darwin Medal from the Royal Society, and
in 1958 Queen Elizabeth created him a Knight of the Empire.

A long-time member and supporter of the United Nations' Educational, Scientific, and Cultural Organization, Sir Julian served as
UNESCO's director general in 1947 and 1948. His forty books include *Evolution in Action, Man Stands Alone, Religion Without
Revelation, Africa View, From an Antique Land, On Living in a
Revolution, Essays of a Humanist, Democracy Marches* and *Man in the
Modern World.* He has lectured on scientific subjects in many cities
of Europe, Asia and the Americas. Married to the former Juliette Baillot
and the father of two sons, Mr. Huxley resides in the City of London.

Man's Soaring Destiny

I believe that life can be worth living. I believe this in spite of pain, squalor, cruelty, unhappiness and death. I do not believe that it is necessarily worth living, but only that for most people it can be.

I also believe that man, as individual, as group, and collectively as mankind, can achieve a satisfying purpose in existence. I believe this in spite of frustration, aimlessness, frivolity, boredom, sloth and failure. However I do not believe that a purpose inevitably inheres in the universe or in our existence, or that mankind is bound to achieve a satisfying purpose, but only that such a purpose can be found.

I believe that there exists a scale or hierarchy of values, ranging from simple physical comforts up to the highest satisfactions of love, aesthetic enjoyment, intellect, creative achievement, virtue. I do not believe that these are absolute, or transcendental in the sense of being vouchsafed by some external power or divinity; they are the product of human nature interacting with the outer world. Nor do I suppose that we can grade every valuable experience into an accepted order, any more than I can say whether a beetle is a higher organism than a cuttlefish or a herring. But just as it can unhesitatingly be stated that there are general grades of biological organization, and that a beetle *is* a higher organism than a sponge, or a human being than a frog, so I can assert, with the consensus of civilized human beings, that there is a higher value in Dante's *Divina Commedia* than in a popular hymn, in the scientific activity of Newton or Darwin than in solving a crossword puzzle, in the fullness of love than in sexual gratification, in selflessness than in purely self-regarding activities—although each and all can have their value of a sort.

I do not believe that there is any absolute of truth, beauty, morality, or virtue, whether emanating from an external power or imposed by an internal standard. But this does not drive me to the curious conclusion, fashionable in certain quarters, that truth and beauty and goodness do not exist, or that there is no force or value in them.

I believe that there are a number of questions that it is no use our asking, because they can never be answered. Nothing but waste, worry, or unhappiness is caused by trying to solve insoluble problems. Yet some people seem determined to try. I recall the story of the philosopher and the theologian. The two were engaged in disputation and the theologian used the old quip about a philosopher being like a blind man, in a dark room, looking for a black cat—which wasn't there. "That may be," said the philosopher, "but the theologian would have found it."

Even in material matters of science we must learn to ask the right questions. It seemed an obvious question to ask how animals inherit the result of their parents' experience, and enormous amounts of time and energy have been spent on trying to give an answer to it. It is, however, no good asking the question, for the simple reason that no such inheritance of acquired characteristics exists. The chemists of the eighteenth century, because they asked themselves the question "What substance is involved in the process of burning?" became involved in the mazes of the phlogiston theory: they had to ask "What sort of process is burning?" before they could see that it did not involve a special substance but was merely a particular case of chemical combination.

When we come to what are usually referred to as fundamentals, the difficulty of not asking the right kind of question is much increased. Until quite recently, among most African tribes, if a person died, the only question asked was, "Who caused his death, and by what form of magic?"; the idea of death from natural causes was unknown. Indeed, the life of the less-civilized half of mankind is largely based on trying to find an answer to a wrong question: "What magical forces or powers are responsible for good or bad fortune, and how can they be circumvented or propitiated?"

I do not believe in the existence of a god or gods. The conception of divinity seems to me, though built up out of a number of real elements of experience, to be a false one, based on the quite unjustifiable postulate that there must be some more or less personal power in control of the world. We are confronted with forces beyond our control, with incomprehensible disasters, with death, and also with ecstasy, with a mystical sense of union with something greater than our ordinary selves, with sudden conversion to a new way of life, with the burden of guilt and sin. In theistic religions all these elements of actual experience have been woven into a unified body of belief and practice in relation to the fundamental postulate of the existence of a god or gods.

I believe this fundamental postulate to be nothing more than the result of asking a wrong question: "Who or what rules the universe?" So far as we can see, it rules itself, and indeed the whole analogy with a country and its ruler is false. Even if a god does exist behind or above the universe as we experience it, we can have no knowledge of such a power; the actual gods of historical religions are only the personifications of impersonal facts of nature and of facts of our inner mental life.

Similarly with immortality. With our present faculties we have no means of giving a categorical answer to the question whether we survive death, much less the question of what any such life after death will be like. That being so, it is a waste of time and energy to devote ourselves to the problem of achieving salvation in the life to come. However, just as the idea of god is built out of bricks of real experience, so too is the idea of salvation. If we translate salvation into terms of this world, we find that it means achieving harmony between different parts of our nature, including its subconscious depths and its rarely touched heights, and also achieving some satisfactory adjustment between ourselves and the outer world, including not only the world of nature but the social world of man. I believe it to be possible to "achieve salvation" in this sense and right to aim at doing so, just as I believe it possible and valuable to achieve a sense of union with something bigger than our ordinary selves, even if that something be not a god but an extension of our narrow core to include in a single grasp ranges of outer experience and inner nature on which we do not ordinarily draw.

But if God and immortality be repudiated, what is left? That is the question usually thrown at the atheist's head. The orthodox believer likes to think that nothing is left. That, however, is because he has only been accustomed to think in terms of his orthodoxy.

In point of fact, a great deal is left.

That is immediately obvious from the fact that many men and women have led active, or self-sacrificing, or noble, or devoted lives without any belief in God or immortality. Buddhism in its uncorrupted form has no such belief; nor did the great nineteenth-century agnostics; nor do the orthodox Russian Communists; nor did the Stoics. Of course, the unbelievers have often been guilty of selfish or wicked actions; but so have the believers. And in any case that is not the fundamental point. The point is that without these beliefs men and women may yet possess the mainspring of full and purposive living, and just as strong a sense that existence can be worth while as is possible to the most devout believers.

I would say that this is much more readily possible today than in any previous age. The reason lies in the advances of science.

No longer are we forced to accept the external catastrophes and miseries of existence as inevitable or mysterious; no longer are we obliged to live in a world without history, where change is only meaningless. Our ancestors saw an epidemic as an act of divine punishment; to us it is a challenge to be overcome, since we know its causes and that it can be controlled or prevented. The understanding of infectious disease is entirely due to scientific advance. To take a very recent happening, so is our understanding of the chemical basis of nutrition, which holds out new possibilities of health and energy to the human race. So is our understanding of earthquakes and storms; if we cannot control them, we at least do not have to fear them as evidence of God's anger.

Some, at least, of our internal miseries can be lightened in the same way. Through knowledge derived from psychology, children can be prevented from growing up with an abnormal sense of guilt and so making life a burden both to themselves and to those with whom they come into contact. We are beginning to understand the psychological roots of irrational fear and cruelty; someday we shall be able to make the world a brighter place by preventing their appearance.

The ancients had no history worth mentioning. Human existence in the present was regarded as a degradation from that of the original golden age. Down even to the nineteenth century what was known of human history was regarded by the nations of the West as an essentially meaningless series of episodes sandwiched into the brief space between the Creation and the Fall, a few thousand years ago, and the Second Coming and Last Judgment, which might be on us at any moment and in any case could not be pushed back for more than a few thousand years into the future. In this perspective a millennium was almost an eternity. With such an outlook no wonder life seemed, to the great mass of humanity, "nasty, brutish, and short," its miseries and shortcomings merely bewildering unless illuminated by the illusory light of religion.

Today human history merges back into prehistory, and prehistory again into biological evolution. Our time scale is profoundly altered. A thousand years is a short time for prehistory, which is thought of in terms of hundreds of thousands of years, and an insignificant time for evolution, which deals in hundred-million-year periods. The future is extended equally with the past; if it took over two billion years for primeval life to generate man, man and his descendants have at least an equal allowance of time before them for further evolution.

Most of all, the new history has been a basis of hope. Biological evolution has been appallingly slow and appallingly wasteful. It has been cruel; it has generated the parasites and the pests as well as the more agreeable types. It has led life up innumerable blind alleys. But in spite of this it has achieved progress. In a few lines, whose number has steadily diminished with time, it has avoided the cul-de-sac of mere specialization and arrived at a new level of organization, more harmonious and more efficient, from which it could again launch out toward greater control, greater knowledge, and greater independence. Progress is, if you will, all-around specialization. Finally, but one line was left which was able to achieve further progress; all the others had led up blind alleys. This was the line leading to the evolution of the human brain.

This at one bound altered the perspective of evolution. Experience could now be handed down from generation to generation; deliberate purpose could be substituted for the blind sifting of selection; change could be speeded up ten-thousandfold. In man evolution could become conscious. Admittedly it is far from conscious yet, but the possibility is there, and it has at least been consciously envisaged.

Seen in this perspective, human history represents but the tiniest portion of the time man has before him; it is only the first ignorant and clumsy gropings of the new type, born heir to so much biological history. The constant setbacks, the lack of improvement in certain respects for over two thousand years, are seen to be phenomena as natural as the tumbles of a child learning to walk or the deflection of a sensitive boy's attention by the need of making a living.

The broad facts remain. Life had progressed even before man was first evolved. Life progressed in giving rise to man. Man has progressed during the million or so years from the first Hominidae, even during the ten thousand years since the final amelioration of climate after the Ice Age. And the potentialities of progress which are revealed, once his eyes have been opened to the evolutionary vista, are unlimited.

At last we have an optimistic instead of a pessimistic theory of this world and our life upon it. Admittedly the optimism cannot be facile, and must be tempered with reflection on the length of time involved, on the hard work that will be necessary, on the inevitable residuum of accident and unhappiness that will remain. Perhaps we had better call it a melioristic rather than an optimistic view; but at least it preaches hope and inspires to action.

I believe very definitely that it is among human personalities that there exist the highest and most valuable achievements of the universe—or at least the highest and most valuable achievements of which we know or, apparently, can have knowledge. That means that I believe that the state exists for the development of individual lives, not individuals for the development of the state.

But I also believe that the individual is not an isolated, separate thing. An individual is a transformer of matter and experience; he is a system of relations between his own basis and the universe, including other individuals. An individual may believe that he should devote himself entirely to a cause, even sacrifice himself to it—his country, truth, art, love. It is in the devotion or the sacrifice that he becomes most himself; it is because of the devotion or sacrifice of individuals that causes become of value. But of course the individual must in many ways subordinate himself to the community—only not to the extent of believing that in the community resides any virtue higher than that of the individuals which compose it.

The community provides the machinery for the existence and development of individuals. There are those who deny the importance of social machinery, who assert that the only important thing is a change of heart, and that the right machinery is merely a natural consequence of the right inner attitude. This appears to me mere solipsism. Different kinds of social machinery predispose to different inner attitudes. The most admirable machinery is useless if the inner life is unchanged; but social machinery *can* affect the fullness and quality of life. Social machinery can be devised to make war more difficult, to promote health, to add interest to life. Let us not despise machinery in our zeal for fullness of life, any more than we should dream that machinery can ever automatically grind out perfection of living.

I believe in diversity. Every biologist knows that human beings differ in their hereditary outfits, and therefore in the possibilities that they can realize. Psychology shows how inevitably different are the types that jostle each other on the world's streets. No amount of persuasion or education can make the extrovert really understand the introvert, the verbalist understand the lover of handicraft, the nonmathematical or nonmusical person understand the passion of the mathematician or the musician. We can try to forbid certain attitudes of mind. We could theoretically breed out much of the human variety. But this would be a sacrifice. Diversity is not only the salt of life but the basis of collective achievement. *And the complement of diversity is tolerance and understanding.* This does not mean rating all values alike. We must protect society against criminals; we must struggle against what we think wrong. But just as if we try to understand the criminal we shall try to reform rather than merely to punish, so we must try to understand why we judge other's actions as wrong, which implies trying to understand the workings of our own minds and discounting our own prejudices.

Finally, I believe that we can never reduce our principles to any few simple terms. Existence is always too various and too complicated. We must supplement principles with faith. And the only faith that is both concrete and comprehensive is in life, its abundance and its progress. My final belief is in life.

Dag Hammarskjold

In our era, the road to holiness necessarily passes through the world of action.

Dag Hjalmar Hammarskjold, eminent Swedish diplomat and for nine years secretary general of the United Nations, proved himself the world's supreme international civil servant in his brilliant thirty-year public career. Since his tragic death in an airplane crash in February, 1961, while on a peacemaking mission to the Congo, the Hammarskjold ideal and influence as "an apostle of quiet diplomacy" has continued to support the cause of world tranquillity, peace and justice. As one New York newspaper editor wrote of him, "To his task he brought the traditions of a nation that has avoided war for 150 years and of a family built upon public service. He is a born peacemaker . . . who has achieved a sort of supreme authority that transcends frontiers and loyalties."

The fourth son of Hjalmar Hammarskjold, prime minister of Sweden during World War I, he was born on July 29, 1905, and brought up in the old university town of Uppsala. Since the first Hammarskjold was knighted for valor in battle by King Karl IX in 1610, at least eighteen members of his family served king and country. In his public career he became Sweden's leading monetary expert, chairman of the Bank of Sweden, and both cabinet minister and deputy foreign minister. In the early 1950s he played an active part in the Organization for European Economic Cooperation and the Council of Europe. In March, 1953, he was chosen unanimously to succeed Trygve Lie as the U.N. secretary general.

Administrative wizard, economic expert, discreet statesman and diplomat, Hammarskjold possessed the qualities needed to become a great United Nations leader. He directed a world-wide staff of seven thousand persons. He participated in the resolution of the Korean, Hungarian and Suez crises, organized and directed the first U. N. Emergency Force to police the Middle East, quietly resisted the Russian campaign to force him from office and substitute a "troika" rule in the Secretariat. In doing "the most impossible job in the world," he found time to visit most of the nations of the world and to supervise establishment of a U. N. Meditation Room.

A bachelor, an intellectual and an ardent mountain climber, Hammarskjold was a member of the Swedish Academy and the Lutheran Church of Sweden. In October, 1964, his diary, *Markings*, was published by Alfred A. Knopf, Inc., revealing the dispassionate diplomat to be an impassioned poet and mystic and recording "a sort of *white book* concerning my negotiations with myself—and with God."

(The Christian credo of Dag Hammarskjold was prepared by the author from his pertinent speeches, statements and interviews.)

To Even Greater Heights

Over the fireplace in my New York apartment hangs a mountain climber's pick given to me by the Tibetan guide Tenzing Norgay, the conqueror of Mount Everest. It is inscribed, "So you may climb to even greater heights." Naturally it is one of my prized possessions, but I mention it only to stress that the qualities required in mountain climbing are just those that I feel we all need today. We need perseverance and patience, a firm grip on realities, clear but imaginative planning, a clear awareness of the objective facts and of the dangers; but the safest climber is he who never questions his ability to overcome all difficulties.

The struggles, aspirations and dangers of mountain climbing find their parallel in the life of men and nations. From generations of soldiers, ministers and government officials on my father's side, I inherited a belief that no life was more satisfactory than one of selfless service to your country—or to humanity. This service requires a sacrifice of all personal interests, but likewise the courage to stand up unflinchingly for your convictions.

From scholars and clergymen on my mother's side, I inherited a belief that, in the very radical sense of the Christian Gospels, all men are equals as children of God, and should be met and treated by us as our masters in God. He who has placed himself in God's hands stands free vis-à-vis men; he is entirely at his ease with them because he has granted them the right to judge. As your place and influence in life enlarges, your responsibility is indeed terrifying. If you fail, it is God, thanks to your having betrayed Him, who will fail mankind.

The Lutheran beliefs in which I was brought up and which, in fact, had given my life direction even while my intellect still challenges their validity, were recognized by me as mine in their own right and by my free choice. Today I can endorse those convictions without any compromise with the demands of that intellectual honesty which is the very key to maturity of mind. I don't know Who—or What—put the question. I don't know when it was put. I don't even remember answering. But at some moment I did answer Yes to Someone—or Something—and from that hour I was certain that existence is meaningful and that, therefore, my life in self-surrender had a goal.

Faith is a state of the mind and the soul. In this sense we can understand the world of the Spanish mystic, St. John of the Cross: "Faith is the union of God and the soul." The language of religion is a set of formulas which register a basic spiritual experience. It must not be regarded as describing, in terms to be defined by philosophy, the reality which is accessible to our senses and which we can analyze with the tools of logic. I was late in understanding what this meant.

The two ideals which dominated my childhood world met me fully harmonized and adjusted to the demands of our world of today in the ethics of Albert Schweitzer, where the ideal of service is supported by and supports the basic attitudes to man set forth in the Gospels. In his work I also found a key for modern man to the world of the Gospels.

But the explanation of how man should live a life of active social service in full harmony with himself as a member of the community of the spirit, I found in the writings of those great medieval mystics for whom "self-surrender" had been the way to self-realization, and who in "singleness of mind" and "inwardness" had found strength to say Yes to every demand which the needs of their neighbors made them face, and to say Yes also to every fate life had in store for them when they followed the call of duty as they understood it. Love—that much misused and misinterpreted word—for them meant simply an overflowing of strength with which they felt themselves filled when living in true self-oblivion. And this love found natural expressions in an unhesitant fulfillment of duty and in an unreserved acceptance of life, whatever it brought them personally of toil, suffering, or happiness.

I know that their discoveries about the laws of inner life and of action have not lost their significance. God does not die on the day when we cease to believe in a personal deity, but we die on the day when our lives cease to be illumined by the steady radiance renewed daily of a wonder, the source of which is beyond all reason.

Several years ago my U.N. executive assistant, Andrew Cordier, and I had the privilege of working with the Laymen's Movement to establish a permanent Meditation Room at the United Nations. It is a place dedicated to silence in the outward sense and stillness in the inward sense. In a room of this kind, in a house of this character, we could not use any of the symbols with which man has been used to link his religious feelings; we had to work on the basis of symbols common to all. In a sense, what I think we had at the back of our minds was something which is said, I believe, in one of Buddha's scripts, that the significance of the vessel is not the shell but the void. This meant that we could perhaps do away with symbols if . . . we achieved purity. It is for that reason that in the center of the room there is a block of iron ore, glimmering like ice in a shaft of light from above. That is the only symbol in the room—a meeting of the light of the sky and the earth.

The original idea is one which I think you will all recognize; you will find it in many great religions: it is the empty altar, empty not because there is no God, but empty because God is worshiped in so many forms. The stone in the center is the altar to the God of all. At the same time, it has strong associations with the cornerstone, the firm element in a world of movement and turmoil. In this house, with its dynamic modern architecture, there are very few things that give you the feeling of weight, solidity and permanence . . . we wanted the massive altar to give the impression of something more than temporary. . . .

In this house we are trying to turn swords into plowshares and we thought we could bless by our thoughts the very material out of which arms are made. Iron ore is a material which represents the very paradox of human life; the basic materials offered by God to us may be used either for construction or destruction. This leads our thoughts to the necessity of choice between the two alternatives. . . .

When we come to our deepest feelings and urgings we have to be alone, we have to feel the sky and the earth and hear the voice that speaks from within us. We tried to create a Meditation Room where men of all kinds and from all regions of the world would have a place where each could find his own God.

In our era, the road to holiness necessarily passes through the world of action. So, once again, you chose for yourself—and opened the door to chaos. The chaos you become whenever God's hand does not rest upon your head.

He who has once been under God's hand, has lost his innocence: only he feels the full explosive force of destruction which is released by a moment's surrender to temptation.

But when his attention is directed beyond and above, how strong he is, with the strength of God who is within him because he is in God. Strong and free, because his self no longer exists.

Before Thee, Father,
    In righteousness and humility,
With Thee, Brother,
    In faith and courage,
In Thee, Spirit,
    In stillness.
Thine—for Thy will is my destiny,
Dedicated—for my destiny is to be used and used up according
    to Thy will.

Marian Anderson

Through the golden moments of musical communion with God, Mother's words still remind me of what should come first: "Grace must always come before greatness."

Marian Anderson, a great lady and a glorious contralto, is the most renowned and honored of American singers in the twentieth century. In her forty years on the concert stage and her regular tours to as many countries, she has sung to an estimated eight million persons. Of her singing, Maestro Arturo Toscanini once said: "A voice like hers is heard only once in one hundred years."

Born of poor, yet devout, parents in Philadelphia's Negro quarter, Miss Anderson first appeared publicly in the Union Baptist Church at age six when she sang "The Lord Is My Shepherd." Before she was ten, "the baby contralto" graduated from the church's junior to adult choir and occasionally substituted for the soprano or tenor soloist. When her father died, twelve-year-old Marian began to sing professionally at church concerts. A Marian Anderson Fund collected by church friends and a music scholarship provided by prominent Philadelphians enabled her to study with the finest teachers before her first prize-winning engagement with the New York Philharmonic Orchestra in 1926.

With her first European concerts in 1930 and the triumphant New York appearances that followed, Marian Anderson began a succession of Continental tours that continue to this day. Europe, Africa, Russia, Japan, Israel, South America, Australia—all saw that rare spectacle, a box-office avalanche. In 1939 alone she gave ninety-two recitals in the U.S., the most intensive concert tour in history. She became the first Negro star at the Metropolitan Opera when she sang the lead in Verdi's *Un Ballo in Maschera* in 1955. As both artist and ambassadress for the U. S. State Depatment, she toured the Far East in 1957, and during President Eisenhower's second term she found time between concerts to serve her country with distinction as a delegate to the United Nations.

Winner of the $10,000 Bok Award, the U. S. Freedom Medal, the Springarm Medal, twenty-four honorary doctorates of music, the Woman of Achievement Award, and countless other honors, Miss Anderson is represented in a mural in the Department of the Interior in Washington, commemorating her Easter Sunday concert in 1939 for seventy-five thousand at the Lincoln Memorial. She has sung three times in the White House, the second time for royal guests from England, King George and Queen Elizabeth. King Gustaf Adolf conferred on her Sweden's "Litteris et Artibus" medal; the Emperor of Japan, the Yukosho medal; Finland, its esteemed Order of the White Rose and the Marshal Mannerheim medal; and other decorations have come to her from Haiti, Liberia, England, France and the Philippines. She is married to the New York architect, Orpheus H. Fisher.

Grace Before Greatness

The longer one lives here on earth, the better one realizes that there is no particular endeavor or thing that you can do alone. To stand on your own, to accomplish some task, to use your voice as I do or even to walk on a stage to perform—it is not of your own doing. Because I have come to realize that God is so great in one's life, I recognize that the "I" in it is very small after all. Out of my mother's deep evangelical faith and out of my own thought and prayer, I know with the biblical prophet: "The eternal God is our refuge and underneath are the Everlasting Arms."

Failure and frustration are in the unwritten pages of everyone's record. I have had my share of them. But my mother's gift of faith repeatedly sustained a life in music which otherwise would have ended long ago. Early in my singing career, for example, I ventured too far ahead and before I was twenty made a premature debut in New York's Town Hall that was a critical fiasco. While waiting in dazed delight to go on, my sponsor said there would be a slight delay. I waited five, ten, fifteen minutes, then peeked through the curtain. The house was half empty! I died inside, but when the curtain went up I sang my heart out. It was no use, for I wasn't ready. The newspaper comments were uncomplimentary and, chastened and disturbed, I returned to Philadelphia.

I did not want to see any music, hear any music or make a career of it. Yet my widowed mother, who had taught me to make my own decisions whenever possible, urged me to "think about it a little and pray about it a lot." For nearly a year, however, I brooded more than I prayed, all the while avoiding my music teacher and rejecting offers to sing at other concerts. As a typical egocentric teen-ager, I wallowed in self-pity.

Yet, my dear Bible-reading schoolteaching mother kept prodding me to pray my way back to life and to the Christ-serving career which she and my many friends believed right for me. Gradually I released my grief and began to pray. And, in those tearful hours, there slowly came the thought that there is a time when even the most self-sufficient cannot find enough strength to stand alone. Then, one prays with a fervor one never had before. From my torment I prayed with the sure knowledge there was Someone to whom I could pour out the greatest need of my heart and soul. It did not matter if He answered. It was enough to pray.

Slowly I came out of my despair. My mind began to clear. No one was to blame for my failure. Self-pity left me. In a burst of exuberance I told my mother: "I want to study again. I want to be the best, and be loved by everyone, and be perfect in everything."

One day I came home from my teacher unaware that I was humming. It was the first music I had uttered at home in a whole year. My mother heard it, and she rushed to meet me, and put her arms around me and kissed me. It was her way of saying: "Your prayers have been answered, and mine have too."

For a brief moment we stood there silently. Then my mother defined the sweet spell of our gratitude: "Prayer begins where human capacity ends," she said.

So my mother gave balance to the home and led us into a rich spiritual life. We knew from earliest childhood that she prayed, and she saw to it that as little girls we said our prayers. As we grew older she always asked, when she tucked us into bed, whether we had said our prayers. If we had not—and we did not know how to deceive her—she would pull back the covers and we would crawl out of bed and get down on our knees to say them.

Good habits can be fine things. If you say your prayers every night there comes a time when they grow more meaningful to you. The child who learns to repeat after his mother, "Now I lay me down to sleep," may get a little thrill out of just saying it, at the beginning. After a time he realizes that he can do nothing about keeping his own soul when he is asleep. As he says, "Now I lay me down to sleep, I pray Thee, Lord, my soul to keep," the realization comes to him that there is Someone else to whom he can commit his soul when he cannot take care of himself.

Although I am now approaching sixty years old and although I have sung for kings and presidents receiving honors far beyond my due, my mother's influence runs through everything I ever wanted to be. I was converted to my Baptist mother's faith and understanding patience long before I could explain either. Living in Philadelphia's Negro quarter, we were poor folks. But there was a wealth in our poverty, a wealth of music, and love and faith. My two sisters, Alice and Ethel, and I were all in the church choir—the junior, not the senior one. There is still a vivid memory of our mother and father, their faces shining with pride, watching us from the front pews. And when I was six I was once fortunate enough to be selected to step out in front of the choir and sing "The Lord Is My Shepherd."

It was a Baptist church we attended in Philadelphia. But my mother taught us early that the form of one's faith is less important than what's in one's heart.

"When you come to Him," she said, "He never asks what you are."

My sisters still attend the Baptist church in Philadelphia. It is a church and a congregation I hold most fondly in my heart for many reasons. These were the people who, years ago, pooled their pennies into what they grandly called "the Fund for Marian Anderson's Future," a gesture of love and confidence impossible to forget in a lifetime. Today, when I come to Philadelphia, I always try to see some of these people who have been so important to me, and though it seldom is possible these days, I love to sing in their choir.

Now in the midst of a farewell tour of the world, I still believe in the basic things mother believes in. Her God is my God. I would not condemn people who do not believe as we do. I feel, however, that each one of us must have something in which he believes with all his heart, so that he need never be absolutely alone. Mother was wise not to try to persuade us to be as she is or to do as she does; her example was such that we wished to follow in her footsteps.

My religion is something I cherish. I am not in church every Sunday, but I hope and believe that I am on good speaking terms with Him. I carry my troubles, and I don't sit back waiting for them to be cleared up. I realize that when the time is ripe they will be dissolved, but I don't mean that one should sit inert, waiting for all things to come from above. If one has a certain amount of drive, intelligence, and conscientiousness, one must use them. Having made the best effort, one is more likely to get a hearing in an extremity.

I believe that I could not have had my career without the help of the Divine Being above. I believe that He put it in the hearts of many people to be kind, interested, and helpful, and to do things that needed to be done for me and that I could not have done for myself. It would have happened anyhow, some might say. I don't believe that it would have happened anyhow.

It is well that there are different roads to faith. Mother's faith has lighted the way for us in all the days of our lives, even the hardest we have gone through. Her day-to-day living and the way she accepted and greeted life and its meaning were the forces that guided us. Today I am blessed, and have been blessed for forty years, with the gift of inspiring people through song. Through the travels and travail, through the applause, the agony, the golden moments of musical communion with God, her words still remind me of what should come first: "Grace must always come before greatness."

Muhammad Zafrulla Khan

Our imperative need is for moral and spiritual values to control the daily increasing stores of power which science is making available to man. The alternative is disaster. For the achievement of this purpose, Islam insists upon firm faith in the unity of God and a clear concept of man's accountability, both here and hereafter, in respect to his conduct.

Sir Muhammad Zafrulla Khan of Pakistan, world-renowned jurist, scholar and international civil servant, serves today as a member and former vice president of the International Court of Justice at The Hague. From 1962 to 1963 he was president of the General Assembly of the United Nations. As foreign minister of Pakistan from 1947 to 1954 he led Pakistan's delegation to the U.N. and represented his government at numerous international conferences.

Zafrulla Khan was born in Sialkot, West Pakistan, on February 6, 1893, and was educated at Government College, Lahore, and at King's College, London. He first practiced law in the Lahore High Court from 1914 to 1935. During this period he also became a member of the Punjab Legislative Council and in 1931 was elected president of the All-India Moslem League. In 1939 Sir Zafrulla headed India's delegation to the Assembly of the League of Nations and from 1941 to 1947 he served as Judge of the Federal Court of India.

Following the independence of Pakistan in 1947, bearded, bespectacled Zafrulla Khan became increasingly helpful to the new nation both at home and abroad. As Pakistan's first minister for foreign affairs, he became especially active in Commonwealth affairs; as chief of Pakistan's first U.N. delegation, he participated in all Assembly sessions and also in the Security Council meetings on the India-Pakistan disputes. In 1961 he was named Pakistan's permanent representative to the U.N. A learned student of the world's great religions and an ardent member of the Ahmadiyyah movement, a missionary branch of Islam, Mr. Khan is the author of *Islam: Its Meaning for Modern Man* and *Islam and Human Rights.*

Islam and the New Era

In November, 1966, I made a special trip from the World Court at The Hague to Washington, D.C., to participate with other religious and cultural representatives in the land dedication ceremony of the Temple of Understanding on the Potomac River. The Temple of Understanding, as its thousands of supporters from every world faith know, is the soon-to-rise, white-marble sanctuary which will symbolize the universal truths of the world's great living religions and provide a serenely beautiful meeting place for their leaders and laity. As both a devout Moslem and a practical Universalist, I felt deeply honored to pay tribute not only to the Temple's long-needed concept of unity underlying diversity but also to the vision of its founder-president, Mrs. Dickerman Hollister of Greenwich, Connecticut.

Men and women of many faiths and cultures gathered together that day in a fellowship of the spirit to witness and participate in the first step toward the fulfillment of a vision vouchsafed to Mrs. Hollister a short while ago. In the welter of today's man-made conflicts which threaten every moment to hurl mankind into the dreaded nuclear holocaust, perhaps it needed the delicacy and penetration of a woman's imagination to grasp the profound truth that man's sole hope centers upon understanding, comprehending and putting into effect the moral and spiritual values which are a true reflection of divine attributes. The pursuit of this great purpose falls within the special domain of religion, and in that domain it is truth alone that counts and has validity. Truth has neither color, nor race, nor blood, nor country, nor nation. Truth is divine, and it is not the monopoly of any, whether of the east or of the west, of the north or of the south. As the Koran states: "To Allah belong the East and the West; whithersoever you turn there is the countenance of Allah. Surely Allah is Omnipresent and All-Comprehending."

All mankind can count itself fortunate that we can now look

forward to the establishment of a center where men and women of faith, vision and wisdom from the corners of the earth may occupy themselves in peace, serenity and the spirit of mutual respect, while fostering the eternal verities, as expounded and set forth in their respective disciplines. Each will carry on his labor of love in complete devotion and utter sincerity, so as to illustrate both by precept and by example the ideals and objectives which he has freely chosen and appointed as his goal. Thus, may those who will have occasion to repair to the Temple's halls and domes seek enrichment of mind and serenity of soul in association with all dedicated servants of God and of humanity.

There are nearly 500,000,000 Moslems today, and most of them recognize that mankind has definitely entered upon a new era. Its outstanding characteristic is the rapid forward march of science and technology. Man's knowledge of, and mastery over, the forces of nature is fast expanding. The prospect ahead is filled with eager hope, but there is also an obverse of fear and dread. All increase of knowledge is an accession of strength and should be welcomed as a divine bounty. The fear results from doubt concerning the application of the vast knowledge to which mankind is becoming heir in daily increasing volume and from apprehension of the almost unlimited power which such knowledge could place in man's hands. Is it possible to ensure that that application will be wholly beneficent in the service of man, so that all fear of misapplication can be eliminated?

Inasmuch as man has been given free choice in these matters, there can be no guarantee, one way or the other, how knowledge and power might be used and applied. It is, however, the province of religion to provide the guidance which will foster beneficence and will at the same time eliminate or reduce to a minimum the fear and dread attendant upon the misapplication of God's bounties.

The imperative need is for moral and spiritual values to control and regulate the application of the daily increasing stores of power which science is making available to man. The alternative is disaster. For the achievement of this purpose, Islam insists upon firm faith in the unity of God and a clear concept of man's accountability, both here and in the hereafter, in respect of his conduct. This would ensure acceptance of divine guidance, and conformity to that guidance would result in righteous action.

Belief in the unity of God means recognition and acceptance of the truth that there is no other being worthy of man's worship and homage. He is the sole and perfect source of all beneficence. Everything else is merely a means which He has created and provided for man's service. He has neither partner nor associate in His Being or in His attributes, and there is none like unto Him. The Koran is very emphatic on that: "He is Allah, the One; Allah, the Independent and Besought of all. He begets not, nor is He begotten, and there is none like unto Him."

The Prophet Mohammed has warned graphically against the trials and tribulations of our present age. When asked about the remedy for such sufferings, he said that it could be found in the opening and concluding verses of the eighteenth chapter of the Koran. The opening verses of that chapter read as follows:

> All praise belongs to Allah Who has sent down the Book to His servant and has not put therein any deviation, He has made it a guardian, that it may give warning of a grievous chastisement from Him, and that it may give those who believe and act righteously the glad tidings that they shall have a good reward wherein they shall abide for ever. . . . So haply thou wilt grieve thyself to death for sorrow after them if they believe not in this discourse. Verily, We have made all that is on the earth as an adornment for it, that We may try them as to which of them is best in conduct, and We shall make all that is thereon a barren waste.

The "grievous chastisement" referred to here may arrive in two stages: "Watch thou for the day when the sky will bring forth a visible smoke that will envelop the people. This will be a painful torment. Then will the people cry: 'Lord, remove from us the torment; truly we are believers.' . . . We shall remove the torment for a little while, but you will certainly revert to your evil courses. On the day when We shall seize you will be the great seizure, then certainly We shall exact retribution."

The true remedy, therefore, for the ills that afflict mankind today and that threaten to overwhelm it tomorrow is for man to turn to God with the single-minded purpose of making his peace with Him, having sincerely determined that in all matters whatsoever his guiding rule shall be: "Thy will and not mine." Truly, mankind stands again on the brink of a pit of fire. God's grace and mercy alone can save it. To win His grace and mercy, mankind must turn to Him alone, the One God, the ever Gracious, the Most Merciful, discarding everything that may ever have been associated with Him, anything that may have displaced Him in men's minds, any being beside Him from whom mankind may at any time have besought protection. There is no other way.

Inasmuch as the indications are that the cataclysm would overtake mankind in consequence of certain causes, the real and effective remedy is the removal of those causes. Once this is done, mankind may be led out of the shadow of the cataclysm into the light. God's purpose is to lead mankind into His grace and mercy. His purpose is not to punish. Misfortunes and calamities follow upon defaults and transgressions, but the gates of God's mercy are ever open, and everyone may enter therein through humble supplication, sincere repentance, and righteous action. Direct communion with God is the spiritual remedy.

God constantly reveals Himself in a new state. All His attributes are manifested continuously. None of them ever falls into disuse. Having revealed Himself as the Creator of nuclear power, He surely could go on to reveal Himself as its guardian and controller, for all is within His power and under His control: "Of Him to beg all that are in the heavens and the earth. Every day He reveals Himself in a different state."

It is only by turning to Him that security may be achieved. He surely has power to inspire the minds of those who are today in control of nuclear power, and are in a position to determine and direct its application, to agree upon measures which would ensure that such power shall be used only for the beneficent service of man, and shall not be employed for his destruction. He also has power to drive away from positions of authority those who continue to resist His will, and to oppose His designs. "Say, O Allah, Lord of Sovereignty, Thou bestowest sovereignty upon whomsoever Thou pleasest; and Thou takest away sovereignty from whomsoever Thou pleasest. Thou exaltest whomsoever Thou pleasest and Thou abasest whomsoever Thou pleasest. In Thy hand is all good. Thou surely hast power to do all things. Thou makest the night pass into the day, and makest the day pass into the night. Thou bringest forth the living from the dead, and bringest forth the dead from the living; and Thou bestowest upon whomsoever Thou pleasest without measure." We must, therefore, turn to Him, to Him alone, the True, the Living, the One God, and humbly beseech Him to make our night pass into day, and to bring us forth alive out of death.

God is mighty and has control and direction over the universe. He causes beneficent results to follow upon human effort which is in accord with His laws. The assurance of the Koran—"a revelation from the Mighty, the One Who blesses human effort with beneficent results"—is a guarantee that the guidance contained therein will not only keep pace with, but will remain ahead of, man's progress in knowledge and science. This guidance proceeds from God's wisdom and is based upon and comprises eternal truth. "The revelation of this Book is from Allah, the Mighty, the Wise. Surely it is We Who have revealed the Book to thee with all truth." God's wisdom has ensured that this guidance shall, in all the contingencies that might arise, prove more than adequate. This follows from God's attributes of perfect power, perfect wisdom, and perfect knowledge.

Pope Paul VI

Blessed are we, if for the Kingdom of God in time and beyond time, we learn to pardon and to struggle on, to work and to serve, to suffer and to love.

Pope Paul VI, slender, ascetic successor to John XXIII and the two hundred fifty-second pontiff in the nineteen-hundred-year history of the Roman Catholic Church, was born Giovanni Battista Montini at Concesio, Italy, on September 26, 1897. The son of a well-to-do Brescia editor and brilliant pupil of the Jesuits and Oratorian Fathers, young Montini became a priest at age twenty-three, a clerk in the Vatican Secretariat at thirty-five and Archbishop of Milan at fifty-seven. From 1936 to 1954, he served in the Secretariat of State as a substitute and pro-secretary under Popes Pius XI and Pius XII.

Now the Vicar of Christ to the world's 500,000,000 Catholics, dark, gentle-voiced Pope Paul has been an ardent scholar, zealous anti-Communist, and observant traveler since he entered the Church. His now famous journeys have taken him from Washington, D.C., to Warsaw and, more recently, from Rome to Jerusalem to Bombay to New York City as supreme pontiff. As humble priest or prince of the Church, the frail yet indefatigable prelate has also been an incessant builder of churches—some seventy alone being built while he was Archbishop of Milan.

The primary purpose and achievement of Pope Paul's apostolic activity has been the continuance of the Vatican Ecumenical Council called by John XXIII. As a result of his skilled, often inspired, leadership of the council's second, third, and fourth sessions, his conciliatory gestures to leaders of both the Christian Orthodox and non-Christian world faiths and his tradition-shattering jet flights to such events as the International Eucharistic Congress in India, the ferment and influence of the Catholic Church have never been at fuller flood tide. Above all today, as it has been the polestar of his forty years of Vatican service, peace and religious unity remain his constant prayer and purpose.

Addressing the sacred college of cardinals on the second anniversary of his pontificate, Pope Paul said: "Like our predecessors, we shall continue to preach peace. We shall continue to work for the Christian peace of Pius XI: the peace of Pius XII based on natural and positive law; the peace of John XXIII rooted in truth, justice, liberty and love. We cannot forget the admonition of Christ, whose Vicar we have been made, 'Let him who is the greatest among you become as the youngest and him who is the chief as the servant.'"

(*The Christian message of His Holiness Pope Paul VI was condensed by the author from his addresses to the sacred college of cardinals and his sermons at the Shrine of Fatima, Portugal, and at Yankee Stadium, New York, New York.*)

Peace on Earth

Our predecessor of glorious memory, Pope John XXIII, in issuing his faith-affirming encyclical, *Peace on Earth,* called all men of good will to "the immense task of restoring the relations of the human family in truth, in justice, in love and in freedom—the relations between individuals, families, intermediate associations and political communities on the one hand and the world community on the other." This is a most exalted task, all will agree, for it is the task of bringing about true peace in the order established by God.

The late beloved pontiff went on to say: "Every believer in this world of ours must be a spark of light, a center of love, a vivifying leaven among his fellow men. And he will be all this the more perfectly, the more closely he lives in communion with God in the intimacy of his own soul. In fact, there can be no peace between men unless there is peace within each one of them—unless, that is, each one builds up within himself the order wished by God. Hence St. Augustine asks: 'Does your soul desire to overcome your lower inclinations? Let it be subject to Him who is on high and it will conquer the lower self: there will be peace in you—true, secure and well-ordered peace. In what does that order consist? God commands the soul; the soul commands the body; and there is nothing more orderly than this.'"

In the first four years of our apostolic activities—as the humble

Vicar of Him whom the prophet called the Prince of Peace—we have expended all our energies to the profound aspiration which we know is shared by all men of good will: the consolidation of peace in the world. These outstanding events, which enable the Church to enter into dialogue with the world in which it exists and labors, included continuation of the Second Vatican Ecumenical Council, the institution of a Secretariat for non-Christians and our pilgrimages of historic stamp to India and the Holy Land, Portugal, Turkey and the United States. These and other similar steps are our way of demonstrating our firm confidence in the all-powerful help of the Lord and in the catholicity of the Church in a period suffused with the spirit of the Council.

For example, in our private reflections we asked ourself why the announcement of these pilgrimages and their subsequent development met with such quick responsiveness and ready approval from all—from the cardinals and the council fathers, from the faithful, from those who, although still separated from this Apostolic See, look to Jesus Christ as the Master and Founder of the one and only Church, and from people belonging to other religious denominations or none at all. It seems that this must be the answer. Our pilgrimages to Palestine and India touched upon and gave concrete expression to a common aspiration toward friendship founded on motives which are quite human, yet at the same time lofty and transcendent.

The religious significance and ecumenical value of journeys to India and Palestine by St. Peter's successor were appreciated by everyone. We were filled with joy and hope by our meetings with Patriarch Athenagoras and the other patriarchs and metropolitans of Eastern Churches—both those which are still united with us and those separated from us. These meetings lent support and encouragement to the movement already under way to establish closer contacts with our separated brothers in a spirit of mutual charity, mutual trust, and better understanding. Hopefully, they represent the prelude to a restoration of unity.

In similar demonstrations of love and respect, we were greeted by the reverent Indian people, by their holy Hindu leaders and by their exalted President Sarvepalli Radhakrishnan. When on one occasion of venerable fraternity, I recited their ancient Vedic prayer, "O Lord, lead us from the unreal to the Real, from darkness to Light, from death to Immortality," we were all near moved to tears.

Now there is need for reflection and work, prayer and study, so that the bright "signs" which have appeared may reach fulfillment; so that the seed sprouting in the once barren soil may blossom forth with the desired fruit.

We shall continue to follow the progress of this complex and difficult question with great spiritual interest, modeling ourself on the spirit of Jesus Christ and remaining faithful to the "depositum" of truths and precepts which He has entrusted to His Church. But we are also prepared to wait patiently and benevolently, until the "hours of God" sound the bells of peace and joy for the Church of the world.

Religion, of its very nature, is a relationship between God and man. Prayer expresses such a relationship in dialogue. Revelation, i.e., the supernatural relationship which God Himself, on His own initiative, has established with the human race, can be represented as a dialogue in which the Word of God is expressed in the Incarnation and, therefore, in the Gospel and in the Church.

Our first intention is for the Church, the Church, one, holy, catholic and apostolic. The Ecumenical Council has revitalized the heart of the Church, has opened up new vistas in the field of doctrine, has called all her children to a greater awareness, to a more intimate collaboration, to a more fervent apostolate.

What terrible damage could be provoked by arbitrary interpretations, not authorized by the teaching of the Church, disrupting its traditional and constitutional structure, replacing the theology of the true and great fathers of the Church with new and peculiar ideologies, interpretation intent upon stripping the norms of faith of that which modern thought, often lacking rational judgment, doesn't understand and doesn't like.

What a delusion our efforts to arrive at universal unity would suffer, if we fail to offer to our Christian brethren, at this moment divded from us, and to the rest of humanity which lacks our faith in its clear-cut authenticity and in its original beauty, the patrimony of truth and of charity, of which the Church is the guardian and the dispenser.

We want to ask of Mary a living church, a true church, a united church, a holy church.

We want to pray together in order that the aspiration and efforts of the Council may find fulfillment through the fruits of the Holy

Spirit, the font of the true Christian life, whom the Church celebrates at the feast of Pentecost.

These fruits are enumerated by the Apostle Paul: "love, faithfulness, joy, peace, patience, kindness, goodness, gentleness and self-control."

We want to pray that the love of God now and forever reign in the world, that His laws guide the conscience and customs of modern man. Faith in God is the supreme light of humanity, and this light not only must never be extinguished in the hearts of men, but must renew itself through the stimulus which comes from science and progress.

This thought, which strengthens and stimulates our prayer, brings us to reflect, at this moment, on those nations in which religious liberty is almost totally suppressed, and where the negation of God is promulgated as representative of the truth of these times and the liberation of the people, whereas this is not so. We pray for such nations, we pray for the faithful of these nations, that the intimate strength of God may sustain them and that true civil liberty be conceded to them once more.

You know that the world is in a phase of great transformation due to the enormous and marvelous progress in the knowledge and in the conquest of the earth and of the universe. But you can easily see that the world is not happy, is not tranquil, and that the first cause of its uneasiness is its difficulty in entering into harmonious relationship, its difficulty in following the paths of peace. Everything seems to lead the world to brotherhood, to unity, but instead the heart of mankind still bursts with tremendous, continuous conflict.

Two conditions, therefore, render difficult this historic situation of mankind: it is full of tremendously deadly armament, and it has not morally progressed as much as it has scientifically and technically.

Moreover, a great part of humanity is still in a state of need and of hunger, while it has been awakened to the disturbing consciousness of its own need and the well-being which surrounds it.

Therefore, we say, the world is in danger. For this reason we have come to the feet of the Queen of Peace to ask her for the gift, which only God can give, of peace. Yes, peace, a gift of God which supposes His intervention, divine, good, merciful and mysterious. But it is not always a miraculous gift. It is a gift which works its wonders in the hearts of men; a gift, therefore, which has need of free acceptance and of free collaboration. I call upon all men to strive to be worthy of the divine gift of peace. Be true to yourselves, be good, wise, open to the common good of the world.

Be magnanimous. Try to see your dignity and your interests not as contrary to but as conformable to the dignity and the interests of others. Do not contemplate projects of destruction and of death, of revolution and of suppression, but think rather of projects of mutual strengthening and of solid collaboration.

Think of the gravity and of the grandeur of this hour, which can be decisive for the history of the present and of the future generations, and begin to approach each other with thoughts of building a new world; yes, the world of true men, a world which can never be without the light of God on its horizons.

Listen to our humble and trembling voice, weigh our words which echo the words of Christ: "Blessed are the meek, for they will possess the earth. Blessed are the peaceful, for they shall be called the children of God."

Behold, my brothers and children, who listen in this hour, behold the immense and dramatic picture which the world and its destinies presents to us. It is the picture which Our Lady opens up before us, the picture which we contemplate with frightened eyes, but ever-trusting knowledge, the picture to which we ever draw near and to which we pledge ourselves, following the counsel which Our Lady gave us, that of prayer and of penance and which God desires, that this picture of the world shall never again have to face wars, tragedies, and catastrophes, but the conquest of love and the victory of peace.

So, in the paper, iron and concrete heart of modern man, the throbbing of human sympathy, of pure and generous affection, of poetry, of things that are fundamental and alive, of love and charity must be reawakened through religion. Christ in His Gospel has spelled out for the world the supreme motive and the noblest driving force for action and hence for liberty and progress: love. The only sound law of life is His Gospel. No one can surpass it, nor can anyone subdue or supplant it. The human person reaches his highest level in Christ's teaching. Human society finds therein its most congenial and powerful unifying force. As St. Paul has told us: "May Christ find a dwelling place through faith in your hearts."

We believe, O Lord, in Thy word; we will try to follow and live it. Now we hear its echo reverberating in the souls of the men of our century. It seems to tell us: Blessed are we, if in poverty of spirit we learn to free ourselves from false confidence in material things and to place our chief desires in spiritual and religious goods, treating the poor with respect and love as brothers and living images of Christ.

Blessed are we if, having acquired the meekness of the strong, we learn how to renounce the perverse power of hate and vengeance. Then we shall have the wisdom of preferring to the fear of armed force, the generosity of forgiveness, the alliance between freedom and work, and conquest through goodness and peace.

Blessed are we, if we do not make egoism the guiding criterion of our life, nor pleasure its purpose, but learn rather to discover in sobriety our strength, in pain a source of redemption, in sacrifice the very summit of greatness.

Blessed are we, if we prefer to be oppressed rather than be the oppressors and constantly hunger for the progress of justice.

Blessed are we, if for the kingdom of God in time and beyond time we learn to pardon and to struggle on, to work and to serve, to suffer and to love.

Nelson A. Rockefeller

The power of love must ultimately triumph in the hearts of God's children.

Nelson A. Rockefeller, thrice elected governor of New York by more than one-half million votes, is the Empire State's forty-ninth chief executive. Under the Rockefeller administration, New York has achieved remarkable gains in the fields of social welfare, public health, government reorganization, business-labor relations, capital-labor relations, industrial expansion, encouragement of the arts, and construction of such highly-praised new institutions as the State University of New York and the State Capitol Government Center at Albany.

Governor Rockefeller was born in 1908 at Bar Harbor, Maine, the third of six children of John D. Rockefeller, Jr., and Abby Aldrich Rockefeller. He is the grandson of the founder of the Standard Oil Company and various Rockefeller philanthropic foundations. Although his service in New York State did not begin until 1956, he has been active in federal government activities for almost thirty years.

In 1940, for example, President Roosevelt appointed him Coordinator of Inter-American Affairs. In 1944–1945 he served as Assistant Secretary of State for American Republic Affairs. In 1950 President Truman named him chairman of the newly created International Development Advisory Board. Among his responsible positions under President Eisenhower were chairman of the President's Advisory Committee on Government Organization; Under Secretary of the Department of Health, Education, and Welfare; and Special Assistant to the President for Foreign Affairs. Mr. Rockefeller's distinguished career has also been marked by his support of countless church, charity, and scientific-educational projects throughout the world.

A Mission of Love

In a speech before the Methodist bishops of New York several years ago, I said that my father, the late John D. Rockefeller, Jr., translated his Christian faith into a personal credo. That credo, to which I subscribe 100 per cent, is as follows:

I believe in the supreme worth of the individual and in his right to life, liberty, and the pursuit of happiness.

I believe that every right implies a responsibility; every opportunity, an obligation; every possession, a duty.

I believe that the law was made for man and not man for the law; that government is the servant of the people and not their master.

I believe in the dignity of labor, whether with head or hand; that the world owes no man a living, but that it owes every man an opportunity to make a living.

I believe that thrift is essential to well-ordered living and that economy is a prime requisite of a sound financial structure, whether in government, business or personal affairs.

I believe that truth and justice are fundamental to an enduring social order.

I believe in the sacredness of a promise, that a man's word should be as good as his bond, that character—not wealth or power or position—is of supreme worth.

I believe that the rendering of useful service is the common duty of mankind, and that only in the purifying fire of sacrifice is the cross of selfishness consumed and the greatness of the human soul set free.

I believe in an all-wise and all-loving God, named by whatever name, and that the individual's highest fulfillment, greatest happiness, and widest usefulness are to be found in living in harmony with His will.

I believe that love is the greatest thing in the world; that it alone can overcome hate; that right can and will triumph over might.

Throughout my own life, these words of my father have been an inspiration—and a challenge. I can find nothing in this statement that I would alter now. For while these are words of personal conviction, they spring from the ancient Judaeo-Christian ethic that has uplifted mankind through the centuries—and is the moral and spiritual basis on which this nation was founded.

It is well to remind ourselves today of this moral base, to draw strength from the wellsprings of our spiritual heritage, as we contemplate the unfinished business of our civilization. And of this unfinished business, nothing is more crucial or fundamental than the final and permanent assurance that our professions of man's equality shall truly have full meaning for every American. For this nation, under God, was founded on and draws its sustenance from the concept of the worth of the individual and the brotherhood of man; indeed, at a time when the strength and endurance of fundamental human values are being tested throughout the free world, it is appropriate and desirable to rededicate ourselves to the dignity and rights of the individual.

As Abraham Lincolin said: "I hold that while man exists, it is his duty to improve not only his own condition but to assist in ameliorating mankind. . . . Let us at all times remember that all American citizens are brothers of a common country. . . ."

As descendants of various races and religions upon whom have fallen the cruel and indefensible blows of ancient prejudice, many know whereof I speak. Yet in our daily lives, we see that the power of law grows steadily stronger in ameliorating these wrongs; we see that the power of persuasion grows ever affirmative; and we know that the power of love must ultimately triumph in the hearts of God's children.

Ours, then, is a mission of love in which all who believe as our forefathers believed, who believe as my father believed, will make common cause.

His Majesty King Mahendra

As a devout Hindu, I know that to gain heaven or hell lies within our own heart and action. Under Nepal's system of partyless democracy the country belongs to all of us, and so it is the responsibility of all of us to take her to the pinnacles of progress and prosperity.

His Majesty King Mahendra Bir Bikrani Shah Deva, forty-eight, light and leader of modern Nepal, has been sovereign of the independent Himalayan kingdom located between China and India since 1955. Under his enlightened rule two five-year economic plans have been carried out, a National Panchayat system of partyless democracy instituted and his nation of twelve million people firmly bound to the world community through membership in the United Nations. The result: a successful royal crusade for reconstruction of his once isolated and stagnant country so "that the will of the people shall, both in legislation and policy, prevail."

King Mahendra was born in Katmandu at the Naran-hiti Palace on June 11, 1920. The son of His Majesty King Tribhuvan, he was trained in the arts of statecraft, brought up in Nepal's official Hindu religion and was married in 1940 to Her Royal Highness Indra Rajya Laxmi Debi Shah who died suddenly a decade later. His marriage to the present Queen Ratna Rajya Lakshmi Debi Shah was solemnized on December 10, 1952, and His Majesty has three sons and three daughters from his late consort.

His Majesty ascended to the throne at a critical period in Nepal's history, soon after the downfall of the Rana regime of hereditary prime ministers in 1951. The revolution was blessed by King Tribhuvan, who granted an interim constitution to the people of Nepal. It was, however, left to King Mahendra to grant the Constitution of 1959, under which nationwide elections were held on the basis of adult franchise, irrespective of race, creed, caste and sex. This was a unique event in the nation's history. The Constitution of 1959, however, had to be withdrawn in 1960 when widespread dissatisfaction was felt in the country with the system of political parties. Hence in December, 1962, another constitution was granted by the King. Under the new system of panchayat democracy, representatives to the one-chamber

National Panchayat (Parliament) are elected through three levels of panchayats respectively at the village, district and the zonal levels. A council of ministers under a chairman is appointed by the King from among the members of the National Panchayat.

Under King Mahendra's rule, Nepal has taken vigorous measures for national economic and social development. Notable progress has been made during the five-year plans in improving transport, communications and education. Nepal has also expanded her foreign and international relations under King Mahendra. Thus Nepal became a full-fledged member of the United Nations in 1955 and has also established diplomatic relations with more than forty countries. Nepal's foreign policy is one of nonalignment. King Mahendra, for example, attended the Belgrade Conference of Non-Aligned States, and has made state visits to India, Ceylon, Chinese People's Republic, Japan, Burma, Pakistan, the U.S.S.R., U.S.A., Israel, and Federal Republic of Germany.

The Kingdom of Sky and Spirit

Nepal is an ancient Hindu nation, and as its king I am by tradition and choice a devout Hindu. Like 500,000,000 other Hindus, I believe in the one Eternal Spirit called Brahman and I believe in the one God's omnipresent trinity, Brahma the Creator, Vishnu the Preserver and Shiva the Destroyer. I believe in—and try to emulate—in my own life the Hindu virtues of self-control, detachment, truthfulness, nonviolence, charity and compassion toward all living creatures. To me, Hinduism is a religion of life, color and joyful feelings which has as its sublime purpose union with God.

Hinduism is the religion of unity, the essential and eventual unity of God and man. Hinduism is the religion of one God and 330,000,000 separate deities or infinite aspects of the Absolute. Hinduism, as my friend President S. Radhakrishnan of India has pointed out, requires every man to think steadily on life's mysteries until he reaches the highest revelation. Hinduism, thus, becomes a universal fellowship that embraces all who accept the law of right, love their fellow men and earnestly seek the truth.

According to Hindu belief, man is the most intelligent and

dynamic creature in the world. He is always moving ahead because constant progress is inherent in his nature. Being zealous for progress, he had been continually opening up new avenues to achieve it in ever-growing degrees. If all the political systems such as autocracy, democracy, monarchy, republicanism, panchayat democracy and the like are the ways and means devised by him at different times and in different climes with a view to achieving complete material happiness, the different religious systems such as Hinduism, Buddhism, Mohammedanism, Christianity and the like are the manifestations of his conscious efforts toward spiritual growth. The test of the superiority of man lies in making the right effort in the right direction in the wilderness of such opposing social systems in order to make a royal road to the goal of all-around well-being. He does not like to go astray by confounding the end with the means, nor does he want to make a wild-goose chase hankering after the impossible things in a foolish way.

"Better late than never" is a saying based on profound human experience, and it is but human nature to mend ways sooner or later when mistakes are realized and make a fresh start again and again with added zeal. This aspect of human life is a very common phenomenon. By dint of this noble virtue, man ever succeeds in achieving higher things in life and leaves footprints on the sands of time for others to follow in. Every student of biology knows that many species of the living things of the past, being unable to adapt themselves to their changed environments, have long since become extinct, and they are remembered at present for their archaeological interest alone. But man is a progressive creature, and nature has made him so.

It deserves repetition here that man can be misled for some time on his march to progress, but sooner or later he realizes his mistakes, gallantly confesses them and veers around to the right course with good grace. This is the difference we find between a man and a superman. This habit of confessing one's weaknesses ennobles the life of a common man, lends him the distinction of being a superman and exalts him to the state of being the man of his age. Rama, Krishna, Buddha, Christ, Mohammed, King Prithivi Narayan Shah, Mahatma Gandhi and a host of others were such supermen. They were fully conversant with the popular feelings of their times, and properly guided them. They were never confused in their objectives. On the other hand, they were ever ready to own their shortcomings, and were resolute in their nobler aims. By way of an example, we can cite an anecdote from the life of Lord Buddha.

In his search for truth, Lord Buddha had at first taken recourse to self-imposed bodily chastisement through voluntary starvation and other penitential exercises, but in due course of time he realized its futility. A mistake was a mistake for him, and he immediately switched over to the simpler and surer method. But this act of his was wrongly interpreted as a sign of fickleness of his character, and thinking him to be only a pretender and imposter, his followers gave up his company. But Lord Buddha never lost sight of his noble objective, went on persevering unswervingly and achieved ultimately the world-resounding success in his altruistic quest of truth. If even after the realization of the futility of his first chosen method, he had stuck to it laboring under the false notion of prestige and fought shy of his followers' criticisms, he would never have achieved any success in his quest; and he would have gone down in history not as the man of his age but as a prince of Kapilavastu only, which he was by birth. Thus the life of Lord Buddha serves as a case history to show that a superman is always willing to admit his failings and discard the unavailing methods in favor of a rational one, and thereby succeeds in leading his generation to the realm of greater light and glory.

Nepal and her king were also confronted with a similar situation toward the close of the year 1960. After the revolutionary change-over of 1951, the Nepalese people were expecting to see the Nepal of their dreams come true under the parliamentary system of government. But even the first democratically elected government of the country failed to deliver the goods. Lawlessness became rampant; looting, arson and murder became the order of the day. Reservoirs and cooling tanks in the country became dumping grounds for the dead bodies of the murdered people. Anarchy was thus reigning supreme from one end of the country to the other. The people of Nepal were savagely disillusioned. The parliamentary system imported from abroad proved to be incompatible with the genius of the Nepalese people. So, in keeping with the spirit of their illustrious ancestors, the nation took a firm step on December 15, 1960, conveying, in unequivocal terms, its determination to achieve its noble objectives of fuller life and wider democracy without undue attachment to the means adopted and found wanting. It was at this time that I initiated in this country the system of panchayat democracy.

Like other countries of Asia and Africa, the problem before Nepal is to telescope within ten or twenty years the progress achieved by other advanced countries of the world in the course of a century or two. This is a problem which cannot be solved without the unified, wholehearted and enthusiastic support and cooperation of the people. And it can no longer be hoped or expected that the people line up with the government, unless they are satisfied that they are in an effective position to express their will and have it carried into effect.

The key to the solution of the problem has been the adoption of the panchayat system. It is a system rooted deep in our historical environment. It constitutes, indeed, a growth, a continuous growth from the time before history was written. Pancha is a mystic number in the legend and literature of Nepal. We speak of Pancha Tattwa, the five constituent elements of the mortal frame; Pancha Indriya, the five terminals of sensation; Pancha Sheela, the five principles of right conduct; Pancha Amrita, the five nectars of votive offering to Shiva; Pancha Rakshya, the five lines of defense against evil; Pancha Bhaladmi, the five persons of genteel birth and upbringing; Sri Pancha, which is variously translated as five times godly or five times gracious.

The panchayat system is pre-eminently suited to foster national unity and whip up public participation on a massive scale in all nation-building efforts from the village upward. Immune from the artificial dichotomy which party government presupposes, the panchayat system provides the structural basis for the evolution of a new national philosophy. The panchayat philosophy's main points may be summarized as follows:

(a) Political equality is the birthright of every citizen.
(b) Economic freedom is the *sine qua non* of individual and collective development.
(c) Individual liberty and dignity of man are at the bottom of our humanistic culture, religion and tradition.

The political aims of the system are to secure the foundation of a democratic system based on and developed from the grass roots, which will ensure and promote the country's nationalism and sovereignty in keeping with the desires and sentiments of the people.

In my fourteen years on the ancient Nepalese throne, I have tried to open the doors of opportunity for our people and to bring about a revolutionary transformation in their lives. Under Nepal's pattern of partyless democracy the country belongs to all of us, and so it is the responsibility of all of us to take her to the pinnacles of progress and prosperity. As a devout Hindu I know that "to gain heaven or hell lies within our own heart and action" and that "to attain the sum of true righteousness, treat others as thou would'st thyself be treated," and finally the "virtue" is spotlessness of mind, all else is mere noise." So humbly we have tried to do.

In conclusion, may I repeat the benediction that Hindus use at the end of many public events and recitals of such epics as the Bhagavad-Gita: "May there be just welfare for the people; may rulers follow the righteous path and protect the world; may there always be good to cows, people and Brahmins; may the entire universe be happy."

Dana McLean Greeley

*The liberal religious vision involves three major elements
—faith, freedom and fellowship. They are the parts of
what the Unitarian prophet William Ellery Channing
called the "one sublime idea" of the dignity of man
under the fatherhood of God.*

Born and bred to liberal Christianity and a world view, the Reverend
Dr. Dana McLean Greeley serves as the first president of the Unitarian Universalist Association. He was elected in May, 1961, at the
time of the formal merger of the Universalist Church of America and
the American Unitarian Association, and was re-elected by the U. U. A.'s
Fourth General Assembly in 1965. Today Dr. Greeley is giving the
unified, swiftly-expanding cause of liberal religion a crusading zeal it
has lacked for decades. He led the Unitarians and Universalists in
their 1968 international observance of the four-hundredth anniversary
of the first proclamation of religious liberty by King John Sigismund of
Hungary, and twice in two years joined a group of religious leaders
in Vietnam in seeking to reduce the terrors and tensions of war.

Dana Greeley was born in Boston and educated at Harvard College
and Harvard Divinity School. His father, a prominent New England
architect, served both as president of the Unitarian Laymen's League
and moderator of the American Unitarian Association, and young Greeley began his ecclesiastical career as president of the Young People's
Religious Union. Before assuming the pulpit of Boston's famed Arlington Street Church in 1935, he held pastorates in Lincoln, Massachusetts, and Concord, New Hampshire. During his twenty-three-year
pastorate at the Arlington Street Church, he also found time to fill
such significant positions as secretary of the American Unitarian Association and president of the Unitarian Service Committee.

Dr. Greeley, who is a leader in civic as well as religious affairs,
was president of the American Unitarian Association before merger
with the Universalists. He also is a past president of the Massachusetts
Council of Churches, the Harvard Divinity School Alumni Association
and the New England Citizen's Crime Commission and serves on the
board of United World Federalists, the Planned Parenthood Federation,
and the Institute on Religion in an Age of Science. His books include
Toward Larger Living and *A Message to Atheists*. Dr. Greeley is married, and his daughter, Faith, is married to the Rev. Carl R. Scovel.

One Sublime Idea

A people without vision will surely perish. We need that vision, and we must not perish. G. K. Chesterton once said that if we only had more visionaries among our statesmen, we might get something really practical done. It is practical to have a dream and then to make that dream come true; and without a dream we have nothing to contribute to our society. It is certainly not practical only to see things and to do things as they have always been seen and done in the past. John on Patmos said, "I saw a new heaven and a new earth, for the first heaven and the first earth were passed away." We need to see a new America and a new world, for the first America and the old world are passing away right in front of our eyes. A century ago George Ripley and the Transcendentalists from Boston had their dream, and they went out to West Roxbury and established Brooke Farm as a noble experiment. They had their own socialist community and their own ideal life. Our Brooke Farm today, however, cannot be on a few acres of land removed from the city; it must be where the people are and must relate to the whole of our modern civilization.

Alfred North Whitehead's definition of religion was that it is the vision of that which is beyond and behind and within the passing flux of immediate things. So, we must have our vision and see a new earth and create in our midst our ideal community. The church is not primarily an institution, and the Unitarian-Universalist free faith is not basically an organization or an association; it is a vision. It is a vision of man and of all of his capacities and infinite worth. It is a vision of God as the creator and source of all life, the God of the ever-expanding and infinitely vast cosmos of ours, and the God of the flower in the crannied wall. It is a vision of the future which must unfold from the present, a vision in which we should place our confidence and a vision for which we should dedicate our energies. It is a vision of the New Jerusalem, or the crowning glory of a great culture.

This liberal religious vision, more specifically, involves three values or major elements in our major religious experiences and idealism: *faith, freedom, fellowship.* They are old words, but they are everlasting words. They are the three parts of what our American Unitarian prophet William Ellery Channing called the "one sublime idea" of the dignity of man under the fatherhood of God.

Faith is the first value. It need not be negative or iconoclastic but can be affirmative. Our liberal faith is a larger faith, not a smaller one. It is more dynamic, not static. It is enlightened and not blind. It is personal and not ecclesiastical. Francis David said four hundred years ago in old Transylvania, when Unitarianism was born there, that "faith is a gift of God," because he believed that we need no intermediaries between ourselves and God and that faith is not ecclesiastical or dogmatic. Jeremiah, in the days of the Hebrew prophets, said, "I will make a new covenant with you, not according to the covenant of old. I will put my law in your inward parts and write it in your hearts, and you shall teach no more every man his nature and every man his brother saying, 'know the Lord,' for they shall all know me, from the least of them unto the greatest of them." Our own prophet, Ralph Waldo Emerson, said very much the same thing in different words: "Trust yourself, every heart vibrates to that iron string." "Faith is a star," as the modern religious writer Roland Gammon has so beautifully illustrated in his book of that title, and it is a bold propeller and an inspiration.

The second value is freedom. I believe in freedom as against predestination. I believe in freedom as against the domination of the individual by society or the enslavement of the individual by society; and I believe in freedom as against one's own appetites and selfishness. Channing said, "I call that mind free which controls the animal appetites and directs its own destiny." Goethe said, "Great men create circumstances even more than circumstances create great men," or that we can shape our world as much as our world shapes us or prove ourselves in some respects to be stronger than the influence of our environment upon us. The great president of Bowdoin College, William DeWitt Hyde, wrote a hymn that Unitarians and Universalists love to sing together: "Since what we choose is what we are and what we love we yet shall be, the goal may ever shine afar, the will to win it makes us free." I believe in freedom for every man, not just for some, or not just for any segment or segments of the human race.

The third value is fellowship—faith, freedom, and fellowship. Independence is a great virtue, but interdependence is an even greater virtue. No man is an island. No church is an island, and no denomination is an island; and no country and no race is an island. New nations today have to achieve their independence and their identity. Hippies are experiencing the same need, as are many blacks; but there is a greater need for the sense of togetherness and for the spirit of love. This means a commitment for fellowship or for interdependence. The great Universalist Hosea Ballou preached the gospel of love in a time when Calvinism was holding this country in an almost iron grip. He believed in a God of love; nothing else can do us any good; and, if we have love, nothing else can do us any harm. Hammurabi, way back before the time of Christ—two thousand years before—gave to the people a new code in which he talked about even justice: "An eye for an eye and a tooth for a tooth and a life for a life." But then the generations and the centuries and even two millennia went by; and Moses liberated his people and led them across the wilderness and received for them two tablets, including a new commandment which said in the language of a prohibition, "Thou shalt not kill." The generation and the centuries went by again, and the Son of a Hebrew carpenter grew up to be what we often think of as the greatest teacher in the history of man. He did not speak of an eye for an eye and a tooth for a tooth; and he did not even phrase his commandment in negative or prohibitory fashion. He said, "Thou shalt love thy neighbor—and thine enemy—as thyself. Thou shalt overcome evil with good." It is a hard law to learn, but I believe we have to learn the art or the law of nonviolence and that it will someday represent the real maturity of man. We do not overcome hate with more hate, but we do overcome hate with love. We must promote fellowship and mutuality of spirit, or brotherhood and love in action. This is mutuality and understanding of one God—and it should exist among all the nations and among all the races of mankind.

Konrad Adenauer

Music, painting, flowers and the practice of a simple Catholic faith have always been private passions of mine.

When Konrad Adenauer, ninety, died in 1966 after fifteen years as chancellor of postwar Germany, he was justly regarded as one of the greatest Germans and one of the greatest Europeans of his time. Founder and shaper of the Federal Republic of Germany, the former mayor of Cologne took over the fatherland at age seventy-three, and in four terms as chief of state led a defeated and despised nation into "the Christian world of the West."

A Rhinelander, a Catholic and a patient pragmatist who was never a soldier, "Der Alte" more than any other German helped turn a nation with little talent for democracy into a functioning parliamentary society. With an extraordinary combination of moral fervor and political acumen, Adenauer revived a shattered Germany both spiritually and economically. He clamped total civilian control on the militarists who had launched five aggressive wars in a century. He became an enthusiastic ally of the West, refusing recognition of East Germany, negotiating a Franco-German treaty, binding West Germany firmly to NATO and the European Common Market.

Konrad Adenauer, for so long the unshakable spokesman of postwar pacifist Germany, began his political career fifty-five years ago as a city official in Cologne. Only after the end of World War II did he attain sufficient prominence to help organize the Christian Democratic Union, a broad people's party composed of workers and industrialists, farmers and craftsmen, Catholics and Protestants. In 1949, under his leadership, the Federal Republic was founded, and he began his still-unrealized drive to reunite Germany. Throughout his distinguished career, Adenauer's philosophy of action and his legacy of achievement emerged logically from a Catholic upbringing rooted in God and conserving of the precious cultural and moral values of the past. Today that a prosperous peaceful Germany moves steadily nearer that ideal is the supreme achievement of their esteemed "Old Man."

Inner Order and Outer Peace

The Holy Night is over. The lights on the Christmas tree are out, the revelry of the New Year is spent. There is stillness all around me. I sit by my home altar alone and quiet. Thoughts and pictures come to my mind, partly the thoughts and pictures from many years ago, thoughts from the years before 1914 when there was real peace, quiet and security on this earth—a time when we didn't know fear. My thoughts wander: the First World War, the first German defeat, the inflation, the slow recovery. All this comes back to me. And again my thoughts wander to the 1930s, the years without freedom, the depressing years of unrestricted nationalism, the drive to power and despotism, the years of the Second World War, the years of death and destruction, the years when fear increasingly gripped mankind.

Then a newer period comes to mind, the postwar time of rebuilding the nation, rebuilding the cultural and political life, rebuilding the economy. But for most men and women, the fear remains and it grows. Security and quiet have disappeared from the lives of men since 1914. And peace? Since 1914, the Germans have not known real peace nor has much of mankind. How many people now living in the world have known a life without fear, a life in peace and security? Before 1914 it was taken for granted, so much so that we did not recognize the value of it or know how to appreciate it.

Isn't it sad, isn't it terrible to think that the majority of the people now living never knew a life free from fear, a life of quiet, peace and security? A long and deep darkness lay over the centuries, a long and deep darkness that was lightened only sparingly and occasionally by God's mercy. But, in spite of it, mankind never gave up the hope that someday a wise power, a power coming from godliness, would shatter the darkness and overcome it. Then came Bethlehem. The Child that would deliver mankind was born in a stall and laid in a cradle by Mary, his mother. The light of the angel led the shepherds to the stall; they kneeled before the Holy One and prayed to Him. The star led the wise men from the Orient to the manger and they gave Him gifts. What wonder! How deep into the history of mankind this event went, this miracle that led mankind to a higher stage of development.

But man is an enigmatic creature. How often he acts against his own better judgment, ignores the truth and the good and commits acts against God. Thus, in the end, it is religion alone that can save men and nations. That is why I tried to infuse the reconstruction of Germany with the Christian spirit. That is why in organizing the Christian Democratic Union in 1945 I asked for an alliance between Catholic and Protestant churches to struggle jointly for the practical realization of Christian principles in public life. I have become firmly convinced that henceforth nations must be governed by godly principles or they shall perish.

All of us, who are involved in the bustling activities of day-to-day living—in business, pleasure, travel, in the hustle and bustle of modern society—must deliberately find time to exercise the power of reflection that we so sorely need today. Rather than despair of oneself, each one should cultivate the society of the self. Music, painting, flowers and the practice of a simple Catholic faith have always been private passions of mine. Today, at this turning point of history, we need more than ever to reflect about ourselves, to work for peace, to consider how the spiritual and aesthetic values of the past can be most usefully applied to the present.

Tomorrow is built upon today, that is true. But today and to-morrow are based on yesterday. Nothing in the world can set this truth aside. All of us ought to reflect about ourselves, also about what lies in the past as well as in the future. Thus, we should evaluate our inner development. Only he leads a conscious life—a life worthy of being called human—who becomes aware of himself. If one does not reflect, one gives up one's own personality and there-fore one's self; then one begins to drift back and forth somewhat like a leaf, aimless and blown by the wind.

Our critical century certainly contains the good and the beautiful, honest effort and honest work. But something seems to have be-come rare among us, something without which a human being doesn't really live. Something has disappeared in us which most people had in the past—the inner order. This is what I think of when I speak of the values of the past. If inner order or equilibrium is missing, so is our inner strength, ease, quiet and contentment.

I am the last person to live in the past and to see only good in it. Mankind must think and move forward constantly and untiringly. My father instilled that in me from my earliest youth, and nowadays parents ought to tell their children this too. But men also must see the danger of their time, the time in which we have been placed on earth, and preserve from the past that which is good. The inner order belongs to the good things of the past. Many people developed this spiritual quality and it gave them the firmness, endurance and inner seriousness that enabled them to endure even in confusing and uncertain times.

Are you now asking yourself what I really mean by inner order? I will try to answer in a sentence: he who can distinguish between good and evil and is absolutely determined to remain loyal to the good has inner order. Much work on oneself and much exercise of will power against bad influences that come both from within and without is needed. Yet, if we do not have inner order, neither acquisition nor enjoyment nor outward success can help us come to inner harmony and with it the attainment of the greatest happiness this life can offer us.

The struggles which have shaken the world during recent years cannot be compared to the wars of nations during past centuries. Those wars aimed almost invariably at the extension of areas of national sovereignty. I don't think the future will see much of that type of war. The great struggles of our time are not concerned with territorial dominion but with the clash of different and opposed ways of life—between democracy, which is ultimately founded upon the Christian concept of individual freedom, and a materialistic conception of the world in which the freedom of the individual is subordinated to a collective whole. These collectivist concepts, whether they are called National Socialism or Communism, are invariably rooted in materialism and therefore must inevitably lead to the totalitarian state.

This struggle has now spread over the entire globe. Europe, and in particular Germany, are placed at the focal point of this conflict. It is a struggle which will continue for many more years, and in my view the world will not finally achieve peace and freedom unless the concept based on Christian principles emerges victorious. Thus, the continuing world conflict today is essentially a conflict between Christianity and Communism.

The modern technical world in which we live, with its cinemas, radio and television, favors development toward a mass society, and this "mass man" will always incline toward materialism. To counterbalance this we need, in all countries, Christian parties which penetrate not only political, social and economic life with a Christian spirit, but, over and above that, aim at creating the essential conditions for a Christian existence of the individual.

Among these essential conditions are a modest measure of property which will relieve the working man of his fear of starvation and misery; an adequate home for the family where the children can grow up in healthy surroundings, in fresh air, light, sunshine and enough space to move in; sufficient leisure and free time: for any true personality needs calm, exercise and rest in order to develop. And, above all, there must be a Christian education of the young.

For the great world struggle between Christianity and materialism is being fought out today in the soul of youth. Unless we succeed in persuading the individual young person to conceive of himself as a Christian personality, with a duty to account for his life to God, we shall have worked in vain.

"Glory to God on high and peace for all men of good will." It is not without reason that this glorious phrase provides the central theme of Christmas. It is not without reason that the paean, "glory to God," comes before the words of peace. Peace is only willed us, peace can only be given us, when we first give glory to God; then inner peace comes to each of us, peace for all of us everywhere. I think that all of us think too little of this truth—that first God deserves to be worshiped. All of us, no matter who we are or what we do, must first honor Him in order that there will be peace for all of us.

In history there are periods of desperate darkness, unrest, disturbance, fear. But again and again the human mind, the human soul has struggled through to light and peace. In truth, there is something wonderful in the strength and the power of the mind and the soul. The human mind and the human soul is not to be defeated because they come from God. Therefore, we must not fail. We must not become discouraged when we think of the things we have lived through and the darkness into which we came. Let us think of the Child in the manger who brought God's Word to man. Let us think of the shining angel; let us think of the star that led the wise men to Him. Let us think of the divine message that Christ brought to us, the Word and the light that He forever brings to our poor humanity.

Glory be to God in the highest! We must worship God each one of us and then the prophecy of the angel will come true: Peace on earth, good will to men!

Linus Pauling

*I believe that there is a greater power in the world than
the evil power of military force, of nuclear bombs—
there is the power of good, of morality, of humanitari-
anism.*

Dr. Linus Pauling, winner of Nobel Prizes for both Chemistry
and Peace and for forty-two years a professor at the California Institute
of Technology, became world-famous as "the chemist's chemist" because
of his pioneering research in the structure and behavior of proteins.
Now a resident fellow at the Center for the Study of Democratic
Institutions in Santa Barbara, California, he divides his scholarly efforts
among the three fields of principal interest to him—science, medicine
and world peace. Among his scores of honorary degrees, prizes and
medals are the 1961 Humanist Award of the Year and the Presidential
Medal for Merit for his scientific contributions in World War II.

Dr. Pauling's early researches were centered about the problem of the
structure of molecules and crystals and the nature of the chemical bond.
For this work he was awarded the Nobel Prize for Chemistry for the
year 1954. In 1934 he and his co-workers began a series of experimental
and theoretical researches in molecular biology and medicine, which in
the course of time encompassed the magnetic properties of hemoglobin,
the three-dimensional structure of protein molecules, the structure of
antibodies and the nature of serological reactions, and the discovery of the
abnormal human hemoglobins that are related to certain diseases.

Dr. Pauling's work to abolish war began in 1945, immediately after
the use of atomic bombs at Hiroshima and Nagasaki, with a series of
public lectures about the nature of nuclear weapons and nuclear war. It
was intensified in 1946, when he became associated with Albert Einstein
and seven other scientists in the Emergency Committee of Atomic
Scientists. During recent years his work for world peace has for the
most part been carried out in collaboration with his wife, Ava Helen
Pauling. Together they have given lectures about peace in most of the
states of the United States and in twenty-five other countries.

Hans Bethe, distinguished physicist of Cornell University, and
former member of the President's Science Advisory Committee, has
said: "It should be realized that the limited test-ban probably would not

exist if it were not for the scientists. Dr. Pauling got the Nobel Prize for his role in this—I think rightly. . . . Pauling certainly had great influence on people both in this country and abroad. Without his awakening of the public conscience on this issue there would not have been any pressure on governments, and there would not have been any test-ban." In addition to scientific articles and books, Dr. Pauling has published about one hundred articles on world peace and banning the bomb, and one book on the subject, *No More War!*

Humanism and Peace

What have we, as human beings, to hope for? We suffer from attacks by the vectors of disease, from accidents, striking with the blind malevolence of chance, from the ills accompanying the deterioration of age; and also, in a sense the most viciously, from man's inhumanity to man, especially as expressed in the evil institution of war.

I believe that we can have hope, and that we can win a great victory not only over the plague of man's natural condition, the physical ills that beset us, but also over the terrible plague of man's oppression by man, over the evil of war.

The world has been changing rapidly during recent decades. This change has involved especially a greater understanding by man of the causes of human suffering. We now know that certain combinations of genes, which in some cases can be predicted to occur with high probability, lead to gross physical or mental defects which cause great suffering for the person who is so afflicted and for his parents and others. We know now that the pool of human germ plasm is continually being changed by gene mutation, and that the natural process of removing deleterious genes from it, in order to preserve its integrity, involves much human suffering.

We are faced with an ethical problem, characteristic of the many that we shall have to face as our knowledge of the nature of human beings and of the world increases. Shall the deleterious genes that exist in the pool of human germ plasm, and that would otherwise continue to increase, be removed by the suffering and death of millions of children, or by a procedure that attempts to recognize them and to prevent the conception of these defective children?

For thousands of years, throughout the entire period for which we have historical knowledge, war has been one of the principal causes of human suffering. I believe that we have now reached the time in the course of the evolution of civilization when war will be abolished from the world, and will be replaced by a system of world law based upon the principles of justice and morality.

In his encyclical letter *Pacem in Terris* Pope John XXIII said:

> Men are becoming more and more convinced that disputes that arise between States should be resolved not by recourse to arms, but rather by negotiation. It is true that on historical grounds this conviction is based chiefly on the terrible destructive force of modern arms; and it is nourished by the horror aroused in the mind by the very thought of the cruel destruction and the immense suffering that the use of armaments would bring to the human family. For this reason it is hardly possible to imagine that in the atomic era war could be used as an instrument of justice.
>
> Nevertheless, unfortunately, the law of fear still reigns among peoples, and it forces them to spend fabulous sums for armaments: not for aggression, they affirm—and there is no reason for not believing them—but to dissuade others from aggression.
>
> There is reason to hope, however, that, by meeting and negotiating, men may come to discover better the bonds that unite them together, deriving from the human nature that they have in common; and that they may also come to discover that one of the most profound requirements of their common nature is this: that between them and their respective peoples it is not fear that should reign but love, a love that tends to express itself in a collaboration that is loyal, manifold in form, and productive of many benefits.

Let us consider the significance of war as a cause of human suffering, in comparison with other causes.

I accept, as one of the basic ethical principles, the principle of the minimization of the amount of suffering in the world. I do not accept the contention that we cannot measure the suffering of other human beings, that we do not know what is good and what is evil.

Even though my relationship to myself is subjective and that to other human beings is objective, I accept the evidence of my senses that I am a man, like other men; I am "fed with the same food, hurt with the same weapons, subject to the same diseases, healed by the same means, warmed and cooled by the same winter and summer; when I am pricked I bleed, as do other men; when I am tickled, I laugh; when I am poisoned, I die." I cannot contend that it is the result of anything but chance that I am I, that this consciousness of mine is present in this body; I cannot in good faith argue that I deserve a better fate than other men; and I am forced by this logic to accept as the fundamental ethical principle the golden rule: "As ye would that men should do to you, do ye also to them likewise."

I know what causes me to suffer. I hope that other human beings will take such actions as to keep my suffering to a minimum. And it is my duty to my fellow men to take such actions as to keep their suffering to a minimum.

We suffer from accidents, from natural catastrophes, from disease, from the ills accompanying the deterioration of age, and also, in a sense the most viciously, from man's inhumanity to man, as expressed in economic exploitation, the maldistribution of the world's wealth, and especially the evil institution of war.

Man has reached his present state through the process of evolution. The last great step in evolution was the mutational process that doubled the size of the brain, about one million years ago; this led to the origin of man. It is this change in the brain that permits the inheritance of acquired characteristics of a certain sort—the inheritance of knowledge, of learning, through communication from one human being to another. Thus, abilities that have not yet been incorporated into the molecules of deoxyribonucleic acid that constitute the pool of human genetic material are not lost until their rediscovery by members of following generations, but instead are handed on from person to person, from generation to generation. Man's great powers of thinking, remembering, and communicating are responsible for the evolution of civilization.

During year after year, decade after decade, century after century the world has been changed by the discoveries made by scientists and by their precursors—by those brilliant, original, imaginative men and women of prehistoric times who learned how to control fire, to cook food, to grow crops, to domesticate animals, and then to build wheeled vehicles, steam engines, electric generators and motors, and nuclear fission power plants. These discoveries provide the possibility of abolishing starvation and malnutrition, improving the well-being, and enriching the lives of all of the world's people.

The effect of the discoveries of scientists in decreasing the amount of human suffering is illustrated by the control that has been achieved over the infectious diseases. In many parts of the world it is now rare for women to die of puerperal infection, for infants to die of diphtheria or scarlet fever, for people to die of diseases such as smallpox or bubonic plague. Cancer remains a cause of great human suffering not yet brought under control; but we may hope that this terrible disease will also succumb in the next few decades to the attack on it that is being made by scientists.

The result of medical discoveries and technological developments have not yet been made available to all of the world's people. Modern means of waging war seem to be more easily available to the underdeveloped countries than drugs, food, and machines for increasing the production of goods.

Our system of morality as expressed in the operating legal, social, and economic structures is full of imperfections, and these imperfections have been accentuated during recent decades. There is great misery caused by the abject poverty of about half of the world's people; yet most of the scientists and technologists of the world today are working to make the rich richer and the poor poorer, or are working on the development and fabrication of terrible engines of mass destruction and death whose use might end our civilization and exterminate the human race.

The already enormous disparity in the standards of living of different peoples has been increasing, rather than decreasing, in recent years. The use of a large part of the world's wealth, $120,000,000,000 per year, for the support of militarism and the failure to stop the increase in the amount of human suffering due to poverty are causing a deterioration in morality, especially among young people.

I believe that it is a violation of natural law for half of the people of the world to live in misery, in abject poverty, without hope for the future, while the affluent nations spend on militarism a sum of money equal to the entire income of this miserable half of the world's people.

Pope John in his great encyclical letter said that every human being is a person, that every man has the right to life, to bodily integrity, to food, clothing, shelter, rest, medical care, and social services, to security in case of sickness, inability to work, widowhood, old age, unemployment, or deprival otherwise of the means of subsistence through no fault of his own; the right to respect for his person, to his good reputation; the right to freedom in searching for truth and in expressing and communicating his opinions; the right to be informed truthfully about public events; the right to share in the benefits of culture; the right to a basic education and to suitable technical and professional training; the right to free initiative in the economic field and the right to work under good working conditions, with a proper, just, and sufficient wage; the right to private property, with its accompanying social duties; the right of residence and of freedom of movement, of membership in the human family and membership in the world community.

Most human beings are denied these rights. It is our duty to work to achieve them for everyone.

Now in working to abolish war and poverty, we are working also for human freedom, for the rights of individual human beings, for the achievement of world morality. This is the only religion for me. As Benjamin Franklin said 175 years ago, in discussing the progress of science, "It is impossible to imagine the heights to which will be carried in one thousand years the power of man over matter. O that moral Science were in as fair a way of improvement, that men would cease to be wolves to one another, and that human beings would at length learn what they now improperly call *humanity.*"

We can no longer afford to evade our responsibilities. The time has come now when morality must win out in the world. The survival of the whole human organism now depends upon whether or not we can work together for the common good.

I believe that we can have hope. I believe that we can win the final victory over the immorality of war, that the nations of the world will give up war, will become moral; that the fine ethical principles that are now accepted by the units of humankind will be taken over also by that whole great organism itself; and that we, all the people of the world, who together constitute this greatest of all organisms, the whole of humanity, the culmination of the great process of evolution, will move forward together into the world of the future, a world of peace and morality and ever-increasing happiness.

Pablo Casals

I believe that every person must act according to the dictates of his conscience. I feel that the capacity to care is the thing that gives life its deepest significance and meaning.

Pablo Casals, now ninety-one, is the world's most celebrated cellist. He is also an ardent peace advocate and practicing idealist who in 1938 attracted international attention when, in protesting the subjugation of Spain by the Falangists, he left his native land never to return as long as Franco remained in power. He now lives in Santurce, Puerto Rico, where he composes, conducts and prepares for the periodic concert appearances which take him to many parts of North America and Europe.

Casals as artist, philosopher and world citizen has earned the admiration of such national leaders as England's Queen Elizabeth, France's General de Gaulle and America's President Kennedy for whom he played at the White House. Yet, for twelve years following his exile from Spain, he gave no public concerts until he performed at a festival in Prades, France, commemorating the two-hundredth anniversary of the death of Bach. This heart-stirring event, in which he was joined by many noted European soloists, led to his establishment of the annual Prades Chamber Music Festivals.

In 1962 Casals organized his own personal Peace Crusade, using his oratorio, *The Manger,* as a central piece for his concerts in many countries and as a musical expression of his devotion to peace among men. In the same spirit, "Pau" Casals became the star and guiding genius of the famous festivals Casals now held every June in San Juan, attracting outstanding instrumentalists, conductors and critics from all parts of the world. Born into a musical family near Barcelona in 1876, he could play the flute, piano, violin and organ when he was five, and shortly thereafter began to compose and sing in the church choir. More than eight decades later this durable, doughty Catalan is still making beautiful music and, together with the former Puerto Rican cello student who is now his wife, they have turned their bustling Caribbean island into a musical mecca for mankind.

Peace Through Music

When one looks about him at the miraculous diversity of our universe—at the miraculous world that each person, each tree, each leaf is—how can one help but believe in something greater than oneself, something that cannot be described. I think if you develop an awareness of what you are, gradually you will find God. I find Him when I awake. I go immediately to the sea and everywhere I see God, in the smallest and the largest things. I see Him in colors and designs and forms. I have the idea of God constantly. I find Him in music. What is this world, what is music but God?

Here in Puerto Rico each morning after I return from the seashore, I have breakfast and immediately afterward I go to the piano and I play two Preludes and Fugues of Bach. I have done that every day of my life for the last eighty-one years. I began to learn to play the piano at four. I knew at ten that Bach existed, and immediately I began to play the Preludes and Fugues every morning without fail, except when I was on a train or a ship and there was no piano to play on. So I see God in Bach. Every morning of my life, I see nature first, then I see Bach. I treat music as something divine, as I treat every human being. Every human being is a miracle. The world is a miracle that only God could make. Think how no two grains of sand are alike, how there is not one voice like another, not one nose like another, how in the millions and billions of living and nonliving things in the universe, no two are exactly alike. Who but God could do that? God cannot die. God *must* be present all the time. Nothing can destroy that. I don't agree with the philosopher Claude Lévi-Strauss that the human race will one day vanish like every other form of life. I can't conceive it. It is an unthinkable thought.

There was a fisherman I knew in San Salvador many years ago. He could not read or write. I learned more from that man than from the philosopher Henri Bergson. Because he lived with nature himself; because he had learned directly from nature and life. I have never believed in great names. I believe in what happens in the whole of life. This is the teacher. This is the conductor. Life is the philosophy to read and adopt. Nature is where I go, without anybody's help but God's. Nature is what has inspired me, what I have learned from and what has been the cause and content of my meditations. Nature has helped me, not the philosophies of the study.

Let me say something on the subject of a man's place in life. It is sometimes necessary to make the humblest people who do the humblest work understand that their work, if done well, is equally necessary for humanity. Not everybody has a special talent, the means of thought and imagination to do what is thought an *important* thing. Those who do the strenuous and less rewarding jobs of life, those who are physically wearied by their work, if they take pride in their work and are conscientious, are as necessary, perhaps more so, than those who, because of some special talent or gift, are thought of as doing superior work. Such workers are entitled to the reward of retirement; but they can always find joy in doing whatever they can to lift their spirit and feel that they are useful. To "retire" is to begin to die.

You ask what my legacy to the world is. It is always the same: the lesson of never underestimating life; of never losing touch with it. To respect and love life in every sense, one's own and that of others. To resist doing things that have no meaning for life. Some time ago, I gave an address at the Manhattan School of Music. Two thousand music students came to hear me, many from other schools. I said to them, as I say to all my fellow men and women: "Do not waste life and love in things you do not feel. Do what you feel, and listen to your conscience. If you do that, you will do right for the world and for yourselves."

The philosopher Bergson once asked me what was my feeling while playing great music like Bach or Beethoven. I said that what I found was that if, after a good performance, I felt satisfied, I had a special feeling which could only be compared to carrying a weight of gold inside me. He was very interested in this remark and whenever we met he used to talk about it. One day he said, "This weight you talk about, is it equal or similar to the one we should feel when we have done a good action?" I also knew the feeling one has after a good action, but it is of a different nature. In that I feel something outside my own self, whereas the one which comes from artistic creation seems to belong to the inner self, as if one's participation had been deeper and more definite. There is another difference between the two sensations: a good action with me is followed by a desire to forget it so as not to lapse into self-admiration, but a successful performance seems to become a part of me even to evoke a feeling of self-recognition.

The miracle of Bach, for example, has not appeared in any other art. To strip human nature until its divine attributes are made clear, to inform ordinary activities with spiritual fervor, to give wings of eternity to that which is more ephemeral; to make divine things human and human things divine; such is Bach, the greatest and purest moment in the music of all time. Yes, Bach is the supreme genius of music. I have reached this conclusion, so easy to state, and of such enormous significance. This man, who knows everything and feels everything, cannot write one note, however unimportant it may appear, which is anything but transcendent. He has reached the heart of every noble thought, and has done it in the most perfect way.

I used to think that eighty was a very old age, but now that I am ninety-one I don't think so any more. There are times when I feel like a boy. As long as you are able to admire and to love, you are young. And there is so much to admire and to love—look at the sea, the sky, the trees, and flowers! A single tree—what a miracle it is! What a fantastic, wonderful, diverse creation this world is! That is the law of nature—diversity. That is why I can never play the same work exactly the same way twice, why each note, even, is a different world. My wife says to me, "You are so excited all the time!" I say, "I have to be excited. How can I help it?" Teachers should teach the richness and diversity and wonder of life. Then there wouldn't be so much *bêtise*, so much stupidity and ugliness propagated.

I haven't changed much, only developed. I think one becomes formed very early; for example, since I was a child, my nature and my outlook have been very much what they are today. As a boy I was strong and daring but not pugnacious. I didn't much like to fight, but when I finally did, it would be with all my conviction. I never enjoyed having toy soldiers, and when my playmates played at war games I would refuse to join in. Even though I am a

Spaniard, I have never cared for bullfighting . . . it revolts me. Nor have I ever liked to hunt any living thing.

All my life, as far back as I can remember, I have hated lies. When I was seven, I had a bad tooth and had to go to the dentist to have it pulled, and I was afraid to go, fearing not the pain particularly but the blood. My father persuaded me, he said it wouldn't make blood. The dentist was a friend of my father's. He, too, assured me it wouldn't bleed. Well, of course it did. I was outraged. "You didn't keep your word!" I exclaimed. To this day I remember how indignant I was that my father and the dentist had lied to me. Parents shouldn't lie to their children, not even when they think it's for their good. Even a little lie is dangerous; it deteriorates the conscience and conscience is eternally important, like love. Something is happening to the world in this regard. We have consciences still, I think, but we don't heed them as we used to. Personally, perhaps, we do, but en masse, no. I remember, when I was a young man, the Dreyfus case. The whole world was concerned over the injustice done to one man. Now we are more callous: millions of people can be killed and we accept it and say it can't be helped.

The criterion of conscience is what will prevail in the end, because the great things of humanity will never change and what we shall always find in artistic creation is the man, the man in flesh and blood and not an abstract creature. Today we still like what is beautiful, even if the works are thousands of years old, like Chinese and Indian poetry. They have the same reason for existing as our true music has. Their life is the same today as in *all eternity*.

I am not a politician. I never have been and do not pretend to be one. I am simply an artist. But the question is whether art is to be a pastime, a toy for men to play with, or if it should have a deep and human meaning. Politics do not belong to an artist but, to my mind, he is under an obligation to take sides, whatever sacrifice it means, if human dignity becomes involved. Besides, the word "politics," if not used in good faith, can cover up much confusion. It may mean the ordinary legislation of each nation, in which I have no right to interfere unless it concerns my own country. But the politics we spoke of [Russia and Nazi Germany] concern the governments which betrayed the general rights of human nature. In this case moral principles are involved which prevail above all frontiers; all men of good will should fight against the violation of these principles.

I have shown you my conception of all art, which should elevate and not degrade us. Considering that an artist is a man, he cannot as a man withdraw from his solidarity with his fellow creatures. When I see innocent blood spilled and the tears of the victims of injustice, it becomes more important to me than my music and all my 'cello recitals!

I am now prepared for everything! Nothing that happens will surprise me. The pursuit of music and love for my neighbors have been inseparable with me, and if the first has given me the purest and most exalted joys, the second has brought me peace of mind, even in the saddest moments of my life. I am every day more convinced that the mainspring of any important human enterprise must be moral strength and generosity.

Hubert H. Humphrey

> *Let us make this hour—history's most shining hour—*
> *shine with goodness. Let us preserve the best of the past,*
> *coloring it, strengthening it. Let us strive on for the best*
> *in the future.*

In eloquent, ebullient Hubert H. Humphrey the United States had the busiest Vice President in its history. He presided over the U. S. Senate, directed the work of a dozen national councils and commissions, traveled on delicate diplomatic missions for President Johnson that took him to South Vietnam, India, Pakistan, a number of Middle Eastern and European countries and the Dominican Republic. A prominent Democrat since his two terms as mayor of Minneapolis, he is hyperactive today in the high councils of the party as he was in the structure of presidential power and decision-making.

Pink-cheeked and peripatetic at fifty-eight, Hubert Humphrey (his first name means "bright spirit") was born in Wallace, South Dakota. The son of a druggist, he earned a degree from Denver College of Pharmacy in 1933, later received a B.A. degree from the University of Minnesota and his Master of Arts from Louisiana State University. Before becoming a crusading "New Deal" politician, Humphrey was a teacher for the WPA in Minneapolis.

Elected mayor of Minneapolis in 1945 and re-elected in 1947, he was elected to the United States Senate in 1948 and re-elected in 1954 and 1960. He was named Senate majority whip in 1961. In 1964 he was elected Vice President for the term beginning January 20, 1965.

During his one term as Vice President, Hubert Humphrey was chairman of the National Aeronautics and Space Council, chairman of the National Council on Marine Resources and Engineering Development, chairman of the Peace Corps Advisory Council, chairman of the Special Cabinet Task Force on Travel USA, member of the National Security Council, and member of the Board of Regents of the Smithsonian Institution. Married to the former Muriel Buck, they have three sons and a daughter and are enthusiastic members of the Chevy Chase Methodist Church in Washington, D.C.

(The Christian credo of Mr. Humphrey was prepared by the author from his pertinent speeches, statements and interviews.)

A Recommitment to Moral Order

These are the most exciting days that man has ever known. Today we are just at the pioneering, primitive stages of our development; we are just on the threshold of man's greatest progress. For, if we are trying to live and grow by the guidelines of our Judaic-Christian religion, we believe in God, brotherhood and the moral order and we believe with Jesus, "Greater things than I have done, ye shall do also."

Because as a Christian Congregationalist I believe in God, man and a moral order in the universe, I also believe in—and work for—world peace through statesmanship, human friendship in a world community, full progress of America's system of private enterprise, recommitment to self-discipline in our personal lives and universal compassion especially for the needy and sick. Religion from my Minnesota boyhood days in church and Sunday school has taught me the sacredness of human life, the worth of every individual as a child of God and therefore my obligation to others. Once we understand that people are in a sense reflections of the Divine, then we begin to understand why people ought to live better, why we believe in equal rights and equal opportunity, why we cherish democracy in the deepest sense as an understanding of man and his relationship to divine Providence.

On April 28, 1964, there was a historic National Inter-Religious Convocation on Civil Rights in Washington, D.C. The next day, I discussed this great occasion in the Senate and cited the "moral dimension" of this issue. Especially, I said of this impressive gathering:

> The religious leaders of America are to be highly commended for their courageous statement in behalf of human rights, freedom, and dignity. It was a beautiful occasion. As the Senators who were there looked toward the interreligious choir, we saw America as it is—people of all races, colors, and creeds, lifting

their voices in song—ancient hymns, beautiful spirituals, and patriotic songs, that tell the story of America's life, faith, and purpose. As I left the auditorium, I said to a friend that that was one of the most moving, inspiring, exciting, and exhilarating experiences of my life.

Whatever our particular spiritual heritage or faith, we are taught the brotherhood of man just as we are taught the fatherhood of God. Thus, I am proud of the thousands of church leaders today—yes, and the tens of thousands of concerned laymen—who are working to make real the goal of human brotherhood.

The Holy Scriptures remind us to "pursue peace"—and mankind has since the beginning of time condemned the horrors of war. If discord and strife, wars and the threat of wars have persisted throughout history, it is perhaps as St. Augustine says: that men make war not because they love peace the less, but rather because they love their own kind of peace the more. Yet men of peace of every kind and every land remember well the year of 1963. For, in that fateful year a venerable apostle of peace left our world, leaving behind a legacy which will endure for years to come. Generations of men—young and old alike—will remember the final testament of that gentle peasant pope, Pope John XXIII, the encyclical *Pacem in Terris*, in which he left to men of all faiths, to men holding many concepts of peace, an outline for peace in our world which can be accepted by all men of good will. And, if our generation can heed the parting plea of this blessed man, generations yet to come may hope to live in a world where, in the words of the late President Kennedy, "the strong are just, the weak secure, and the peace preserved."

We Americans build peace whenever we help anybody with our voluntary religious, nonsectarian groups around the world. We build peace with an exchange of teen-agers. We build peace with the 4-H Club exchange. We build peace in the United Nations. And we must win that peace. Man cannot live through nuclear holocaust. The same man who has developed instruments of total destruction —and we now have them I can assure you—is the same man who can develop the instruments to build a better world.

Here, then, is my message for all people everywhere who have the future in their hands: Be men and women of compassion . . . of courage . . . of perseverance. Devote yourselves to the search for justice . . . and for peace. As the Holy Bible tells us: "And beside this, giving all diligence, add to your faith, virtue; and to your virtue, knowledge; and to your knowledge, temperance; and to your temperance, patience; and to your patience, Godliness; and to your Godliness, brotherly kindness; and to your brotherly kindness, love."

The greatest need of the hour is for builders of a still better tomorrow. We need additional men and women in every community eager to build all that is good, beautiful and noble. The Great Architect created a world in which men could build happy lives for themselves and their children.

God gave us a soul with which to achieve life's highest values. He gave us a brain with which to conquer problems, split the atom, race to the stars, construct cities, banish want, heal the ill. Step by step, mankind has climbed up the ladder of civilization. Now we can see heights we have never before dreamed of attaining.

We of the United States enjoy more blessings than any other people. Most of these blessings did not come easy. From the days of the wilderness onward, Americans had to make sacrifices. Generation after generation had to win and rewin our blessings, fight and die for them when our land and our freedom were imperiled.

Americans—like all other peoples—are the heirs of a universal heritage—the Judaeo-Christian ethic. We are the beneficiaries of many great advances in many lands, over many centuries. But we are the special heirs of the builders, protectors of this continent, this Republic. They were patriots and statesmen—inventors and scientists—humanitarians and crusaders—spiritual leaders, philosophers and educators, soldiers, sailors, marines and aviators—both known and unknown. They gave us—preserved for us—great ideas and ideals.

They gave us a Constitution which is "the most wonderful work ever struck off at a given time by the brain and purpose of man," as Gladstone said. They gave us—protected for us—productive industries and fruitful farms, superb transportation, the best of schools, libraries, parks, playgrounds, hospitals, entertainment—comforts and conveniences.

Our goal is a just and enduring peace. It is a peace with honor. It cannot be a peace of betrayal, of surrender or of violation of our convictions or our commitments. We seek not a sterile peace—

the mere absence of war—but a creative peace. We seek to build bridges of friendship across gaps that separate nations. We seek works of peace—international teamwork for health, for research, for education, for knowledge, for schools, for culture.

We seek to make of our own land a still brighter beacon for a world that is still partially in darkness. There is so much for each of us to do—on our street, in our neighborhood, our town, city, region, nation—to build, to improve—to perfect. Every thinking citizen can rejoice in our historic opportunity. We have the chance to serve—not merely ourselves—but others, as well. We have given generously toward this end. No land has been more selfless toward a stranger or toward a former foe.

This nation, said President Lyndon B. Johnson, in his State of the Union message in 1965, was ". . . never meant to be an oasis of liberty and abundance in a worldwide desert of disappointed dreams. Our nation was created to help strike away the chains of ignorance and misery and tyranny wherever they keep man less than God means him to be."

Man was made in the image of his Maker. Man can serve other men to a greater extent than ever before—or can destroy other men in unprecedented numbers.

We are determined that the awesome powers of the twentieth century shall be used for good. Arnold Toynbee said that our age can be remembered ". . . not for its horrifying crimes nor its astonishing inventions, but because it is the first generation since the dawn of history in which man dared to believe it practical to make the benefits of civilization available to the whole human race."

Many benefits must still be made more available to our own people. Look around you. Great as our progress has been, many tasks are undone, many preparations for the future still to be made. We must provide for our growing population. They will number 400,000,000 in the next half-century, including over three-fourths in urban areas. Meanwhile, we must make our cities more livable, safer, healthier, quieter, more comfortable. We must beautify our once-green landscape. We must clean the air and the streams.

We must wage to victory the war against poverty—helping the less fortunate to rise—to the greatest extent by their own efforts. We must wage unceasing attack on disease and disability—on pain, suffering and premature death. We must combat injustice, redress grievances, right wrongs. Where there is suspicion among groups, we must encourage trust. Where there is hatred, friendship. Where there is fear—faith.

What, then, is our goal?

Our American author, Thomas Wolfe, expressed it: "To every man his chance, to every man regardless of his birth, his shining golden opportunity—to every man the right to live, to work, to be himself and to become whatever thing his manhood and his vision can combine to make him."

Who can better serve these and other causes than they who have pledged themselves to brotherhood? They whose creed is good deed—in the name of God and humanity. They to whom purity is not just a symbol, but enduring practice, to whom charity is not an empty token, but the essence of conviction, to whom building is not just a hope, but a part of their fraternal mission.

Fortunately, we have many brotherly Americans, many human builders, but we do need more. We need more builders of the basic institutions of our civilization—the home, the church, the school, the civic and fraternal organization. We need more builders who will ask each day, "What can I do to add to the well-being of my family, of my loved ones, to the children of my neighborhood and town and, yes, to the stranger—near or far?"

We need men and women who will act upon that question and who will serve with joy. We need men and women, great of heart, great of stature to build—what our President has so well termed—a truly Great Society. "Give me men to match my mountains" is the saying of our great American West.

Let us match and exceed our past achievements. Let us make this—history's most shining hour—shine with goodness. Let us preserve the best of the past—enhancing it, strengthening it. Let us strive on for the best in the future. Let us so live that future generations will say of us: "They were builders. We are blessed by what they did and by what they believed. They were true to the needs of their time. They were faithful to those who followed after them."

The Dalai Lama

*He who destroys life, who speaks untruth, who takes
what is not given him, who goes to another man's wife,
even in this world digs up his own root.*

His Holiness, the Dalai Lama, Tenzin Gyatso of Tibet, is the fourteenth
incarnation in the line of the Dalai Lamas. The spiritual and temporal
head of the Tibetan nation since his sixteenth birthday, he was forced
to flee his capital city of Lhasa in 1959 to escape abduction and
murder at the hands of the invading Red Chinese armies. Now thirty-
three and living in exile with eighty thousand other refugees out of
which fifty thousand are in India, he has become the heroic symbol of
resistance to the Communist attempt to annihilate a peace-loving people.

The present Dalai Lama or Precious Protector of the Tibetan tradition was chosen to succeed his predecessor, the thirteenth Dalai Lama,
at the age of three when learned lamas were led by profound signs
and omens to his remote village. During the 1950s, as both temporal
and spiritual head of his six million Tibetans, he revitalized Buddhism
in his country, pressed for modern social and technological reforms
among his people, attempted repeatedly to achieve a just and friendly
relationship with the aggressive Chinese threatening his nation.

Today, from his current residence in northwestern India, the smooth-
faced, bespectacled holy leader works day and night directing Tibet's
government-in-exile. Care for the dispossessed remnants of his people—
their shelter, food, work, education and medical care—preoccupies him
constantly as does his meetings with U.N., governmental and press
representatives to carry his "fire alarm" call to all the world. His daily
routine consists of prayer and meditation for the well-being of all living
beings and study in Buddhist philosophy. Speaking to the free world
the Dalai Lama says: "Ever since my arrival in India, I have been
receiving every day sad and depressing news of the suffering and in-
human treatment of my people. I have heard almost daily, with a heavy
heart, of their increasing agony and affliction, their harassment and
persecution and of the terrible deportation and execution of innocent
men and women. These have made me realize forcibly that the time
has arrived when, I must not keep silent any longer but must frankly tell
the world the truth about Tibet and appeal to the conscience of all peace-
loving and civilized nations for help."

Toward Limitless Light

On March 17, 1959, at four o'clock in the afternoon two mortar shells were fired into the Norbulingka Palace at Lhasa as evidence of the Chinese intention to use military force to subjugate Tibet to their purpose. The Dalai Lama had endeavored to maintain friendly relations with China since its Communist government forced me to sign the so-called Agreement of 1951 under threat of invading armies. Although an agreement between two independent and sovereign states, the Chinese deliberately pursued a policy of action opposed to the very conditions they themselves had laid down, and began a reign of terror which finds few parallels in the history of Asia. Thus, after nearly a decade of trying to calm his own people while entreating the occupying Chinese militarists to a policy of conciliation and friendliness, the Dalai Lama realized at last that any hope of serving his people by remaining in Tibet was shattered. Accordingly, I and my government secretly departed the summer palace just before midnight and started the dangerous descent into India.

As Tibet's spiritual and political leader, the Dalai Lama tried repeatedly during the 1959 crisis to negotiate with the Chinese aggressors to save my venerable country from war and bloodshed. Nothing availed. The Chinese even tried to trick me into attending a "tea party" at their Lhasa headquarters but tens of thousands of loyal Tibetans encircled the palace for twelve tumultuous days and nights to protect me. Disguised as a poor lama or priest and accompanied by only a retinue of officials, I made my way through this human wall to eventual safety in India—but only after three weeks of tortuous travel across the high Himalayas, down twisting mountain trails plunging nineteen thousand feet, crossing the flood-swollen Kyichu and Tsangpo rivers into the Assam plains.

Today in this Buddhist land of lamas, farmers, and peace-loving families, a nightmare of terror and tyranny prevails. The Chinese

Communists have undertaken a policy of the complete extinction and absorption of the Tibetan people; crimes against humanity and religion multiply. To date, thousands of innocent men, women, and children have been murdered en masse, and the massacres continue daily. According to a Chinese document, only in central Tibet alone, over eighty-seven thousand Tibetans were massacred within the short period from March, 1959, to September, 1960. Thousands of monastaries have been razed to the ground and their sacred images and articles ruthlessly destroyed. Tibetan men and women by the thousands have been dragged from their homes and forced into Red Chinese slave-labor gangs; children in large groups at a time are shipped by the truckload to work on collective farms in China. Life and property are no longer safe and Lhasa, capital of the state, is now a dead city.

Tibet is a land of religion; living in the presence of the majestic Himalayas, the Tibetans long ago found it natural to be religious. The Dalai Lama is a bikkhu (a mendicant) wedded to the dharma of peace and freedom and dedicated to the welfare of his people who have been entrusted to his care. As the Lord Buddha has spoken, "Let him advise, instruct, and dissuade one from evil. Truly pleasing is he to the good, displeasing is he to the bad."

All that the Dalai Lama wishes to make clear is that since my country embraced Buddhism, they have been wedded to the doctrine of peace and good will. They have lived for centuries in friendly relations with all their neighbors. They have had no unholy desire for expansion or conquest. They have lived in peace and their earnest desire is to live in peace. The long and honored relations between India and Tibet have always been on a friendly basis. Ideas and concepts of religion and culture have brought them together and cemented this relationship. The Tibetans have also lived on terms of friendship and amity with the British government in India, the government of Russia, and the governments of all the Americas. They have had, therefore, no feeling of enmity or hatred against any foreign country. Even today they do not cherish any ill feelings against the people of China. It is no doubt true that the recent happenings in Tibet have created the deepest feelings of hatred and resentment against the Chinese authorities in Lhasa, but the fact remains that they are peace-loving people and cherish no ill will or anger against any other people or nation.

In a speech last November to the World Fellowship of Buddhists during their Seventh General Conference held in Sarnath, India, I said:

> The continents separated by great oceans and high mountains have been brought closer and closer to each other by the present-day technological development. This has made us feel that the world is growing smaller, making it possible for us to come closer to understand each other. Close exchange of philosophical and religious ideals between West and East is highly important. Because in the course of thousands of years in evolving culture of a country, factors typical to that particular country have considerably influenced it in shaping it, which in turn has molded the religion introduced to that country. We should understand the good things that every country has, to contribute for this further propagation of the dharma and should exchange our valuable experiences with each other.

In this atomic age, material progress is touching the highest watermark, and it has been providing excellent means to give mundane pleasure to the human beings. But everybody knows that material progress alone cannot give us absolute pleasure and happiness. Along with the material progress there should also be a parallel improvement made in our mind. Regard for individual's self-respect, kindly treatment and affection for living beings, practice of patience and such like magnanimous principles should be developed. Unless this balance is proportionately maintained, instead of providing pleasure and happiness, the material progress will give rise to nothing but terror and unbearable disaster. For these reasons, the Dalai Lama conceived how important it is to inculcate and promote ideal principles of religion in the human mind.

Nowadays every possible measure is being taken in this world for disarmament and reducing the tension of war. If, I, a humble Buddhist bikkhu, am permitted to say so, the situation of this world, whether peaceful or sanguinary, is essentially the creation of the mind. Therefore, if everyone earnestly determines to raise the standard of one's moral principles, the Dalai Lama knows there is the possibility of having true pleasure and happiness in this world.

Improvement in the mind can be done only by following the deep meanings of philosophical and religious teachings—teachings in harmony with the realities of this world. Buddhist doctrine emphasizes faith in rational knowledge and spiritual experience consistent with the principles of factual things. Hence, I believe it is highly essential to give due attention to reasoning.

Today two different interpretations are advanced in explaining away the outlook of a single phenomenal object. The scientists with advanced technology described it in one way and Lord Buddha, to whom we owe our deep gratitude, with His transcendental *jnana*, described it in another way. But, in my humble opinion, results obtained by these two processes are identical. Thus, the Doctrine, which is not only consistent with the factual things but which gives benefit for now and ever, should be further promoted. To uphold it and continue it is the most proper responsibility of us who are the followers of Lord Buddha.

Incidentally, it is evident to all of us that, when Buddhism was first introduced in various parts of the world, there were many gurus and learned scholars of various names and races, functioning during different periods, introducing different aspects of the Doctrine under different titles and languages and script and so on. In our Tibet alone there are many different varieties of this kind. However, it is the same INDIA—from where we all obtained the same Buddhism taught by the same Gautama Buddha. It is, indeed, a matter of great joy and inspiration to remember this fact.

Therefore, it is the Dalai Lama's submission that we Buddhists of different countries having different languages and literature should gradually have a clear understanding of each other, and should endeavor to follow intimately the essence of the paramount teachings of our Lord Buddha for putting them in actual practice.

The Dalai Lama concludes with sincere prayers wishing for the dharma, based on pure reasoning, to prosper and last forever to heal the wounds of humanity caused by intolerance and conflicts and let peace and happiness reign in this world and the innumerable worlds beyond.

Elmer G. Leterman

The dictionary is the only place where success comes before work.

Nobody in America asks "Where's Elmer?" any more—Elmer Leterman, that is. Everybody knows he is at the top, acclaimed across the land as the number one salesman in the United States. A master insurance executive for more than forty years and a masterful friend of the great and near-great from New York to Honolulu, balding, cherub-faced Elmer Leterman has sold more than two billion dollars' worth of group-insurance policies in his career. More than that, in his skillful blending of salesmanship and showmanship, he has mastered the art of human relations, and thousands of persons are the happier for it every day, everywhere.

America's fabulous "Giveaway Man" has built his fame and fortune on one principle: the more you help others, the more you help yourself. Born in Charlottesville, Virginia, and bred to a commercial career by a Jewish storekeeping father, young Elmer at fourteen slipped the harness of home and high school to take a clerk's job in nearby Baltimore. By the time he was nineteen, he was making twenty-five thousand dollars a year as a woolen goods salesman, and immediately after World War I he opened his own insurance office in New York City. With sales topping ten million dollars the first year and with a pride of friends that included Al Jolson, Mary Pickford and Jack Dempsey, Leterman early perfected the sales-and-service philosophy that was to assure his personal and professional success. A soft-sell specialist and Beau Brummell dresser, he first sells himself and that supreme sale is based on a genuine love of people, a flair for imaginative favors and a genius for bringing together other executives for *their* benefit.

Today, full of years (sixty-nine) and honors (typical is the *Forbes* magazine accolade as "One of America's Twelve Master Salesmen"), ebullient Elmer Leterman still runs his $200,000,000-a-year insurance company, Leterman-Gortz Corporation, from an office high in Rockefeller Plaza. He lunches every day at Manhattan's swank Four Seasons, inviting to his poolside table such prominent friends and peers as TV star Ed Sullivan, minister Norman Vincent Peale, raconteur Harry Hershfield, U. S. Senator Jacob Javits, ex-heavyweight champ Gene Tunney and bridge expert Charles Goren. In recent years he has written his phenomenal philosophy of selling into a number of best-selling books which include *Personal Power through Creative Selling, How Showmanship Sells,* and *The Sale Begins When the Customer Says No.*

Casting his bread upon the waters of friendship and broadcasting "the brain sell techniques" which have made him world-famous only serve to polish a lost literary art which is Leterman's favorite hobby—writing epigrams. In the high French tradition of a Montaigne or a Rochefoucauld, he composes an annual of axioms which distill the life of selling and the selling of life. Letergrams to remember include "It is good to see through a thing, but it is better to see a thing through"; "Only a mediocre person is always at his best"; "A smile creates happiness in the home, good will in business and welcome in friendship"; "Luck is what happens when preparation meets opportunity"; "Courtesy is free, give it generously"; "A friend is a present you give yourself"; "A man's greatest strength develops at the point where he overcomes his greatest weakness"; "Personality can open doors, but only character can keep them open."

Salesmanship + Showmanship = Success

My religion is the Ten Commandments, and I try to follow them in my professional, social and family life. My philosophy is the golden rule, and I try to keep my brother's need and welfare before me in my daily rounds. I was born a Jew in Charlottesville, Virginia, before the turn of the century and am proud of my Jewish spiritual heritage. Today I don't wear it on my sleeve, but in my heart.

In historic old Charlottesville I lived surrounded by history without knowing it. Thomas Jefferson's storied Monticello stood nearby on its magnificent grounds. Edgar Allan Poe had walked its streets while attending the University of Virginia (we just called it "the University"). My father's grand old department store occupied a niche on Main Street; here I often clerked after school and often listened to my father read from the Torah. There was no synagogue in Charlottesville in those days so, in addition to my religious training at home, I was allowed to attend the Methodist Church Sunday school and even on occasion a Catholic Church Mass!

To this day in memory, Charlottesville remains a magical town to be born and brought up in. Several years ago when an old friend, the famed *Saturday Evening Post* writer, Pete Martin, and I returned home together, we reminisced long and lovingly about such local landmarks as Vinegar Hill, Miss Becky Lee's kindergarten and Mr. Jefferson's mountain "escape hatch" through which he supposedly fled the approaching British redcoats. As we lingered near the site of our fathers' Main Street stores, I recalled that my dad's favorite lifeline for me had been the maxim: "Do what is right and fear no one."

In life's school of hard knocks, however, my real religion soon became work. In fact, work in my book is a form of worship; there is no substitute for work. In my own case out of necessity, I never finished high school but went to work at age fourteen for eight dollars a week. From the first I loved selling and, by the time I was twenty, I had arrived in New York and was earning twenty-five thousand dollars a year—as an insurance salesman. In selling people insurance, I always tried to become genuinely interested in them and help them solve their problems. Sales ability gets a customer; service ability keeps him.

The dictionary is the only place where success comes before work. In all creative selling, work is the beginning, the middle, and the end of success. He who does not work will not sell. He who sells will produce sales in direct proportion as he works. He who works will demonstrate how seriously he wants to succeed by how much he works.

Three little words sum up what has lifted most top men above the crowd: "and then some." They did all that was expected of them—and then some. They did as much as anybody else in the same line or the same outfit—and then some.

The soldier who gets the decoration is the one who performs "above and beyond the call of duty." He is a good soldier—and then some. The rewards of the market place go to the men in peaceful pursuits who display the extra that in a soldier makes the hero.

Many fail to recognize opportunity because its favorite disguise is hard work. "I never did anything by accident, nor did any of my inventions come by accident," said Thomas Edison. "They came by hard work."

The following story will illustrate just what Edison meant.

The Edison and Bell interests were once locked in a tight competitive struggle in England. Edison had the transmitter rights for a telephone system and Bell had the receiver rights. Neither could move without cutting the other's throat. There had to be a consolidation, but who was going to control it? As a practical matter the Bell interests had the advantage in the situation. Accordingly they presented a consolidation plan which would bring them the larger share of the profits. Edison's English agent, at his wit's end, sent the agreement to Edison with a recommendation that he sign it.

Edison went into action. He cabled his agent: "Do not accept terms of consolidation. I will invent a new receiver and send it over."

"Then," said Edison, telling the story afterward, "I set to work."

In three weeks he invented a new receiver. It was better than Bell's. In a few more weeks he had six hundred made. He put them along with a body of men trained to make and handle them, on a fast liner. They started to install them immediately on their arrival in England. This brought Bell around. Edison and Bell were consolidated on equal terms soon afterward.

The answer Edison gave to a situation that apparently had no answer was, "Then I set to work." It is the password that answers every challenge of every sentinel guarding every road of opportunity. *The climb to the top is a walk-up, never a walk-over.*

Let me give you two statistics on salesmen to bring out how this applies full force to them. Twenty insurance companies were asked to state the distinguishing good qualities of their four hundred most successful salesmen. The answers put good character at the top of the list. But immediately after that was, "willingness to do a full day's work." Alongside that put this story dealing with all kinds of salesmen. The members of the Chicago Sales Executive Club were asked to answer a questionnaire about their hiring and firing practices. Their replies showed that of 624 salesmen discharged by them, one out of every three got his walking papers for "lack of industry." In plain words, he did not work.

Years ago, for example, John McGraw, the fighting Oriole who became manager of the Giants and the terror of the National

League, gave me the biggest scare of my life. I was a young salesman pioneering group insurance and group insurance was new then. I was beating my brains out to find a way to make the public conscious of it. I needed a headline.

One day I got an idea. America is full of baseball fans. A baseball club is a group. I could enlist America's favorite sport to get attention for group insurance if I could sell a policy to a baseball club. I asked a friend who knew baseball to help me. He called me one day to meet him at a certain place. The address did not register with me. So, I was totally unprepared when I met him to find myself ushered into the presence of McGraw, the legendary tough man of the diamond. I was so overwhelmed that all I could do was to stutter a few incoherent words, and get out.

Later, I screwed up my courage to make another appointment with him. He was pretty gruff, but he listened. Finally he said: "Bring in your policy, young man. We'll make this a policy to be remembered." He made a production of signing it—right out on the diamond of the Polo Grounds in front of the crowd at the big-league game of May 19, 1930.

A man's greatest strength develops at the point where he overcomes his greatest weakness. You may be saying: "I am shy. I am tongue-tied. I am not good-looking. I am unsure of myself."

Here is good news for you. What you now think is your greatest handicap, work can change into your greatest asset. This may sound to you like whistling in the dark. It is not. Work can change an original imperfection into something near perfection.

We have a beautiful illustration of this in one of the great men of our time. Winston Churchill started out in life with a speech defect. He knew he could never have the career he wanted unless he corrected it. He concentrated on it. Precisely because he gave this weakness his greater attention and handled it more carefully than any other one detail of his life, he developed such skill in speaking that he was universally hailed as one of the great orators of his day. Where he was inferior he achieved his greatest superiority.

I feel so strongly about this changing of weakness into strength through work that I have made a hobby of collecting examples of it. You can guess the reason. When I started out in life I had the will to be a salesman, but I had no college education. I had no illusions about being handsome, I was no natural charmer. I needed encouragement. I found it by studying examples of people who turned their weaknesses into strength. I got my education from them. I made it a point to have people with brains around me. I studied the good manners of people at ease in the world. I applied to my work everything I could learn from everybody.

Here is a short rundown of some of the men who have inspired me—men who had demonstrated that greatness consists in overcoming natural weaknesses and handicaps.

Demosthenes, the Churchill of ancient Athens, began life with a stammer. Homer, the poet of a sunny world, was blind. Both Frederick the Great and Napoleon, commanders of men, were small and unimpressive in build. Socrates and Michelangelo, exponents of beauty, were both ugly in appearance. Byron, the romantic poet and lover of perfect form, was lame from birth.

If you have the will to be a salesman, but feel some sense of inferiority holding you back, don't run away from it. Face it. Don't be afraid of it. Spell it out. Go to work on your weakness. Keep working on it. There will come a day when you will be strongest where now you think yourself most likely to fail.

Whether he is extraordinary or inferior, one truth applies to every man in his job: *There is no substitute for work, and work can solve any problem.*

Never mind yesterday. Never mind tomorrow. Do today's work today.

Reinhold Niebuhr

Every possible peril and anticipated evil cannot destroy the faith, that the love of God gives meaning to life.

Reinhold Niebuhr, scholar, teacher and former dean and vice president of Union Theological Seminary in New York City, has commanded the world's respect for three decades as America's pre-eminent Protestant theologian. Born in Wright City, Missouri, in 1892 and graduated from Yale Divinity School in 1915, Dr. Niebuhr accepted a call to the Bethel Evangelical Church in Detroit and during a long, eventful pastorate achieved national recognition as a defender of labor and a critic of motordom's "economic royalists." While a socialist, pacifist and "social gospel" Christian in his early years, he became progressively dis-illusioned with Marxism and Fascism and by 1940 backed U.S. entry into World War II from a position of Christian realism.

Over the years, the intense stern-visaged Christian philosopher has written polemics, led causes, analyzed modern man's plight as few Western sages have been able to do. As always, he upholds "the glory of the incorruptible God" as against "the image of a corruptible man." In 1939, for example, Dr. Niebuhr became the fifth American to deliver the Gifford Lectures at Edinburgh University, drew the biggest crowds in Gifford history. In 1949 he served as a member of the U.S. delegation to UNESCO in Paris. In 1959 he spent a year at Princeton's Institute of Advanced Studies to write a book on the ethics of foreign policy. All during this period he taught at Union as a professor of philosophy and applied Christianity, and edited the crusading Protestant publication, *Christianity and Crisis*, which he helped found.

Now in semiretirement as Union's professor emeritus of ethics and theology, the seventy-six-year-old Protestant pundit still engages in a multitude of religious and scholarly activities designed to direct man's faith to what alone can give ultimate meaning to life. He has recently been a visiting professor on the Princeton, Columbia and Harvard University campuses. He contributes regularly to *Christianity and Crisis* and other religious journals. The recipient of eighteen honorary college degrees, he was awarded the Grand Cross of the Order of Merit from Germany in 1960, the American Liberties Medallion from the American Jewish Committee in 1962 and the U. S. Medal of Freedom from President Johnson in 1964. Dr. Niebuhr's twenty published books include *Faith and History*, *Moral Man and Immoral Society*, *The Nature and Destiny of Man* and *The Structure of Nations and Empires*.

Christianity and Crisis

There is an essential nature of man to which man must conform. A part of that essential nature is his freedom, for which love is the only law. Over the years, I have come gradually to realize that it is possible to look at the human situation without illusion and without despair only from the standpoint of the Christ revelation of love. At the summit of that love is a self-giving affirmation of the being and well-being of another; reason, or man's self-awareness in the moment of self-transcendence, always has an inchoate knowledge that love is the law of human life. This awareness is accentuated, clarified and made full by the revelation.

The motive and direction of Christian love is essentially sacrificial. Indeed, the primary meaning of love is to be found in self-sacrifice, even as love must be regarded as the final flower and fruit of justice. Without an element of heedless love, every form of mutual love would degenerate into a calculation of mutual advantages, and every calculation of such advantages would finally generate resentment about an absence of perfect reciprocity.

The relation between sacrificial love and mutual love contains the issue of the relation between the eschatological and the historical in a nutshell. Love, heedless of the self, must be the initiator of any reciprocal love. Otherwise the calculation of mutual advantages makes love impossible. But heedless love usually wins a response of love. That is a symbol of the moral content of history. But this response cannot be guaranteed, as modern thought sought erroneously to guarantee it. That is symbolic of the "tragic" dimension of history and a proof that the meaning of life always transcends the fulfillments of meaning in history. That is why Christian faith is eschatological and has a touch of "otherworldliness," which one cannot eliminate by trying to contain all facets of meaning in the processes of history.

All who have become Christian will find their own convictions formed by the witness of the whole Christian church through the ages, beginning with the witness of Scripture. A responsible theologian, as distinguished from an irresponsible speculator, will think and live within the discipline of this church, though he will feel free to correct what seem to him to be errors of the past.

The trouble with religious naturalism is not only that it obscures the whole mystery of the divine, the mystery of creativity and grace, but that it also falsifies the whole drama of human history with its increasing heights of good and evil and in the paradoxical relation of persons to this drama. For persons are both the creatures and the creators of this process.

I believe that there is a "biblical" faith of great consistency and uniqueness which must be distinguished from both classical rationalism and Oriental mysticism. Every religious or philosophical faith is an existential commitment. This commitment must not be restrictive so that it would prevent us from recognizing truth and grace in other lives with other commitments. I believe that the Christian faith illumines the truth about man and God; about man's freedom, responsibility and sin; and about the grace which makes the freedom tolerable and which overcomes the sin.

I have spent a good part of my life validating the love ethic as final on the one hand, and trying to prove on the other hand that it must and can include all the discriminate judgments and commitments which we may broadly define as commitments in the cause of justice. That these commitments may involve us at times in war, and that at all times they involve us in moral ambiguity, must be recognized if an ethic of justice is not to degenerate into a merely political ethic. On the other hand, I am certain that an ethic of love which dispenses with the structures and commitments of justice is ultimately irrelevant to the collective life of man.

The most basic need of the human spirit, as I see it from my vantage point of seventy-six years, is the need for security, and the most fundamental problem of religion is the problem of meeting this need. In a true religion, faith in the ultimate meaningfulness of existence, grounded in a God who transcends the caprices and contingencies of the physical order and who is capable of overcoming the chaos created by human sin, is the final security of the human spirit. In false religion this ultimate security is prematurely appropriated and corrupted so that it assures man peace in his sins and not through the forgiveness of his sins. To understand the importance of this distinction it is necessary to analyze the whole imperiled nature of the human enterprise.

Man's insecurity lies first of all in the determinate and finite character of human existence amidst the immensities of the physical world and the caprices of nature. When he surveys the heavens, the work of God's hands, the moon and the stars which He hath ordained, he is overcome with a sense of his own insignificance: "What is man that thou shouldst be mindful of him?" The summer's heat and the winter's cold, the capricious storm or the equally unpredictable attack of unseen disease germs, may destroy his life. To the perils of the natural order must be added the perils of the social order. At any moment man may become the victim of the greed, the cruelty, and the thoughtless passions of his fellows. The fury of war may claim his life. He is, as was St. Paul, "in peril by land, in peril by sea, in peril of false brethren." Unable to live without a sense of the meaningfulness of his existence, his confidence in meaning is constantly imperiled by the chaos which threatens to engulf him. The chaos may be represented by the capricious forces of nature which seem to take no account of his significance, his hopes and his dreams. In the words of Goethe: Die Elemente Hassen das Gebild her Menschenhand. [Nature abhors the products of man's creation.] Or the chaos may erupt out of the sinful forces of his society; for all human society seems but a tentative peace and uneasy armistice between conflicting interests and passions.

In consequence of these perils the need of security is a basic need of human life. I remember how wonderful was the experience of my boyhood when we ran to the barn, warned by ominous clouds of an approaching storm, and then heard the wind and the rain beating outside while safe and dry under the eaves of the haymow. The experience had actual religious overtones. The safety and shelter of the haymow were somehow symbolic of all security against dark and tempestuous powers. The words of the Psalmist, committed to memory in confirmation class, achieved a sudden and vivid relevance: "Thou shalt not be afraid for the terror by night; nor for the arrow that flieth by day; nor for the pestilence that walketh in darkness; nor for the destruction that wasteth at noonday. There shall no evil befall thee, neither shall any plague come nigh thy dwelling." This word of the psalm is, incidentally, a perfect illustration of all the illusions which may arise from an ultimate religious faith. When faith in an ultimate security is couched in symbolic expressions which suggest protection from all immediate perils, it is easy to be tempted to the illusion that the child of God will be accorded special protection from the capricious forces of the natural world or special immunity from the vindictive passions of angry men. Any such faith is bound to suffer disillusionment. Nor does it deserve moral respect.

Stoic indifference toward the varying vicissitudes of mortal existence is preferable to lobbying, with whining entreaties, in the courts of the Almighty, hoping for special favors which are not granted to ordinary mortals or to godless men. The ultimate security of a noble faith lies in the assurance that "all things must work together for good," but not that all things are of themselves good, or that the faithful will escape vicissitudes which are of themselves evil rather than good. Those who know and love God understand that the meaning of life lies rooted in a power too great and good to be overcome by the momentary anarchies of history or by the periodic suggestions of chaos and meaninglessness which arise from man's strange relationship to nature's blind and morally indifferent forces. St. Paul expresses this idea perfectly in a glorious passage in Romans: "For I am persuaded, that neither death, nor life, nor angels, nor principalities, nor powers, nor things present, nor things to come, nor height, nor depth, nor any other creature, shall be able to separate us from the love of God, which is in Christ Jesus our Lord." Every possible peril and evil is anticipated—and discounted, because it cannot destroy the faith that the love of God gives meaning to life.

During my pastorate of thirteen years in Detroit, for example, the city expanded from a half to a million and a half population. The resulting facts determined my development more than any books which I may have read. For on the one hand, my congregation grew from a handful to eight hundred souls; on the other hand the social realities of a rapidly expanding industrial community, before the time of the organization of the workers, and under the leadership of a group of resourceful engineers who understood little about human relations, forced me to reconsider the liberal and highly moralistic creed which I had accepted as tantamount to the Christian faith. In my parish duties, I found that the simple idealism into which the classical faith had evaporated was as irrelevant to the crises of personal life as it was to the complex social issues of an industrial city.

The church is a curiously mixed body consisting of those who have never been shaken in their self-esteem or self-righteousness and who use the forms of religion for purposes of self-aggrandizement; and of the true Christians who live by "a broken spirit and a contrite heart." Whether we belong to this latter group, which makes up the true but invisible church, no one but God can know. Facing the test of death is obviously more important than I had imagined in the days of my simple moralism. But I have noted that defiance of malignant evil, involving the peril of death, is also a test which proves some obscure saints to be true conquerors, while others less obscure may fail mysteriously to pass the test. Indeed, one must come to the conclusion that none of us can be certain whether we have the faith or the courage to pass any final test.

I have only recently come to realize fully why the dramatic-historical account of the Bible should give a truer view of both the nobility and the misery of man than all the wisdom of scientists and philosophers. The fact is that the human self can only be understood in a dramatic-historical environment. Any effort to coordinate man to some coherence, whether of nature or of reason, will falsify the facts; because the self's freedom, including both its creative and destructive capacities, precludes such coordination.

There is a dimension of human existence which makes all purely rationalistic interpretations, not to speak of purely naturalistic ones, inadequate. That is the dimension of the eternal in the human spirit, which reveals itself in the capacity of the self to transcend not only the processes of nature but the operations of its own reason, and to stand, as it were, above the structures and coherences of the world.

It has become progressively clear in my mind, since I have written my several books and taught for several decades at Union Theological School, what line the apologetic venture of the Christian church should take. I hope to follow out this line in the years of activity still allotted to me. We must make it clear that the concepts of both personality and history are ontologically ambiguous. Personality, whether God's or man's, is defined only in dramatic and historic encounter. Though these dramatic and historical media of personality are not inherently "irrational," they are not subject to the ordinary "scientific" tests of rational intelligibility. Nothing in history follows as it does in nature or reason, "in a necessary manner." The personality is bound by historical destiny rather than by natural or ontological necessity; the truth in Christ cannot be speculatively established. It is established only as men encounter God, individually and collectively, after the pattern set by Christ's meditation. The encounter between God and man, as the encounters between men in history, must be by faith and love and not by the discovery of some common essence of reason or nature underlying individuals and particulars.

Thus, a genuine Christian apologetic must be prepared to bring the judgment of Christ to bear as rigorously on the household of faith as upon the secular and the pagan world.

U Thant

The United Nations provides the principal hope of collective mankind even as personal religion provides the principal hope of individual men and women.

The U.N.'s U Thant, the third secretary general of the United Nations, succeeding Dag Hammarskjold and Trygve Lie, today more than deserves his accolade as the world's No. 1 schoolmaster, civil servant and crusader for peace. Filling what Mr. Lie called "the most impossible job in the world" for his second full term, the serene, smiling-faced Burmese statesman pursues an unrelenting course of international travel as he practices his personal art of quiet diplomacy among the 125 U.N. nations. A dynamic United Nations, he believes, constitutes humanity's only hope for survival.

An ardent Buddhist even while a sophisticated politician, U Thant ("U" is a title of respect rather than a first name) personifies the hopes of hundreds of millions as he pleads, prods and leads the parliament of man in trying to solve a planet of problems extending from the Middle East to the Far East, from Cyprus to the Congo, from South Africa to Vietnam. In mounting his immense assault on war, disease, ignorance, pestilence and famine, he often occupies his U.N. thirty-eighth-floor command post ten to fourteen hours a day. He directs the daily activities of an international army of civil servants, supervises a score of specialized agencies ranging from UNICEF to UNESCO and attends all significant sessions of the Security Council and the General Assembly. Traveling to more than half of the U.N.'s member countries during his two terms in office, the secretary general made repeated personal efforts in America, Europe and Asia to end the war in Vietnam. Like the schoolteacher he was in his native land, he frequently scolds member delegations as well as entire nations for their failure to "respect the high purposes and principles of the U. N. Charter."

U Thant was born in January, 1909, in Pantanow, Burma, where his father owned a rice mill. Educated at National High School and at University College in Rangoon, he later served as headmaster of the high school, as a member of the Council of National Education, and as secretary of Burma's Education Reorganization Committee. In 1947 he was appointed press director for the government of Burma, later serving as director of broadcasting and secretary for special projects under the prime minister. As his diplomatic career developed, Mr. Thant became the principal adviser to his former college friend, U Nu, the first prime minister after Great Britain granted Burma its independence. He became head of the Burmese delegation to the U.N. in 1957 and in 1959 was named a vice president of the General Assembly's fourteenth session. The recipient of a dozen university degrees and special titles, the secretary general is the author of *The League of Nations, Toward a New Education* and *History of Post-War Burma.*

(*The Buddhist credo of U Thant was prepared by the author from the secretary general's pertinent speeches, statements and interviews.*)

Light on the Path

We live in a world of noise, yet our conscience is called the still, small voice. As my predecessor Dag Hammarskjold once pointed out, "We all have within us a center of stillness surrounded by silence." Unless we heed our own conscience, we shall continue to be attracted by what is loud and garish and lose our sense of values. If there is no peace in the world today, it is because there is no peace in the minds of men.

It is important, therefore, that all of us should determine to set aside some time each day to commune with ourselves, to talk with our own small voices, to devote certain precious minutes to thoughts of peace and good will. The General Assembly of the United Nations begins and ends each session with one minute of silent prayer. That is a good example for all of us to follow in our daily lives. "Life's real treasure," as the Buddha tells us, "is that laid up through charity and piety, prayer, temperance and self-control."

In my home country of Burma, as in many Far Eastern lands, Buddhism is the great living religion of the people, and it is my own faith. Buddhism as a system of mental and moral training stresses Four Noble Truths: the existence of pain, the cause of pain, the cessation of pain and the Noble Eightfold Way that leads to its cessation. This Noble Way, which when followed faithfully leads to the extinction of the petty, ego-centered self and the attainment of the liberated, blissful permanent state of being called *nirvana*, consists of the following proven practices: right view, right intention, right speech, right action, right livelihood, right effort, right mindfulness, right concentration.

Nirvana is the Noble Truth of the stopping of suffering or becoming. But, because when it is reached, craving detaches itself, it is called renunciation, surrender, release. "Is nirvana extinction?" Visuddhimagga asks. "No . . . because it is without source, it is unaging and undying. Because there is no source, no aging or dying, it is permanent. Because it is attainable by means of special cognition perfected by unfailing effort, because it was spoken of by Buddha, because it has existence in the ultimate meaning, nirvana is not nonexistent."

My religion has always been precious to me and it still is my mainstay in the demanding work here at the U.N. My formal Buddhist training began with my very religious mother who, thank God, is still living back home in Burma; at first, strictly ritualistic and traditional, my religious awareness grew more and more mystical until today my morning and evening meditations are as essential to my well-being as breathing. Although life in our modern complicated, high-speed age is a far cry from my untroubled boyhood in a tiny Burmese town, the light of religion alone can show us the true way. In fact, I deeply believe that even as the United Nations provides the principal hope of collective mankind so religious faith provides the principal hope of individual men and women.

My youthful dream, as expressed by Buddha in the *Metta Sutra*, is still my valid workday philosophy: "May all living human beings be happy and at their ease! May they be joyous and live in safety! All beings, whether weak or strong, in high, middle or low realms of existence, small or great, visible or invisible, near or far away, born or to be born, may all beings be happy and at their ease! Let none deceive another, or despise any being in any state; let none by anger or ill will wish harm to another. Even as a mother watches over and protects her only child, so with a boundless mind should one cherish all living beings, radiating friendliness over the entire world."

In Asia, where Buddhism is one of the dominant religions, we attach much more importance to the mind than to the body, and still much more importance to the spirit than to the mind. Traditionally, the aim of religion and education in Asia has been—I stress the word "traditionally"—to discover what is the truth, to discover truth inside of us, to learn to understand the extraordinary moral and spiritual qualities of man. In other words, the traditional aim of education and culture in Asia has been, throughout the centuries, the discovery of oneself, and to try to understand the spiritual qualities such as humility, compassion, reverence for old people, and so on. In the West, the stress has been on the development of the intellect, if my interpretation of Western educational aims and ideals is correct. There is too much stress on the intellectual development of man. The aim of education in the West—when I say West, of course, it applies to the United States of America, western Europe, and other countries of Europe, too—the aim of education in the West has been, and still is, to create doctors, scientists, engineers, to discover outer space, to fly to the moon, Mars and the stars, while at the same time the development of the spiritual qualities of man is more or less ignored.

The doctrine taught by Gautama Buddha, which is called dharma, or universal principle of truth, is at once philosophy, science, ethical teaching and the supreme way to spiritual perfection. It is all these things and more. It is different from the other religions of the world, as it has features not to be found in any of them, while at the same time it is independent of many ideas that are commonly thought to be essential to religion (for instance, the idea of a creator-God and the principle of the soul). Such concepts do not find any place in Buddhism.

Buddhism offers to the world absolute truth; a rational explanation of the mysteries of life, of good and evil and the problem of suffering; and a way by which the ultimate reality—nirvana—can be reached. It teaches, above all, a universal compassion, to be extended to all living beings, irrespective of their status, race or creed. All sentient beings are involved in suffering; all are struggling in a dark ignorance that blinds them to the truth of their own nature and the laws that govern their existence. It is through the ignorance of the law of karma that men do evil to one another, and thus to themselves. If each of us were to realize that whatsoever he does to another he does in effect to himself, through the law of reciprocal action, this world would become a happy and peaceful place. There would be no more crime, no more injustice, no more wars and no more hatred between one nation and another. But it is in the nature of samsara that we shall never be able to produce a perfect paradise on earth; all we can do is to mitigate the suffering whenever possible, strive to make our fellow men a little happier—no matter how bad their karma may be—and at the same time seek to purify and ennoble ourselves. This is the only certain way to happiness, in this life and in lives to come.

I believe that it is only in the dharma (the absolute truth) that we can hope to find a solution to the problems that beset us. It is only there that we can find a justification for our inherent belief in a moral order in the world—and a basis for right action, inspired by love and compassion in our relations with our fellow men. The dharma teaches us that violence will not resolve any of our conflicts. Similarly hatred and greed will only breed more hatred and greed.

One of the doctrines of Buddhism has a direct relevance to present-day conditions. It is the doctrine of selflessness or non-egoism. To be egoistic is to be blind to the needs, and the reality, of others. In addition, egoism is bad for oneself because it does not exist for long by itself. It becomes, in course of time, the parent of the twin sins of pride and prestige. If there is one lesson that history teaches us, it is that wealth and power, pride and prestige, are not only transitory but even illusory.

Another doctrine of Buddhism is the universal principle of metta —unbounded love and compassion for all living creatures. Buddhism teaches that the principle of nonviolence should extend not only to other human beings but to all living things.

I have dealt very briefly with some important principles of Buddhism which I believe are relevant to the human condition today. The universal principle of truth is obviously the most basic of them. So many of the problems that we face today are due to, or the result of, false attitudes—some of them have been adopted almost unconsciously. Amongst these is the concept of narrow nationalism— "my country, right or wrong." It is lack of truth in international relations that leads to the conscious or unconscious adoption of double standards. It is therefore essential that, in international relations as in human relations, we should practice, as we preach to others, the universal principle of truth.

The doctrine of karma, the principle that every action has a reaction, obviously has a direct application to international relations.

The U.N. Charter calls on us to practice tolerance and live together in peace with one another as good neighbors. This is the practical application of the principle of reciprocity.

The principle of nonviolence is also a basic concept of the Charter. One of the most fundamental principles to which member states have committed themselves is to refrain in their international relations from the threat or use of force. History teaches us that no durable solution can be found for any human problem except by persuasion and by common consent. The use of violence is double-edged, as violence is bound by the doctrine of reciprocal action, to provoke violence in turn. Before long, we find that the rule of law has given place to the law of the jungle. We have therefore to go back to first principles and to observe the Charter commitment regarding the nonuse of violence or the threat of violence in international relations.

The doctrine of non-egoism is equally important in international relations. Today we have in the world two superpowers, a number of major powers and a very large number of smaller nations. It is understandable that the major powers should pursue objectives which seem to them to be in their own national interests; but they should not be blind to the existence of a larger goal, the common interest of all countries, large and small, in the survival of the human race. They should, at least occasionally, pause to reflect on the course of history, which has seen the rise and fall of so many great empires. Generations to come will judge the conduct of those in positions of authority today by the effect that their actions had on the course of human peace and progress. If they wish to have an honored place in human history they must appear as men of peace and not as mere victors in war.

The law of love and compassion for all living creatures is again a doctrine to which we are all too ready to pay lip service. However, if it is to become a reality, it requires a process of education, a veritable mental renaissance. Once it has become a reality, national as well as international problems will fall into perspective and become easier to solve. Wars and conflicts, too, will then become a thing of the past, because wars begin in the minds of men, and in those minds love and compassion would have built the defenses of peace.

Bertha Holt

Fear not; for I am with thee. I will bring thy seed from the East, and gather thee from the West. . . ."

ISAIAH 43:5

Mrs. Bertha Holt, American Mother of the Year in 1966 and "Woman of the World," especially embodies the virtues of universal motherhood so essential to the new age of mankind in the universe. A vivacious Oregon homemaker and mother of six children, this mild-mannered, sparkling-eyed Christian lady slipped into immortality in the 1950s by becoming the unexpected "grandmother" of thousands of Korean orphans. The Holt Adoption Program, conceived and initiated by her husband Harry and by Mrs. Holt in 1955, resulted in the first shipment of homeless Korean children being brought to the United States to the Holt farm near Eugene, Oregon. Under their direction, additional planeloads of the tragic offspring of American G.I.'s and Korean mothers as well as entirely Korean children, continued to arrive until today more than four thousand destitute Asiatic boys and girls have been placed in American homes in fifty states.

As a result of this Christian good-will project, Mrs. Holt was selected by the American Mothers Committee for the highest womanly honor in the world—Mother of the Year. Citing Mrs. Holt for expressing the motherly traits of affection, patience, courage, cheerfulness, kindness, and understanding, the Committee praised its selfless exemplar for demonstrating in her life and work the precepts of the golden rule. Today, in the recent death of her husband, Mrs. Holt is the chairman of the board of the Holt Adoption Program in the United States, takes personal interest in its Korean Orphanage housing more than 650 children in Seoul, and brings her personal witness of God's love to church and civic groups in all parts of America. Her daughter, Molly Holt, is orphanage director, and Mrs. Holt goes to Korea herself two or three times annually.

Mrs. Holt, born in Des Moines, Iowa, is a graduate of the University of Iowa and a graduate nurse. In recognition of their lifesaving mission to the racially-mixed orphans of Asia, she received on behalf of her husband the two highest honorary medals that the Republic of Korea can bestow on a foreign citizen. Believing that all things are possible with God, she not only maintains her lovely Oregon farm home where she is raising her "second" family, now teen-agers, but also assists the American Mothers Committee in its program of training the mothers of preschool-age children in various U.S. cities. In the words of Dr. Bob Pierce, President of World Vision, which encouraged the Holts' first trip to Korea, "humble, considerate Bertha Holt is typical of the noble mothers who have worked so hard to make America a sanctuary for family life."

Seed from the East

Although all human beings are weak, with God all things are possible. As a happy, unusually active Oregon family, therefore, our knees repeatedly touched the floor asking in prayer the following request: "Heavenly Father . . . if it be Thy will, give us some way of serving Thee; a humble way, a way of Thine own choosing that will glorify Thy name. We petition Thee through Thine own Son, our Savior and Lord Jesus Christ. Amen."

In the year of 1955, the Lord answered our prayer in a most wonderful way. It was that momentous year that God—working through a human agency, World Vision—first brought to our attention the sad plight of thousands of Asian children left homeless by the Korean war, and inspired my husband and me to bring eight of these children to our farm home for a decent upbringing. Thus was born the Holt Adoption Program which to date has resulted in four thousand Korean orphans finding happiness in American homes in fifty states and several foreign countries.

Although my husband died in Korea in 1964 in the loving service of these unloved Amerasians (half American because many of them have unknown U.S.-G.I. fathers), I constantly thank God for the April day in 1955 when he first spoke to me about the sublime idea welling up within him. As a farm family with our own six children it was our custom when we had finished our evening meal for Harry to read a chapter from the Bible. It was a sweet time of fellowship for the family during which we all came to know and love the common bond we feel in our Lord. I felt then and still do that families who do not share a Christ-centered life are missing a great source of pleasure and love. I also believe there would be few divorces in America if families shared the reading of God's Word, and prayed together concerning whatever their troubles might be. I can testify from years of sweet communion with God that He never fails.

On Friday, April 15, Harry voiced the burden on his heart.

"I've been thinking I'd like to go to Korea."

"I know. I've been hoping you'd go."

For a moment he just sat quietly and looked out the window. Then he spoke again.

"Every night when I go to bed, I see that movie we saw of the destitute orphans all over again. It doesn't make any difference where I am or what I'm doing, I think about those kids over there. I look out here at this beautiful playground God has so generously given us and something inside of me cries out at the thought of those poor little babies starving to death or being thrown into dumps to be gnawed by rats."

Again there was silence but I knew he had more to say and would appreciate saying it as he felt it. So I just sat still and listened.

"I think we ought to adopt some of the G.I. children."

"That's the way I feel, too."

"How many do you think we could take care of?"

I knew what I wanted to say. I had thought of it many times and I felt like bursting out with the number eight. Somehow, I lacked the courage. I knew Harry had thought long and hard about the matter, too, and I had no idea of the number he felt would be right. Finally I answered in a far-off squeaky little voice.

"I suppose we could care for six."

"Oh my . . . we have plenty of room for eight . . . or ten . . . or even more.

I felt a sudden, joyful release. Now I knew that Harry's number even surpassed mine . . . and then I heard him continue to say, "Suzanne and Linda's bedroom is big enough for two or more beds. We can put cots in some of the other bedrooms; and the game room can be partitioned off along that ceiling beam to make a double bedroom."

As I listened to Harry repeat almost word for word the very things I had told myself could be done, I realized that God was working in our hearts. Only God could bring about such a miracle. Simultaneously and without discussion, a highly unusual decision had been made within both our hearts.

"I suppose ten would crowd us quite a bit," he said. "I guess we'd better make it eight."

Always before, when we considered some undertaking for Harry, we were concerned about his weak heart. This time, however, neither of us gave it one thought. We knew that when the Lord told him to go to Korea, He would also give him the strength to do it. And so it turned out, although a nerve-racking half-year was to go by before our air-borne bundle of little Koreans could be brought home by Harry from Seoul.

The next few months, filled with heart-stirring activities at home, were also marked by calls and correspondence between us and national and international figures. We kept in touch with Dr. Bob Pierce, the dedicated minister and president of World Vision, about ways and means to enter war-torn Korea. Even while running the farm and teaching our ever-growing Bible class, Harry made periodic trips to Portland and San Francisco to obtain a passport and visa, clothes, supplies and vaccinations for typhoid, typhus, cholera and smallpox. We besieged our great Oregon Senator Richard Neuberger to sponsor a bill permitting us to bring eight G.I. children from Korea; we even wrote President Eisenhower asking him *please* to sign our precious bill when it passed the Senate—which he did! Finally, after intensive weeks of preparation and briefings by the cooperative Korean Consulate, Harry boarded a big Pan-Am plane at Portland International Airport for the first leg of the trip to Hawaii.

There were no tears, just good-bye kisses all up and down the line, when the clipper's door closed and the four-motored ship took off and disappeared into the clouds. A farmer was on his way to Korea. A fifty-year-old farmer with a scar on his heart was saying, "Yes, Lord . . . here am I."

As we might have foreseen had we been more sophisticated, Harry was to spend all summer in Korea fighting the confusion, disease, red tape and tragic aftermath of war before he could even select and ready "our" eight orphans for the journey to America. Perhaps the anxieties and elations of those long days can best be suggested by excerpts from several of his letters.

For example, a typical letter from Seoul, dated June 15, 1955, reads as follows: "Dear Bertha and all: You must not worry about things over here. This is the Lord's work and it will be done in His way. Just pray He will keep me in His will. I feel there is much more involved than just the adoption of our own children. Each child has a special need. The exact number of these children is not known. I have heard anywhere between 750 and 2,500. They're still coming in to the homes. Undoubtedly many are still hidden by their mothers.

"I have selected four of ours. They are at the hospital in Seoul. There are two more I hope to get shortly. They're in Taegu and their names are Robert and Mary. I'm having quite a time with the Korean nurses. Every time one of the children starts crying, some nurse picks him up and holds him. They did it all day yesterday and then last night the kids were wild. I'd chase one nurse out and two would take her place. Finally I had to get the head nurse, Miss Bourns, and she managed to keep them out. They probably think I'm a cruel man. But . . . the kids were asleep in about five minutes.

"A report has come in that there are fifteen to twenty mixed-race children in Inchon. That's a port city on the Yellow Sea about twenty miles from here; the place where MacArthur landed his troops when he took Seoul. From what I understand, the children are roaming the streets and they're being mistreated. We may go there tomorrow and see what we can find. With all my love, Daddy."

Another letter, written ten days later, read: "Dearest Bertha and all. World Vision, Inc., is going to build a reception center here in Seoul for mixed-race children. Such a building is desperately needed. Its existence could save lives. If these small unfortunates are to be adopted in the United States, they must be gathered from all over the country and nourished back to health. Believe me, I wish it were ready now so that our children could be there.

"I hope to have our children all together by next Wednesday. It may seem like a slow process but I want to avoid being hasty. I might select the wrong ones. I am slowly proceeding with the belief that if I do not have the ones God wants me to have, He will, in some way, overrule. The eight I have selected include two babies—a boy—and a little girl, Judy. Helen and Paul are each about a year. Christine and Mary are about two years old and the two other boys,

Robert and Joseph, are between two and three. They all have to remain in the hospital for their tests and inoculations.

"I don't want you to worry about what I am about to tell you. I relate these things, so you will know better how to pray. In the ward next to us, children are dying all the time, mostly from starvation but there is disease, too. They are abandoned babies. There is one little colored child I am afraid will die tonight. Pray for these children. Pray for ours. Today I asked for a special nurse and got one. We have shut the door between our room and the ward in an effort to protect these few from disease. How I wish I had a place for them to play. Oh, if God by His grace will only let me bring these little ones to our home! Poor little kiddies no one ever wanted . . . until now. How can we thank Him for the Christian people over here who have labored so unceasingly to keep the children alive."

So went the tenor of every letter. All we could think of was having Harry and the children home. The dolls' dresses were finished. The nursery bathroom was well equipped; diapers, baby oil, cotton and two of those old-fashioned round things with an enamelware clatter. (These and two aristocratic modern ones sat in a row in the bathroom . . . all waiting to serve the same humble purpose.) In the basement, rows of canned goods lined the shelves. Freshly canned peaches stood cooling in a long sparkling row. Our Sunday clothes had come back from the cleaners and as nearly as we could determine . . . we were ready for A-day.

At last it came—noon, October 14, 1955, sunny and warm, the Portland airport swarming with newsmen, photographers and hundreds of spectators. At home, we had been getting used to cameramen and flashbulbs and I knew Harry, who normally avoids all publicity, had been getting the same treatment from Seoul to Tokyo to Honolulu. Then suddenly, my daughter Wanda shouted, "The plane . . . there it comes! See it swinging in to land!"

We watched the giant craft as it sped silently along its approach to the runway. In my view finder on my camera I carefully led the plane's approach as it taxied to where we stood. As the engines sputtered and died, I thought of a certain blind man who was lying on his bed back in Eugene. I remembered what he said: "We mustn't forget to thank *Him*."

And I bowed my head: "Dear heavenly Father . . . Thou hast

kept Thy promise. Thou hast brought his seed from the East. We give to Thee all the thanks and praise and glory. In the name of our Lord Jesus Christ, Amen."

As I opened my eyes I saw the portable ramp being moved up to the door of the plane. In moments now the passengers would be coming down the stairway to the ground. Photographers were jockeying for position. A huge truck with a giant tripod and camera and sound machine moved up close to the plane. I felt like I wanted to cry aloud for them not to become so interested in the miracle that they overlooked the One who had made it possible. How it must break God's heart to see the unconcern of man.

A small head appeared in one of the windows. Wanda pointed and shouted, "Christine! Christine!" Suddenly months of anticipation became a reality. Christine's sober little face was looking out on a new world. To see her was joy unspeakable. And then we saw Harry! There he was at the top of the ramp. For a moment I was somewhat taken aback by the deep furrows in his face. Never had I seen him look so tired. His clothes were all crushed and wrinkled from the burden of travel. But oh, it was good to have him home.

The officer told me we could go up the ramp so I led the way. I wanted to grab Harry and greet him, enthusiastically, with a kiss. But Harry had never been demonstrative in public . . . and there must have been a thousand pairs of eyes glued on us at the moment. Would he object? Suddenly it was like "The Farmer in the Dell." The farmer took his wife and for a brief, joyous moment there were only two people in the world.

But from inside the plane there rose the hum of happy voices. Dr. Pierce, who had flown to Hawaii to accompany my husband home, stood looking on with deep feeling but then for the first time I saw the children themselves—all bundles of lovable humanity— Bobbie and Betty and Christine and Helen and Paul and Nathaniel and Mary and Little Joe. Once inside our car, I slipped off my shoes and leaned back to relax. I felt a tender satisfaction. Behind me were eight precious God-given babies. Beside me was my husband, exhausted but safe . . . and he, too, was very, very happy.

December 31 is not only the last day of the calendar year, but it is also Harry's and my wedding anniversary. This particular year we were celebrating our twenty-eighth. There were presents from the children and the usual big box of candy from my husband. He has never failed to remember. The day was filled with events of an ordinary nature. We continued to circulate between the babies and the stacks of letters. There was little opportunity to reminisce, which was fine with us, because we firmly believe that the future is much more interesting than the past.

I was ready for bed but I still had to make the usual rounds and turn off the lights. As I went through the living room I noticed the chairs and davenport arranged in a circle. This was a leftover from the noisy falling-down game that had taken place a few hours earlier. There were the usual items of apparel scattered about. I picked up a green boot, which belonged to Joe; and a brown boot owned by Christine; and in the library I found a black one belonging to Nat and one of Mary's red ones. On the table in the library was a box of neatly piled letters, all addressed and stamped for mailing to couples all over America who wanted to adopt Korean orphans.

In the nursery I heard Betty making contented grunts. Harry had given her her bottle. He had carefully covered each child but I still went from bed to bed just to make certain. I guess I repeated the job simply for the sake of satisfaction. There was a great deal of it in caring for our new brood of children—the first of many to be brought to U.S. homes. I remembered what Harry said: "Folks think we've done such a noble thing. They just don't know how much fun it is." And he was right. It is eight times as much fun to cover eight children as to cover one.

I left the boots in the nursery closet and turned off the hall light. From there I went to the nursery bathroom and was happy to see Linda had done her job well, too. The round enamelware was shining brightly and the room had a slight smell of Lysol. Barbara's neat piles of tomorrow's clothes lay in the clean, dry bathtub. There were four piles of girls' clothes in the tub, and there were four stacks of boys' clothes on the edge. Feeling grateful, I switched off the last light.

If the Lord should come tonight, we would have one ear uncovered to hear His triumphant shout; if He tarried, we would be ready for the morning.

Once again, my knees pressed the floor.

"Dear gracious heavenly Father . . . we thank Thee for giving us a way to serve Thee; a humble way, perhaps, but a good way. A way of Thine own choosing.

"Give us wisdom . . . and grace . . . and whatever else it takes to raise our family for Thee."

Charles H. Malik

There are three main things that we must do. We must relearn the meaning of love and sacrifice. We must strengthen the ties that bind us to our fellow creatures everywhere. And we must more diligently seek the knowledge of God.

Widely admired as a statesman and scholar and as an effective mediator between East and West, Dr. Charles H. Malik of Lebanon, since attending the United Nations organizational conference in San Francisco in 1945, represented Lebanon at virtually every General Assembly session until 1958, and served the organization as chairman of the Human Rights Commission, president of the Economic and Social Council, president of the Security Council, and finally, in 1958–1959, as president of the General Assembly. Between 1956 and 1958 he served Lebanon as its minister of foreign affairs and national education. Now on leave from his long, distinguished government service, Dr. Malik is distinguished professor of philosophy and chairman of the department at the American University of Beirut, Lebanon.

His renown as scholar and teacher complements his influence as statesman and Christian public servant. Over a span of four decades, Professor Malik taught physics and mathematics at the American University of Beirut, worked for both the Rockefeller Foundation and Al-Hilal Publishing House in Cairo, taught philosophy at Beirut and at several universities in the United States, represented Lebanon diplomatically in Washington and in the United Nations, and served Lebanon as its foreign minister. He is a member of a dozen or more American and European learned societies, has been decorated by a dozen Near Eastern, European and Latin American governments, and has been awarded more than forty honorary degrees from American, Canadian and European universities and colleges. His two recent books are *Christ and Crisis* and *Man in the Struggle for Peace,* and he has published numerous essays and articles on social, political, philosophical and religious themes, in American, European and Near Eastern journals. He has lectured widely throughout Canada and the United States.

An outstanding leader among the Arab bloc nations, Charles Malik's father and mother, Dr. Habib Khalil and Zarifi Malik, raised him in the Greek Orthodox Church, which has been the faith of the Maliks probably since the foundation of Christianity. Charles Malik was born in 1906 in Bitirram, El-Koura, Lebanon. In June, 1941, he married Eva Badr. They have one son, Michael Habib.

Dr. Malik's schooling progressed from the American Missionary School in Tripoli, through the American University of Beirut, to a doctoral degree in philosophy at Harvard University in 1937. Malik became first an educator at the American University of Beirut in 1927. In 1945 he began a distinguished career in the service of his country when he became the first minister to the United States from Lebanon. That lofty service to Lebanon—and to all humanity—ended with his return to his first love, education and thought.

Will the Future Redeem the Past?

All Western civilization is based upon Christianity. The very fact of freedom grew out of it, as well as that which we call conscience. Our laws and morals are the formal expression of the Judaeo-Christian ethic, of Mosaic law, enriched by Roman law—the eternal truths of good and evil whether expressed in the Bible, the Magna Charta or the Declaration of Independence. Born in Lebanon and brought up in the Greek Orthodox Church, I view the decisiveness of the present moment in history as consisting in a life-and-death struggle between international Communism and the rest of the world, especially the Western world, and in the Western world, especially the United States. Because of my personal knowledge of the West's ultimate positive values, I range myself wholly on the side of the West, despite its many mistakes, imperfections and failures.

The complacent attitude, the lukewarm faith, the sinful selfishness so typical of millions of Western citizens no longer suffice. Something infinitely more humble, more profound, more positively outreaching is required if Communism is to be checked, the godless won, the world's starving fed. The truths of faith, freedom, brotherhood and good works belong to our gospel and we must "go and teach all nations." If we execute this commandment, we would embark on a revolution more profound than Communism, for the unbridgeable difference is that Communism is based on hate, Christianity on love.

But what is pre-eminently at stake in Mediterranean-Western civilization today is its human and universal elements. It is man who is denied; it is the affirmation that there is nothing that binds and cements all men into one family that is the prime danger; it is the fragmentation of humanity into endless exclusiveness, whether national or cultural or racial or economic, that poses the deepest challenge. Western civilization is doomed unless, jolted out of its complacency, self-satisfaction, and sense of apartness, it rediscovers and reaffirms what is genuinely human and universal in its own soul. This means not only economic and technical sharing with Asia and Africa, but intellectual, moral, and spiritual sharing. What is supremely good must be good for all. Those who keep on repeating, as though they discovered a transcendental wisdom, that their ideas, their way of life, their civilization, are "not for export," but only their industrial products, do not know that they are thereby digging the grave of their civilization and the grave of their way of life. Those who come to Asia and Africa and tell them: "You stay where and what you are and we stay where and what we are; we have nothing to give save our goods and gadgets," little know that the day will come, and perhaps is already here, when Asia and Africa will turn upon them and spit in their face. Man can live without goods and gadgets but he cannot live without something human and universal that joins him to his fellow men. A civilization in which the human and universal has atrophied can relate itself to others only through force, and force is not an enduring mode of relation, and it can always be broken by force. I am saying that Western civilization need not be doomed at all because no civilization conceived and developed the human and universal more than it did.

Most certainly it is not a question of "imposing" anything on anybody; what is genuinely human and universal is never imposed; it is awaited, welcomed, and embraced. What is nonuniversal in your civilization you may keep to yourselves: nobody wants it. Not until the businessman from Manchester or Detroit and the peasant from Iran or India can come together on a much deeper basis than the exchange of goods and money can the West really begin to have a chance in the ferocious competition going on at present for the heart and soul of Asia and Africa. Asia and Africa do not want to deal only with businessmen: they crave for human and spiritual fellowship. There is no exchange of soul, there is no sharing of life and ideas, there is no community of spirit, there is no fellowship of man with man. This is Asia's and Africa's deepest challenge of the West: what have you to give me, not of your trinkets, but of your mind, not of the external husks of your life, but of the substance and marrow of your soul? Indeed they mutely ask the West: Do you still *have* a soul?

If there were no universal and human elements in Western civilization the thing would be hopeless. But it happens that the deposit of humanity and universality in this civilization is the richest in the world. The civilization at whose heart pulsate Aristotle and Augustine and Aquinas and Dante and Newton and Shakespeare and Pascal and Kant and Lincoln, the civilization which has been blessed and transformed by Christ, needs only a mighty hand to shake it out of its slumber. And once shaken, once really awakened to the world responsibilities which it and it alone can shoulder, there is nothing it cannot dare and do.

So today we must awaken and respond to the current challenges with daring, depth and wisdom. I believe that the nations which are heirs to the Judaeo-Christian tradition are in difficulty because the three great sources of leadership in the Western world, the Church, the government and the university, have not been living up to their responsibilities.

The church has always been the keeper of men's conscience, the guardian of morals, the vigorous and suffering witness to God. If the people grow selfish, or materialistic or lazy, it is the duty of the church to point an accusing finger, to insist on drastic and immediate change; and above all, it is the duty of its ministers to be a living example themselves of this change. This the church has *not* been doing, not with the indignation, eloquence and authority that are needed; not with the incarnate goodness that Christ meant the church to be; not with His Cross. And so we have fallen into sin—the sin of materialism, of selfishness, of lust, of sloth, and of atheism itself.

Spiritual leadership is essential because the spiritual is far more important than the material in world affairs. I can assure you that the greatest thing to come out of America has been the American missionary effort: the quiet, selfless men and women who left the comfort and security of their homeland to bring the gospel of *Jesus Christ* to less favored nations. In China, in India, in Africa, in the Middle East and in hundreds of far-off places, these obscure missionaries have been far more effective ambassadors than any of the diplomats or moneymen or the agricultural experts or the industrial technicians. And why? Because they represent the best of the original American dream: the selflessness, the idealism, the belief that all men are brothers under the Fatherhood of God, the urge toward something real and wonderful, above sense, above man, and above the world.

This is the spirit that must be reawakened in America, and in the Western world. It is the role of the church to awaken it.

It is also the task of government. The elected representatives must come to realize that the other peoples of the world are more hungry for understanding than they are for any factory-made gadgets. What is needed today is a global Lincoln, a man of depth and compassion, a man of sorrows and suffering, a man who will be followed because the living universal in him appeals to the craving universal in all men. We have had no such leader. As a result, we have not had the unity among the Western allies that is essential if we are to win the cold war.

And the university is to blame. It stresses technique and narrow specialization, and the splitting of atoms as well as of words. It misses *the whole,* which is before and after all technique and all splitting. In the spiritual departments that form the character and the mind, principally philosophy, history, literature and the plastic arts, what do we have? We have analysis and fragmentation, we have formalism and formlessness, we have cleverness and the reduction of man to something unhuman or subhuman, we have flight from essence, from wholeness, from being. And even the analysis is usually of petty things, such as "this is red," hardly of truth and being and God and the final things, because once you embark on "analyzing" these things, you stop "analyzing" altogether, you cease to place yourself above them, you cease to be able to control them, you find yourself shabby and soiled, tarnished and unprofitable, you become in fact humbled into their slave; and the philosopher must always be on top, always in control, always immaculate, always the master. The commanding word of truth is lacking; in fact truth itself is held in derision. There is no positive correlation between the place and power of America in the world today and what the philosophers are spinning out in their private dreams. And the soul of youth goes on parched, soured, rebellious, profoundly unhappy.

Each of us is held within the orbit of a vast complex that includes family, neighbors, friends. If one individual makes a conscious effort to raise his moral standards, or learns the value of sacrifice, or falls on his knees seeking the face of God, this has its effect on the whole complex. If a leaven of individuals change, the entire structure changes.

You must strengthen the government by using your influence and your vote. You must demand more leadership from your church, not by carping and caviling from outside, but by total and joyous identification with all its problems and trials. A revolution must stir in the universities to the end that man, truth, the spirit, reason, God find their rightful place therein. You must learn to trust your instincts; your instincts tell you that love is stronger than hate, that justice is better than injustice, that the individual human person is more important than the state, that freedom is worth fighting for, that above the confusion of daily living there is a God who watches and who cares.

The tendency today to put bodily comfort or material welfare ahead of the things of the spirit is a historical sign of decay—in nations or in peoples. The early Christians profoundly distrusted comfort. They knew that the body is weak and easily spoiled, that it can become addicted to luxuries, and go on demanding them at any price. To combat this weakness they often resorted to harsh penances, self-imposed disciplines designed to strengthen the will and to keep it wide-awake. We of the twentieth century have almost forgotten how to deny ourselves anything, and the results grow more apparent day by day. And yet a single act of self-denial or self-mortification can, in faith, bring untold blessings upon the soul.

Finally, we must hold fast to our Judaeo-Christian religious heritage. This heritage embraces everybody in perfect good will and love; that is why we need not be ashamed or apologetic about it at all. In all other systems man is somehow diminished. In Christianity, God became man: think of the great honor to us weak men! Indeed, if you ask yourself honestly what it is that you wish to preserve in "our way of life," you will find that the things you value most are based squarely on the bedrock of religion. Honor. Duty. Justice. Freedom. Tolerance. Charity. Truth. Reason. Love. Sharing. Repentance. These are all either direct Christian values or values appreciated and respected and preserved by Christianity. Does it not follow, then, that if we are to preserve them, we must actively return to Christ as our Lord and Saviour, and therefore as the guide for everyday living?

Christ Himself was forever counseling His followers not to concern themselves with personal comfort or prosperity, not to lay up treasure on earth, not because these are not important, but because there is something infinitely more important. "Seek first. . . ." Judged by material standards, His life was a failure. And yet He was able to say: *"Be of good cheer, I have overcome the world."*

And so it seems to me that there are three main things that we all must do. We must relearn the meaning of love and sacrifice. We must strengthen the ties that bind us to our fellow creatures everywhere, including the soil and the earth, including the dumb brutes. And we must more diligently seek the knowledge of God.

If we do these things, if it is God's will that we do them, we may yet see a mighty spiritual revival in our time, and the dark tide of materialism, atheism and Communism, which now seems so menacing, will pass like a shadow from the face of the earth, and from the memory of man.

Arthur Michael Ramsey

The supreme fact towering above all else today is the unceasing intercession of the Lord God in human affairs.

The Most Reverend Dr. Michael Ramsey, elected the one-hundredth Archbishop of Canterbury and Primate of all England in 1961, emerges ever more impressively on the world scene as a master mover of Christian unity. A distinguished scholar, theologian and preacher, Dr. Ramsey is one of the six presidents of the World Council of Churches. As both pastoral archbishop and world churchman, he brilliantly fulfills his stated ambition—"to bring the Christian message home to people everywhere by preaching, teaching, writing and by using radio, television and personal influence in every way."

Dr. Ramsey first attained world-wide attention in 1954 when as Bishop of Durham he attended Queen Elizabeth II during her coronation service at Westminster Abbey. In 1956 he led the first delegation of Anglican churchmen to Moscow for conference with the Russian Orthodox Church, and in 1961 in his first overseas mission as archbishop he addressed the Third World Assembly of the World Council of Churches in New Delhi. In 1962 he visited the Ecumenical Patriarch in Constantinople. Again in 1966, in the furtherance of Christian unity, he made his dramatic visit to Pope Paul VI in Rome where the two church statesmen committed their communions to "a serious dialogue which, founded on the Gospels and on the ancient traditions, may lead to that unity in truths for which Christ prayed."

Dr. Ramsey, born on November 14, 1904, and a debating society president at Cambridge University, comes from a family with traditions of the Christian ministry on both sides—his grandfather was a Congregational minister, while the maternal grandfather was an Anglican clergyman. His first parish church was at Liverpool, his first teaching assignment was at the Theological College of Lincoln, and his first bishopric was at Durham. As Archbishop of Canterbury, Dr. Ramsey is entitled to a seat in the House of Lords. England's number one churchman is the author of a number of theological works, and holds honorary degrees from Cambridge, Edinburgh, Durham, Leeds and Hull universities as well as universities in the U.S. and Canada.

Spirituality and the Modern World

Today any nation or group, any church or individual, feels at times helpless amid the violence of the world and the intractability of human affairs. What can we do? Does anything that we do really signify anything? We answer from one side of the Christian hope that every single act of charity or justice has its part of that training of souls for eternity which is the Creator's first and final purpose for human beings. We answer also, from the other side of the Christian hope, that every single act of charity or justice witnesses to the supreme worth of the individual man and woman in this world and serves, even though we may not quite see how, the victory of our Creator's purpose here on earth.

Today, as Christian people from every part of the world and from many different traditions, begin everywhere to work for unity, the supreme fact towering above all else is the necessary intercession of our Lord in human affairs. The seventeenth chapter of the Gospel of St. John is the utterance, amid the historical crisis of the world's salvation, of this intercession, which is everlasting. Our Great High Priest—Christ—is interceding. And for what does He pray? That His disciples may be one, that they may be sanctified, that they may be sanctified in truth. Unity, holiness, truth; as the prayer is indivisible, so the fulfillment is indivisible too. It is useless to think that we can look for unity in Christ's name unless we look no less for holiness in His obedience and for the realization of the truth which He has revealed.

Yet the modern world, which pursues its own brand of unity in a secular way, does not hear the call to holiness and does not care for the truth in Christ. Longing for peace, it desires that men and nations should be joined to each other and the forces which separate them be removed; at the same time the world, which remains shocked when the church fails to manifest unity, persists in its terrible rejection of the divine truth and holiness underlying unity. Thus, the task of unity among ourselves is inseparable from our bringing the everlasting gospel of God to the nations. No less necessary is it for the church to meet the contemporary scientific culture, and to go out to succor those who are in hardship and distress.

There is the presence in the world of a modern, scientific, technological culture, so different from the older culture of Athens, or Oxford or Cambridge. Can our theology ignore this scientific culture? I can think of theologies whose nature it would be to say, "Yes, we can ignore it." But such is not the nature of Greek theology or of Anglican, wherever the Greek spirit has influenced it. The divine Logos, working in all the created world, author of all truth, the inspirer of all knowledge properly so called, is working within the scientific methods of our time. If we shrink from saying this, we may be in danger of being false to the teaching of the Fathers. If we do say this, the theologians will be conversing not only with one another in the ecumenical exchange but with every sort of other academic discipline, not least those which seem most modern. The theologian will best teach when he is ready to learn and to receive wherever the divine wisdom is the teacher.

There is the distress of nations through poverty and hunger, and the distress of races through the lack of brotherhood between them. Here we can listen again to the prophetic words of St. Chrysostom that it is vain to come to the altar in the Eucharist unless we go out to find the altar which is identical with the poor brother: "This altar thou mayest see everywhere lying both in lanes and market places, and thou mayest sacrifice upon it every hour. When thou sees a poor brother reflect that thou beholdest an altar." St. Chrysostom knew the very rich and the very poor within his own city. Today there are countries relatively prosperous and countries of deep poverty. The succor of the homeless and the refugees is a very part of our search for unity in Christ.

The church of God will therefore go out both to learn and to use whatever the divine wisdom discloses in the modern world, and to meet the agonies which are in the world. It can do this with conviction, because it knows the truth about the world and the truth about itself. The *world* is a place where Christ by His death and resurrection has won a cosmic victory: it is in His hands already, and all unseen His power draws it into unity: that is the orthodox faith of Christ victorious, as the Fathers and the Liturgy attest. The *church* is a body where, amidst its many sinful and fallible members, Christ is present as the church's inward life; and the portion of the church on earth is ever one with the church in paradise and heaven.

So, for each one of us, Christian spirituality means the relation of a man or a woman to the Holy Spirit of God, the Spirit bestowed by Jesus Christ after His death, resurrection and ascension. It is the mission of the Holy Spirit to indwell the Christian, influencing his entire life; and when a Christian is called a spiritual person it does not mean that his own spirit matters more than his body but that his whole being—body, soul, and spirit—is responding to the gracious rule of the divine Spirit within.

Now, if that be the essence of Christian spirituality, it clearly has many facets. As the Spirit is the spirit of truth, spirituality includes knowledge of the faith and of God who is the end of the faith. So too, because the Holy Spirit is the spirit of love, spirituality expresses itself in all the practical energies of Christian brotherhood and service. So too is spirituality inseparable from prayer and worship. It is the Spirit who enables the Christians to cry "Abba, Father," bearing witness with their spirits that they are sons of God. The worship of Christians is always to be "in spirit and in truth." It goes with a sacrificial self-consecration to God. The adjective "holy" itself speaks of that Godward consecration. Jesus consecrated Himself in the offering on Calvary that the disciples might in turn be consecrated. The Christians are a holy priesthood "to offer up spiritual sacrifices," and they are enabled to do so inasmuch as Christ "through the eternal Spirit offered Himself without spot to God."

It is, however, possible to say that the last of those aspects of spirituality, namely worship, is primary and definitive, the key to the unity of all the aspects. Spirituality refers to a man's relation to God and it is the recovery in man of his basic and elementary relation to God the Creator. Man was created in God's own image, after God's own likeness in order to come to the perfection of fellowship with his Creator, a fellowship which the biblical verb "to glorify" describes: a fellowship in which man reflects the character of his Creator so far as a creature can do so, humbling himself deeply before his Creator in utter dependence and awaiting the open vision of Him in heaven. That is the chief end of man. And when man, redeemed by Christ, is given the Holy Spirit to rule his life he is enabled to recapture the elemental relation of child and creature. The Holy Spirit is the Spirit of our present sonship, and he is no less the Spirit who anticipates within us the glory of heaven. That is why St. Peter calls him "the spirit of glory," and the author of the Epistle to the Hebrews calls him "the powers of the world to come."

To say all this is to say that the worship of God is itself the inner core of Christian spirituality; the heart, the mind, and the will directed toward the glory of God as man's goal. Every time that a Christian lifts up his soul to God in desire toward Him he is, however faintly, realizing that fellowship with the Creator for which he was created, and he is, in a tiny and yet significant way, anticipating the goal of heaven. Thus regarded, spirituality is no escape from the world. It is lived out in all the complexities of our social life, in family, city, country, industry, culture, joy, and sorrow; for it is the spirituality of a man, and a man is involved in all these things. It is inseparable from service, love, duty, the molding of the common life. Yet in deep-down essence it is the spirit of worship. Allow me to quote some words of a former Archbishop of Canterbury, William Temple. He said: "It is sometimes supposed that conduct is primary, and worship helps it. That is incorrect. The truth is that worship is primary, and conduct tests it."

H. L. Hunt

I believe in God, America, and freedom. In any age, a man needs at least as much pride as humility in order to be a happy, constructive, useful citizen. Only by letting our own people be truly free, by giving them more pride in themselves and in their accomplishments, can we defeat the tyrannies of our time.

Haroldson Lafayette Hunt of Dallas, Texas, is said to be the richest man in America and in the world. An authentic, independent billionaire in Texas and Louisiana oil wealth alone, he also has business interests in such diverse fields as cattle, timber, pecan groves, food and drug processing plants, and real estate in twenty states and Canada, Africa, and the Middle East. As founder and president of the Hunt Oil Company, he is the country's biggest independent oil producer, with a reputed weekly income of one million dollars—after taxes.

But tall, erect, cherub-faced H. L. Hunt at seventy-nine is rich in more than money and the things money can buy. Thrifty and industrious, he works hard each day—and "has a good time doing it"—on the multifarious operations of his oil, cattle and real-estate empires. Dedicated to fighting godless Communism and preserving freedom for all, he spends more and more of his time, talent, and money in furthering the cause of liberty. The daily public affairs radio program, "Life Line," which the Hunt companies and 188 other business concerns sponsor, is heard on 501 stations across America. "Life Line" presents a nondenominational religious message each Sunday.

The youngest of eight children born to a Vandalia, Illinois, farmer and grain speculator, Hunt, a brilliant student, was tutored at home, a not unusual practice at that time. He went with an older brother and sister to take a written exam for high school and passed easily. His education continued in the school of hard knocks—as a cowboy, lumberjack, prospector, Western farm worker; with time out to attend Valparaiso University, after passing an entrance examination. In the early 1920s he made the first of his fabulous oil strikes in Arkansas, Louisiana, and Texas. A nationalist in politics, Hunt calls himself a "Constructive" and deplores the title "conservative," declaring there is nothing conservative whatsoever in his thinking or philosophies. The international oil magnate spent $3,500,000 sponsoring the radio program "Facts Forum," which was suspended in 1958. He encouraged his sons to buy eleven million acres of speculative oil land in Libya, and has written such drum-and-bugle battle cries as *Alpaca, Fabians Fight Freedom, Why Not Speak, Hunt for Truth, HLH Columns, Weekly Strength, Right of Average,* and *Alpaca Revisited.*

Mr. and Mrs. Hunt are members and regular attendants of the First Baptist Church in Dallas, the nation's largest and wealthiest Baptist church. They live graciously, but not ostentatiously, in a white-pillared Mt. Vernon, a slightly larger replica of George Washington's famous home, appropriately set on a graceful rise of land at the edge of White Rock Lake. An American flag, a symbol of the land he loves so dearly, is raised and lowered each day on a tall flagpole on the front lawn. Seven of Hunt's children are associated with him in his far-flung business activities, altogether affording employment to nearly six thousand persons.

Men, Money and the American Dream

I believe in God, in patriotism and in the personal enterprise system which has made our nation great. I work hard every day in the battle to preserve our freedom, under whose banner all citizens are privileged to worship in a church of their choice, pursue a means of support for which they have qualified, and advance with the opportunities earned.

I was born on a farm in Illinois, in a house famous before the Civil War, known as the Reed House. Our farm was located about eighteen miles north of Vandalia, the state capital of Illinois when Abraham Lincoln served in the state legislature. I was the youngest of eight children born to Ella Rose Myers Hunt and Haroldson Lafayette Hunt, an ex-Confederate cavalryman. My mother had been a teacher in Murfreesboro and could read the Bible in Greek. I listened to her Bible stories, reading the Bible and relating her experiences in the Civil War while with her father, Captain Myers, chaplain of a Union regiment.

I went to California when sixteen years old and worked on the Jimmy Irvine San Joaquin Ranch, headquartered about twelve miles east of Santa Ana. The next spring I was in San Francisco and barely escaped being shanghaied onto a whaling ship. I once worked as a lumberjack in the San Francisco National Timber Reserves for the Saginaw Manistee Lumber Company from Michigan. A week before the great earthquake and fire in San Francisco I went to Reno, Nevada, to try out for a semiprofessional baseball team which was being formed there. I was in the wheat harvest in Saskatchewan and Alberta and in the fall of 1907 I left the wheat harvest in the Dakotas to go to Indiana.

My father often told me of fighting in the battle of Ditch Bayou, Arkansas, about ten miles west of Greenville, Mississippi, while he was serving four years in the Confederate Army. He spoke reverently of the richness of the soil near the battlefield. When I was twenty-two, I went from our cattle-feeding farm twenty miles north of Vandalia, Illinois, to Chicot County, Arkansas, and bought about one thousand acres of land, partly wooded, near Ditch Bayou for fifteen dollars per acre. Some plantations had sold for one hundred dollars per acre before the Civil War.

It had been thirty-five years since the area had overflowed, but a few weeks later at planting time the Mississippi River levee broke, and my plantation was inundated for three months. I tried for a late corn crop, but a plague of cutworms followed and destroyed the young corn seedlings.

The next season another overflow of the Mississippi lasted three months and the third year, 1914, my cotton crop was good for a bale per acre. World War I began, and the price dropped to a tragic twenty-five dollars per bale. In 1917 we had a similar overflow, and I finally was impressed that probabilities are not always dependable. In 1918–1919 I made paper profits buying and selling plantations and timberland near Lake Village, Arkansas, and Lake Providence, Louisiana.

Oil was discovered in Arkansas in 1921 by a sensational gusher blowing wild. This was about sixty miles from where I lived, and the price of cotton was very, very low. I went to the oil boom at El Dorado, Arkansas. By 1930 I had about one hundred oil wells and bought the discovery property from C. M. (Dad) Joiner who had discovered the great East Texas oil field. I was lucky, thrifty, and persistent and, under our justly famed personal enterprise system, those qualities paid off.

Today that freedom is threatened by enemies within and without. Those who mourn because they believe that freedom has no future, like those who rejoice for the same reason, forget one of freedom's profoundest truths. Liberty is not a child of fortune but rather, as has often been true throughout history, good fortune has softened, cheapened, and weakened the spirit of liberty until that priceless gift was lost.

Instead, liberty is the child of adversity. Liberty was won by the early Greeks in desperate struggle against the mighty empire of Persia which ruled all the rest of the then known world. Liberty was won by the early Romans in desperate struggle against the empire of Carthage. Freedom to worship was won by the first Christians after terrible persecutions at the hands of the rulers of an older, corrupted Rome.

Our own liberty in America was won, not in a dazzling charge on a spectacular battlefield, but in the silent snows and the bitter endurance of Valley Forge; just as it was saved, a century and a half later, by saddened stouthearted men who would not give up in the rotting jungles of Guadalcanal. When men, absorbed in pointless pleasure and ruthless power, forget freedom, it will die in their hearts, but live again all the more splendidly in the hearts of those who learn by adversity what freedom really means.

I like to speak of freedom. And as I constantly mention freedom, every time that I utter that inspiring word I mean justice, liberty, integrity, fairness, joy, and every other good term and thought in which freedom can be expressed to make and keep a better world for all.

Love of freedom is the extreme opposite of bitterness or "hate." Love of freedom means that you have the highest respect for your fellow man and want to give him every possible chance to make good in the world, to do whatever he most wants to do and to live the kind of life he wants to live, so long as he injures no other person. Love of freedom is the most constructive attitude a man can have. That is why the best name for freedom's active friends is not "right-wingers" or "conservatives," but "Constructives." But if we are to earn the right to call ourselves, and to be called, Constructives, we must stress what we are *for* much more than what we are against.

It is not sufficient just to be for freedom. We must know why we are for it.

Freedom may, and should, inspire our souls. But if we do not use our heads we will never keep it.

Freedom is not good simply because we are used to it or happen to like it. It is not good just because our Founding Fathers, great as they were, loved it. To take freedom for granted or by custom is a contradiction in terms and we will not keep it long on those terms.

Freedom is good because it makes possible a man living the kind of life proper to men. A beast of burden can do the work of a slave. A lion, a tiger or a shark can plunder and destroy. The leader of a band of baboons can rule by force.

But man has a reasoning mind and a constructive will. He can use that mind and will, to build a better life for himself and everyone around him. So long as there is freedom, those men who do use their minds and will in this way will succeed.

But when freedom is destroyed, men are crushed and reduced to hopeless, endless labor or savage marauding.

Freedom gives every man a chance, and the most competent and diligent, the best opportunity to succeed. Centralized power gives nobody a chance, except those who are a part of the ruling machinery, and they soon become potential dictators.

Freedom and force are enemies; they cannot coexist.

There is a familiar story about a man who never wasted words, and who always used them so that nobody could be quite sure just where he stood on any issue where there was dispute. One day this man was asked his opinion of sin. After thinking a long time and weighing his words carefully, he answered: "Well, I'm agin it."

Nothing is easier than being against sin; but as your clergyman will tell you, nothing is harder than living in righteousness. In the same way, nothing is easier than being against all the forces in the world that work to destroy freedom; but to be against these forces is not enough.

"Never in our history has the need been greater for constructive action from all ages on behalf of freedom." So often I am asked if an individual American, one person, can do anything really effective in the fight to save freedom. My answer is always the same; it is always affirmative.

This one person can start out by resolving that he—or she—will never go to sleep at night without having spent ten minutes that day to advance the cause of freedom. If two-thirds of all Americans

would do this every day, we would be giving a total of twenty
million hours each day to the spread of faith in God and the
preservation of liberty. That would save our freedom, our churches,
and our nation.

Alexis de Tocqueville, after a visit to the United States, was
asked what in his opinion made America great. He replied that he
had seen much of America, had seen the great cities, the busy
factories, the fertile farms. He was deeply impressed by their importance. But, he believed, the greatness of America lay in the faith
of her people. The churches of America, he said, are everywhere,
and America was great because America was good.

This happened in the nineteenth century. The years since have
brought many changes. But they have not changed the truth that
America's greatness must grow out of her goodness—out of the faith
of our people is a deep and abiding love for liberty. That is our
tradition.

America has now reached the place where the road divides. It is
not an unmarked trail, like the proud pioneers pondered and then
summoned courage to make a choice on which to stake the contents
of their canteen, and the only lives they had. Rather, it is a well-
marked crossroad that has been traveled many times by many
people. The road signs are in large letters and easy to read. The
pages of history interpret them in clear and unmistakable language
so all may understand. Many civilizations have been lulled by the
sedatives of prosperity, apathy and fear, until the point of no return
has been reached down the socialist fork of the road, and the further
stretches of this road are strewn with their wreckage.

It is too late not to try, but not too late to win. Let us take hold
and restate our position and adopt the constructive measures
necessary for the preservation of freedom. The rights we as Americans enjoy have been purchased at a price dear to all who have
gone before us. We are blessed with the greatest freedom ever
known by man. Our faith has sustained this nation throughout
many conflicts. We shall not falter nor fail. Let us join in preserving
our glorious land which God has so richly blessed, for as we stand
together with God, we will never be alone. We shall then become
part of the true hope of freedom throughout the world. Let us unite
in a supreme effort to learn the truth and keep America free!

Jiddu Krishnamurti

To see the false as the false, to see the true in the false, and to see the true as the true—it is this that sets the mind free.

Jiddu Krishnamurti, born in South India in 1895, was hailed from his youth as a Buddha-inspired prophet whose destiny it was to save mankind. Yet, as a young man surrounded by admiring throngs, he rejected the avatar's adulation and chose the role of teacher who points men the way to self-awareness and spiritual freedom. For four decades now Mr. Krishnamurti has traveled and lectured in many countries in Asia, Europe and the Americas.

Krishnamurti, who was educated in England, now lives in Ojai, California, where he writes, teaches and counsels hundreds of visitors from all parts of the world. Not believing in organizations or schools of thought, he discourages disciples and creedal cults from forming around him; rather, he holds, spiritual growth is an individual matter and liberation can be achieved only through self-realization and the elimination of all that is unreal or unessential in one's consciousness.

Krishnamurti's writings include *Commentaries on Living, Talks at Ojai, The First and Last Freedom* and *Think on These Things*. Of him and his profound understanding of life, critic Frances Hackett has written: "I feel that, as with non-Euclidean geometry, he has hold of a major secret. I think of him as one of half a dozen up-above-self people on whom I look, and to whom I look up, as emancipated . . . he is no other than he seems, a free man, one of the first quality, growing older as diamonds do but the gemlike flame not dating, and alive in all his works."

Reform, Revolution and the Search for God

Real culture is neither a matter of breeding, nor of learning, nor of talent, nor even of genius. It is the timeless movement to find happiness, truth, God. I have only one thought and that is to liberate men from their own prejudice, from their narrow-mindedness and their limitations. I say there is a way of living intelligently, happily and without conflict. I do not propose to give you a system, but to place before you certain ideas so that you may find out for yourselves how to think truly.

Real uniqueness lies in the personal discovery of what is true and being in that discovery. The uniqueness, joy and liberation which comes from this discovery is not to be found in the pride of possessions, of name and fame, of physical attributes and tendencies. True freedom comes through self-knowledge which brings about right thinking; through self-knowledge there is the discovery of the true which alone puts an end to our ignorance and sorrow. Through self-awareness and self-knowledge peace is found, and in that serenity there is immortality.

Amidst so much confusion and sorrow in the world today it is essential to find creative understanding of ourselves, for without it no relationship is possible. Only through right thinking can there be understanding. Neither leaders nor a new set of values nor a blueprint can bring about this creative understanding; only through our own right effort can there be right understanding.

How is it possible then to find this essential understanding? From where shall we start to discover what is real, what is true, in all this conflagration, confusion and misery? Is it not important to find out for ourselves how to think rightly about war and peace, about economic and social conditions, about our relationship to our fellow men? Surely there is a difference between right thinking and right or conditioned thought. We may be able to produce in ourselves imitatively right thought, but such thought is not right thinking. Right or conditioned thought is uncreative. But when we know how to think rightly for ourselves, which is to be living, dynamic, then it is possible to bring about a new and happier culture.

I would like to develop what seems to me to be the process of right thinking so that each one of us is truly creative, and not merely enclosed in a series of ideas or prejudices. How shall we then begin to discover for ourselves what is right thinking? Without right thinking there is no possibility of happiness. Without right thinking our actions, our behavior, our affections have no basis. Right thinking is not to be discovered through books, through attending a few talks, or by merely listening to some people's ideas of what right thinking is. *Right thinking is to be discovered for ourselves through ourselves.*

Right thinking comes with self-knowledge. Without self-knowledge there is no right thinking. Without knowing yourself, what you think and what you feel cannot be true. The root of all understanding lies in understanding yourself. If you can find out what are the causes of your thought-feeling, and from that discovery know how to think-feel, then there is the beginning of understanding. Without knowing yourself, the accumulation of ideas, the acceptance of beliefs and theories have no basis. Without knowing yourself you will ever be caught in uncertainty, depending on moods, on circumstances. Without knowing yourself fully you cannot think rightly. Surely this is obvious. If I do not know what my motives, my intentions, my background, my private thoughts-feelings are, how can I agree or disagree with another? How can I estimate or establish my relationship with another? How can I discover anything of life if I do not know myself? And to know myself is an enormous task requiring constant observation, meditative awareness.

This is our first task even before the problem of war and peace, of economic and social conflicts, of death and immortality. These questions will arise, they are bound to arise, but in discovering ourselves, in understanding ourselves these questions will be rightly answered. So those who are really serious in these matters must begin with themselves in order to understand the world of which they are a part. Without understanding yourself, you cannot understand the whole.

Self-knowledge is the beginning of wisdom. Self-knowledge is cultivated through the individual's search of himself. I am not putting the individual in opposition to the mass. They are not antithetical. You, the individual, are the mass, the result of the mass. In us, as you will discover if you go into it deeply, are both the many and the particular. It is as a stream that is constantly flowing, leaving little eddies and these eddies we call individuality but they are the result of this constant flow of water. Your thoughts-feelings, those mental-emotional activities, are they not the result of the past, of what we call the many? Have you not similar thoughts-feelings as your neighbor?

So when I talk of the individual I am not putting him in opposition to the mass. On the contrary, I want to remove this antagonism. This opposing antagonism between the mass and the you, the individual, creates confusion and conflict, ruthlessness and misery. But if we can understand how the individual, the you, is part of the whole, not only mystically but actually, then we shall free ourselves happily and spontaneously from the greater part of the desire to compete, to succeed, to deceive, to oppose, to be ruthless, or to become a follower or a leader. Then we will regard the problem of existence quite differently. And it is important to understand this deeply. As long as we regard ourselves as individuals, apart from the whole, competing, obstructing, opposing, sacrificing the many for the particular or the particular for the many, all those problems that arise out of this conflicting antagonism will have no happy and enduring solution; for they are the result of wrong thinking-feeling.

Now, when I talk about the individual I am not putting him in opposition to the mass. What am I? I am a result; I am a result of the past, of innumerable layers of the past, of a series of causes-effects. And how can I be opposed to the whole, the past, when I am the result of all that? If I, who am the mass, the whole, if I do not understand myself, not only what is outside my skin, objectively, but subjectively, inside the skin, how can I understand another, the world? To understand oneself requires kindly and tolerant detachment. If you do not understand yourself, you will not understand anything else; you may have great ideals, beliefs and formulations but they will have no reality. They will be delusions. So you must know yourself to understand the present and through the present the past. From the known present the hidden layers of the past are discovered and this discovery is liberating and creative.

To understand ourselves requires objective, kindly, dispassionate study of ourselves, ourselves being the organism as a whole: our body, our feelings, our thoughts. They are not separate; they are interrelated. It is only when we understand the organism as a whole that we can go beyond and discover still further, greater, vaster things. But without this primary understanding, without laying the right foundation for right thinking, we cannot proceed to greater heights. To bring about in each one of us the capacity to discover what is true becomes essential, for what is discovered is liberating and creative. For what is discovered is true. That is, if we merely conform to a pattern of what we ought to be or yield to a craving, it does not produce certain results which are conflicting, confusing, but in the process of our study of ourselves we are on a voyage of self-discovery which brings joy and harmony.

There is a surety in negative rather than positive thinking-feeling. We have assumed in a positive manner what we are, or we have cultivated positively our ideas on other people's or on our own formulations. And hence we depend on authority, on circumstances, hoping thereby to establish a series of positive ideas and actions. Whereas if you examine you will see there is agreement in negation; there is surety in negative thinking, which is the highest form of thinking. When once you have found true negation and agreement in negation then you can build further in positiveness.

The discovery that lies in self-knowledge is arduous, for the beginning and the end is in us. To seek happiness, love, hope, outside of us leads to illusion, to sorrow; to find happiness, peace, joy within, requires self-knowledge. We are slaves to the immediate pressures and demands of the world and we are drawn away by all that and dissipate our energies in all that and so we have little time to study ourselves. To be deeply cognizant of our motives, of our desires to achieve, to become, demands constant, inward awareness. Without understanding ourselves superficial devices of economic and social reform, however necessary and beneficial, will not produce unity in the world but only greater confusion and misery.

Many of us think that economic reform of one kind or another will bring peace to the world; or that social reform or one specialized religion conquering all others will bring happiness to man. I believe there are something like three hundred or more religious sects in this country, each competing and proselytizing. Do you think competitive religion will bring peace, unity and happiness to mankind? Do you think any specialized religion, whether it be Hinduism, Buddhism or Christianity, will bring peace? Or must we set aside all specialized religions and discover reality for ourselves? When we see the world blasted by bombs and feel the horrors that are going on in it; when the world is broken up by separate religions, nationalities, races, ideologies, what is the answer to all this? We may not just go on living briefly and dying and hope some good will come out of it. We cannot leave it to others to bring happiness and peace to mankind; for mankind is ourselves, each one of us. Where does the solution lie, except in ourselves? To discover the real answer requires deep thought-feeling and few of us are willing to solve this misery. If each one of us considers this problem as springing from within and is not merely driven helplessly along in this appalling confusion and misery, then we shall find a simple and direct answer.

In studying and so in understanding ourselves there will come clarity and order. And there can be clarity only in self-knowledge which nurtures right thinking. Right thinking comes before right action. If we become self-aware and so cultivate self-knowledge from which springs right thinking, then we shall create a mirror in ourselves which will reflect, without distortion, all our thoughts-feelings. To be so self-aware is extremely difficult as our mind is used to wandering and being distracted. Its wanderings, its distractions are of its own interests and creations. In understanding these—not merely pushing them aside—comes self-knowledge and right thinking. It is only through inclusion and not by exclusion, not through approbation or condemnation or comparison, that understanding comes.

A lady once told me that she had practiced meditation for a number of years and presently went on to explain that a certain group of people must be destroyed for they were bringing misery and destruction to man. Yet she practiced brotherhood, love and peace, which she said had guided her life. Do not many of you who practice meditation talk of love and brotherhood, yet condone or participate in war, which is organized murder? What significance then has your meditation? Your meditation only strengthens your narrowness, ill will and ignorance.

Those who would understand the deep significance of meditation must begin first with themselves, for self-knowledge is the foundation of right thinking. Without right thinking how can thought go far? You must begin near to go far. Self-awareness is arduous; to think-out, feel-out *every* thought-feeling is strenuous; but this awareness of every thought-feeling will bring to an end the wandering of the mind. When you try to meditate do you not find that your mind wanders and chatters ceaselessly? It is of little use to brush aside every thought but one and try to concentrate upon that one thought which you have chosen. Instead of trying to control these wandering thoughts, become aware of them, think-out, feel-out every thought, comprehend its significance, however pleasant or unpleasant; try to understand each thought-feeling. Each thought-feeling so pursued will yield its meaning; and thus the mind, as it comprehends its own repetitive and wandering thoughts, becomes emptied of its own formulation.

The mind is the result of the past, it is a storehouse of many interests, of contradictory values; it is ever gathering, ever becoming. We must be aware of these accumulations and understand them as they arise. Suppose you have collected letters for many years; now you look into the drawer and read letter after letter, keeping some and discarding others; what you keep you reread and again you discard till the drawer is empty. Similarly, be aware of every thought-feeling, comprehend its significance, and should it return reconsider it for it has not been fully understood. As a drawer is useful only when empty so the mind must be free of all its accumulations for only then can there be that openness to wisdom and the ecstasy of the Real. Tranquillity of wisdom is not the result of an act of will, it is not a conclusion, a state to be achieved. It comes into being in the awareness of understanding.

Meditation becomes significant when the mind-heart is aware, thinking-out, feeling-out every thought-feeling that arises without comparison or identification. For identification and comparison maintain the conflict of duality and there is no solution within its pattern. I wonder how many of you have really practiced meditation. If you have, you will have noticed how difficult it is to be extensively aware without the narrowing-down of thought-feeling. In trying to concentrate, the conflicting thoughts-feelings are suppressed or pushed aside or overcome and through this process there can be no understanding. Concentration is gained at the expense of deep awareness. If the mind is petty and limited, concentration will not make it any the less small and trivial; on the contrary it will strengthen its own nature. Such narrow concentration does not make the mind-heart vulnerable to Reality; it only hardens the mind-heart in its own obstinacy and ignorance and perpetuates the self-enclosing process.

When the mind-heart is extensive, deep and tranquil there is the Real. If the mind is seeking a result, however noble and worthy, if it is concerned with becoming it ceases to be extensive and infinitely pliable. It must be as the unknown to receive the Unknowable. It must be utterly tranquil to receive for the being of the Eternal.

Awareness is the process of freeing the conscious mind from the bondages which cause conflict and pain and thus making it open and receptive to the hidden. The hidden layers of consciousness convey their significance through dreams and symbols. If every thought-feeling is thought-out, felt-out, as fully and deeply as possible, without condemnation or comparison, acceptance or identification, then all the hidden layers of consciousness will reveal themselves. Through constant awareness the dreamer ceases to dream, for through alert and passive awareness every movement of thought-feeling of the open and hidden layers of consciousness is being understood. But if one is incapable of thinking-out, feeling-out every thought completely and fully then one begins to dream. Dreams need interpretation and to interpret there must be free and open intelligence; instead, the dreamer goes to a dream specialist, thus creating for himself other problems. Only in deep extensive awareness can there be an end to dreams and their anxious interpretation.

Right meditation is very effective in freeing the mind-heart from its self-enclosing process. The open and hidden layers of consciousness are the result of the past, of accumulation, of centuries of education, and surely such an educated, conditioned mind cannot be vulnerable to the Real. Occasionally, in the silence after the storm of conflict and pain, there comes inexpressible beauty and joy; it is not the result of the storm but of the cessation of conflict.

The mind-heart must be passively still for the creative being of the Real.

Is there a possibility of finding enduring joy in this life? There is, but to experience it there must be freedom. Without freedom, truth cannot be discovered; without freedom, there can be no experience of the Real. Freedom must be sought out: freedom from saviors, teachers, leaders; freedom from the self-enclosing walls of good and bad; freedom from authority, imitation and the mind-conditioning accumulations of the past; freedom from the petty, ego-bound self, the cause of conflict and pain.

The unity of man is to be found only in Love, in the freedom and illumination that Truth brings. This oneness of man is not to be established through mere economic and social readjustments. The world is ever preoccupied with these superficial reforms; it is ever trying to rearrange its values within the pattern of craving and acquisitiveness and so brings disaster upon itself. We hope that outward revolution, outward change of values will transform man; they do affect him, but greed, acquisitiveness and the search for gratification at lower levels continues. This endless, mindless and purposeless movement of acquisitiveness cannot at any time bring peace to man, and only when he is free of it can there be creative being.

You must become both master and pupil in search of truth. You must make your own approach directly to the Divine without the conflict of example, comparison or opposites. In trying to comprehend the outer world, one comes at last to the inner; and that inner, when properly pursued and rightly understood, leads to the imperishable Supreme which we call God. In the realization alone, peace and order come to the self and to the world. In this bliss of the Real, the experiencer and the experience cease. A mind-heart that is burdened with the memory of yesterday cannot live in the eternal present. Mind-heart must die each day in order to discover eternal Being.

Mohammed Ayub Khan

Our faith in Mohammed and in Allah will be proven only when we make the human qualities of the Prophet be the pattern of our practical daily lives. I pray to God that He may give to all of us—and to all mankind—the inclination and ability to do so.

Mustachioed Field Marshal Mohammed Ayub Khan, sixty-one, now serving his second term as president of Pakistan, has emerged during the 1960s as one of the outstanding statesman-soldiers of the Far East. Devout, dynamic and long admired for his distinctive leadership of the Pakistani Armed Forces, General Khan became his nation's first commander-in-chief in 1951 and added the cabinet post of minister of defense in 1954. On February 17, 1960, he was sworn in as the first democratically-elected president of the newly constituted Moslem state.

In addition to his military genius, which has been apparent from his World War II role as a regiment commander on the Burma front to his skilled direction of Pakistan's elite land and air forces in the 1965 attack on Pakistan by India, President Khan also played an integral part in drafting his country's first constitution and in establishing its various democratic agencies and institutions. A deeply religious Moslem and avid student of the Koran, the England-educated militarist urges Islam's precepts of duty, charity, industry and progress upon his swiftly-evolving land and himself tries to model his life after the sacrificial example of the Holy Prophet. Among his own diverse and demanding duties, Khan serves as president of the Pakistan Moslem League.

Mohammed Khan was born in Behana, India, on May 14, 1907. Educated at a Moslem university and widely traveled while in his teens, he received his military training at Royal Military College in Sandhurst, England. In line with Indian custom in the 1920s, he first served with the Royal Fusiliers and later with the 14th Punjab Regiment. From a World War II battalion commander, he rose rapidly in the ranks of the new Pakistan military; in 1948 he was promoted to major general and appointed the first commander of the East Pakistan Army; two years later he became the first Pakistani commander-in-chief. His presidential rule has been distinguished by progressive social and political reforms, the planning of a new capital at Islamabad and the building of Asia's first Institute of Nuclear Science and Technology.

Science, Survival—and Islam

Pakistan was established on the basis of religion. We demanded Pakistan for the preservation of our religion and culture, and Allah, in His bounty, granted us the boon of Pakistan.

Our people are perhaps the most religious-minded in the Moslem world. But modern education and enlightenment are spreading day by day. In the last century, our so-called religious scholars thought that safety for Islam lay in depriving the Moslems of the knowledge of English, history and the new sciences. If, however, Islam is the true religion of Allah and its principles are correct and everlasting, then Islam does not stand in danger from modern education or new ideas. It is the coward and the liar who are afraid. The truth, or those who are on the side of truth, should not be afraid of the advent of new sciences or new ideas.

It is not the correct way to combat new science and new ideas by confining ourselves within the limitations of our knowledge and keeping away from all outside influences. The correct way is that we should study the new sciences and new ideas. Our religion ordains that we accept a good thing, wherever it may be found, and whatever is wrong, we must counter it and prove that it is wrong. Because Islam is a religion of progress, there is nothing in the Koran and the Sunna which stands in danger from the new sciences or the new ideas. In fact, the Koran repeatedly appeals to us to make use of our own reason and intellect. The Holy Prophet himself opened the gateway of *Ijtihad*.

Therefore, it is the moral and national duty of our religious scholars and of our alert citizenry to prove the everlasting principles of Islam by applying them to the needs and requirements of the present day. The only result of uncompromising adherence to trivialities or outmoded ideas, which no longer hold good, would be that future generations would become irreligious and godless.

It is a paradox of the present age that much of our anxiety, as indeed much of our hope, is focused on science and technology.

The spectacular advances made by science have placed terrifying powers in the hands of man which, if unleashed, may mean his self-destruction. At the same time, only science and technology can ensure the deliverance of large parts of the world from poverty and hunger.

The modern age is the age of science and the universal civilization of science. Anyone desirous of leading an honorable life today cannot escape the use of this new civilization. It particularly applies to the newly emerging nations. These nations have two objectives in view:

1. To reap the benefits of their independence by translating it into human happiness through scientific progress; and

2. To defend their independence by means of power generated through their efforts with the help of science.

They could not but recognize the present age as the age of science whose immediate children are technology and industrialization. The quicker they enter the age of science, the better. They are in a desperate haste to achieve advancement and progress through science.

It has been long known that in Pakistan we wanted to establish an Islamic way of life. This way of life must relate to the realities of life or this ideal will remain a mere slogan and deception. The Islamic way of life means scientific advancement and progress coupled with Islamic religious principles. We want to remain spiritually and morally human beings and not become machines!

The modern scientist is well aware of the fact that circumstances have placed him at the center of things and that he is closely associated with the processes which determine the fate of the world. The scientist of the atomic age has a unique perception of the predicament of mankind which seems to have awakened in him a profound moral sense and concern for the future of humanity. Indeed, that is why more and more scientists have, in the recent past, spoken of the conscience of the world.

It is true that the scientist cannot isolate himself completely from the ethics of the society that he belongs to. As such, he cannot choose not to go on making stronger and stronger contributions to national defense in spite of a certain philosophical uneasiness about it. But there is hope in the fact that the modern scientist is showing an increasing preference for the role which calls him to harness human knowledge for the preservation of peace, for succor of those in distress, for the amelioration of the world's poor and needy. The greatest image of our times is that the multitudes in Asia and Africa, who have recently won independence, are now being borne forward by the high tide of aspiration for a better life. They are engaged in a titanic struggle against poverty, hunger and disease, and they know that their lot can be improved only by the superior knowledge which science and technology bring to them.

There have been momentous periods in history when mankind drew its purpose and strength from the personalities of moral teachers who dominated the landscape of human civilization. Such humane thought and interpretation of the mysteries of mind and soul are no less important today than they were yesterday. But today, and in the future journeys of man's mind, guidance must also come from another source—from the vigor of the scientist-philosopher. He must now come forward to play a vital role in the evolution of the new humanism, which paves the way for a nation's onslaught on the fundamental problems of human existence the world over.

Some fourteen hundred years ago, Islam emerged on the scene as a great blessing. It was a dynamic and progressive movement that reshaped the entire pattern of life and gave a new meaning and purpose to man's endeavors. So long as this movement remained part and parcel of life itself, the followers of Islam continued to perform such memorable deeds in the world of science and practical knowledge as had no parallel in history.

Unfortunately, with the passage of time, the Moslems at large sought to concentrate more on the dogmatic aspects of islam and less on its inherent greatness as a movement. This resulted inevitably in a widening gap between life and religion which continues to affect our lives today. Islam came into being essentially to reduce this gap, but it is an irony of fate that its followers themselves were caught in the yawning gap. The miracle of Islam was that it destroyed idolatry, and the tragedy of the Moslems has been that they rendered religion into the form of an idol.

The noble life of the Prophet Mohammed, however, was a model for all people and for all times. It was not the life of just one human being; it was the idealization of all humanity. The world has not produced any other person who could blend within himself so much of grace, sublimity and beauty. Although every moment of the Prophet's life lays down a pattern for us, I should like to draw your attention to two of its particular facets.

Many people are well aware of Arabia's condition in the seventh century when the Holy Prophet began to spread the teachings of Islam. There was no government; there were no laws and no courts. There was neither a police force to protect the people nor an army to defend them. Everywhere might made right. Whoever had the strength and the sword did just what he liked. In the midst of this rule of the jungle, the Prophet raised his lone voice of truth and righteousness. He stood unshakable in the face of bitter opposition, persecution and tribulations until at last the forces of evil were routed and truth prevailed.

It is easy to talk of these noble precepts, but to emulate them is far more difficult. Today you have every kind of facilities for the protection of your life and property. Besides the police and the army there are all sorts of legal institutions—courts, high courts, supreme courts. But in spite of all these facilities, how many people are there who have the moral courage to speak the truth and act upon it even in the most trivial matters of everyday life? Right before your eyes crimes like black-marketeering, bribery and corruption are committed daily.

You suffer in silence, and it may be you talk about them and criticize them in intimate circles, but you do not come out and lodge complaints against the defaulters because you do not wish to offend anyone!

This attitude is diametrically opposed to the one taught to us by the Prophet of God. Remember that angels from heaven are not sent to reform a nation, nor is it pleasant to give warnings of punishment time and again to that end. Whosoever disciplines himself along lines of truth and honesty—and perseveres on this right path under all conditions—then he alone would be offering implicit obedience to the Holy Prophet. Without this you may be called the Prophet's people but not his true and faithful followers.

The second point I wish to draw is the Holy Prophet's untiring energy and his abiding sense of duty. Today things have come to such a pass that the more power and authority one gets, the more inactive and luxury-loving one becomes. One's chief concern is that one may continue to enjoy power and position, while others may sweat and toil. Today, one is less conscious of one's duties and more anxious to achieve personal gains and comforts.

You and I are, after all, ordinary men. Pakistan is just one country. To me the entire world-system is insignificant before the eminence that God bestowed upon His Prophet Mohammed. God not only made him His Messenger but also called him the Saviour of Humanity, and repeatedly conveyed to him the message of his success and salvation. There can be nothing greater than this for man on earth. Nevertheless, the care and conscientiousness with which the Holy Prophet discharged his worldly and heavenly duties are unique for all times.

One day the Holy Prophet returned home after a day's strenuous routine of prayers and preaching. He was extremely worried and tired. That day his enemies had greatly tortured him. That had scattered thorns in his way, thrown stones at him, and hurled taunting remarks. With the day's strain heavy on him, he was about to retire for rest when someone brought the news that a caravan had halted behind a hill, a few miles from Mecca. The Prophet at once rose up to go and convey to the travelers the Word of God. A few of his followers humbly protested, saying he was tired after the day's work and could very well attend to the newcomers on the following morning.

The Prophet replied: "Who knows but I may die before morning comes; or that the caravan may leave during the night. In that case, my duty to God will not have been discharged."

Such realization of one's responsibility was given only to the Prophet. But those who are so fortunate as to be the followers of the Prophet owe it to their faith to attend to their duties with entire devotion, energy and honesty. The ills of the present have only one antidote—hard work, honest work, clean work. There exists no other miracle that can bring meaning to the life of an individual or of a nation.

It is easy to recite the Koran and be called a Moslem. It is not difficult either to recite Darood and Salaam to show one's belief and faith in the Prophet of God. But it is action that finally counts. Our faith in Mohammed and Allah will be proven only when we make the human qualities of the Prophet the pattern of our practical daily lives. I pray to God that He may give to all of us—and to all mankind—the inclination and the ability to do so.

Albert Schweitzer

To the man who is truly ethical, all life is sacred.

Dr. Albert Schweitzer, long revered as "the Great Man's Great Man" and "the Number One Man in the World," died in 1965 shortly after celebrating his ninetieth birthday hard at work in his jungle hospital near Lambaréné, West Africa. So for the past fifty years, had this living flesh-and-blood saint spent every birthday and almost every other day feeding, housing, clothing and curing sick natives—"to pay back the greatest debt of Western civilization." To most of mankind, his humanitarian life had become the inspiring embodiment of his Christian faith and love.

One of the most extraordinary men of the twentieth century, Alsace-born Albert Schweitzer progressed from a sickly, yet happy, childhood through the study of philosophy and theology at the University of Strassburg to a richly creative career before he was thirty. The son of a Protestant pastor, he became an Evangelical Lutheran minister; a lover of music and the organ, he gained renown as a concert organist and wrote an unsurpassed book on the music and genius of Bach; an avid Bible student and mystical believer, he produced the most revolutionary book on Christ ever written—*The Quest of the Historical Jesus*. In the high tradition of Kant and Spengler, he emerged as a philosopher and metaphysician who thought and wrote deeply about the crises of his epoch.

World-famous as a musician, author, theologian and biblical scholar, Schweitzer suddenly turned his back on the world's dazzling rewards, studied tropical medicine and at age thirty-eight became a medical missionary to the downtrodden Negroes of Equatorial Africa. Since his arrival in Gabon where he had to perform his first operations in a hen-house, the white-maned St. Francis-like doctor gradually cleared the jungle, erected hospitals, set about curing ailments from dysentery to tuberculosis. When Schweitzer won the Nobel Peace Prize in 1953, he used the forty thousand dollars prize money to enlarge the hospital leper colony.

Honored by all races and religions as one of the world's greatest humanitarians, Dr. Schweitzer was awarded the Goethe Prize, the Paracelsus Medal and nearly fifty honorary degrees from leading universities. His twenty-one published books include *African Notebook*,

Out of My Life and Thought, and *The Philosophy of Civilization*. More than the honors bestowed or the praise proffered by the civilized world, Dr. Schweitzer's living memorial remains the thousands of bodies healed and spirits lifted by a modern saint to whom "ethics is nothing more than reverence for life."

Reverence for Life

It was the dry season in usually wet Equatorial Africa and slowly we crept upstream, laboriously feeling for the channels between the sandbanks of the Ogooué River. Lost in thought, I sat on the deck of the barge, struggling to find the elementary and universal conception of the ethical which I had not discovered in any philosophy. Sheet after sheet I covered with disconnected sentences, merely to keep myself concentrated on the problem. Late on the third day, at the very moment when at sunset we were making our way through a herd of hippopotamuses, there flashed upon my mind, unforeseen and unsought, "Reverence for Life." The iron door had yielded: the path in the thicket had become visible. Now I had found my way to the idea in which world- and life-affirmation and ethics are contained side by side! Now I knew that the world-view of ethical world- and life-affirmation, together with its ideals of civilization, is founded in thought.

Thus, to me, ethics is nothing else than reverence for life. Reverence for life affords me my fundamental principle of morality, namely that good consists in maintaining, assisting and enhancing life, and that to destroy, to harm or to hinder life is evil. Affirmation of the world—that is, affirmation of the will to live which appears in phenomenal form all around me—is only possible for me in that I give myself out for other life. Without understanding the meaning of the world, I act from an inner necessity of my being so as to create values and to live ethically. For in life-affirmation and in ethics, I fulfill the will of the universal will to live which reveals itself to me. I live my life in God, in the mysterious ethical divine personality which I cannot discover in the world, but only experience in myself as a mysterious impulse.

The idea that men should ever be favored by being free from the responsibilities of self-sacrifice as men for men is foreign to the ethic of reverence for life. It requires that in some way or other and in something or other we should all live as men for men. Therefore, search and see if there is not some place where you may invest your humanity. From my childhood up, for example, I was troubled about my right to happiness as a matter of course and about the pain which prevails in the world around us. As long ago as my student days, it struck me as incomprehensible that I should be allowed to live such a happy life while I saw so many people around me wrestling with care and suffering. Out of the depths of my feeling of happiness, there gradually grew up within me an understanding of the saying of Jesus that we must not treat our lives as being for ourselves alone.

While at the University of Strassburg and enjoying the happiness of being able to study and even to produce some results in science and art, I could not help thinking of others who were denied that happiness by their material circumstances or their health. Then, one brilliant summer morning during the Whitsuntide holidays, I awoke with the thought that I must not accept this happiness as a matter of course, but must give something in return for it. That morning, with the birds singing outside, I settled that I would consider myself justified in living until I was thirty for science and art in order to devote myself from that time forward to the direct service of humanity. I had found the answer that lay hidden for me in Jesus' saying: "Whosoever shall save his life shall lose it, and whosoever shall lose his life for My sake and the Gospels shall save it."

After a half-century in Africa, I still remain convinced that truth, love, peaceableness, meekness and kindness are the violence that can master all other violence. Whatever you have received more than others in health, in talents, in ability, in success, in pleasant childhood, in harmonious conditions of home life, all this you must not take to yourself as a matter of course. You must pay a price for it. You must render in return an unusually great sacrifice of your life for other life.

When I am asked what modern thinkers influenced my life and philosophy, I invariably name two—the great German author Goethe and the selfless Hindu saint Gandhi. Goethe's message to the men of today is the same as to the men of his time and to the men of all times: "Strive for true humanity! Become a man who is true to his inner nature, a man whose deed is in tune with his character." Likewise, Gandhi, who was the most Christian Hindu of the century, once acknowledged that he got the idea of ahimsa or non-violence from the commandments of Jesus: "But I say unto you that ye resist not evil," and "Love your enemies . . . pray for them who despitefully use you and persecute you, that ye may be the children of your Father which is in heaven." In both, the ethic of inner perfection is governed by the principle of love.

Anyone who has recognized that the idea of love is the spiritual beam of light which reaches us from the Infinite, ceases to demand from religion that it offer him complete knowledge of the supernatural. He ponders, instead, on the great questions: what is the meaning of evil in the world; how in God the will to create and the will to love are one; in what relation the spiritual and material life stand to one another; and in what way our existence is transitory and yet eternal. But he is able to leave these questions on one side, however painful it may be to give up all hope of answers to them. In the knowledge of spiritual existence in God through love he possesses the one thing needful. "Love never faileth," says St. Paul.

It is this principle of love that we have tried to practice in succoring the Negroes of West Africa. For example, when some poor moaning creature is brought to me with an inflamed appendix or a strangulated hernia, I lay my hand on his forehead and say to him: "Don't be afraid! In an hour's time you shall be put to sleep, and when you wake you won't feel any more pain." When the operation is finished, in the barely lighted dormitory, I watch for the sick man's awakening. Scarcely has he recovered consciousness when he stares about him and exclaims again and again: "I've no more pain! I've no more pain! . . ." His hand feels for mine and will not let it go.

I then begin to tell the patient and the others who are in the room that it is the Lord Jesus who has told the doctor and his wife to come to Gabon, and that white people in Europe and America give them the money to live here and cure the sick Negroes. Then I have to answer questions as to who these white people are, where they live, and how they know that the natives suffer so much from sickness. The African sun is shining through the coffee bushes into the dark shed, but we black and white sit side by side and feel that we experience the meaning of the words: "And all ye are brethren." Would that my generous friends in Europe and the United States could come out here and live through one such hour!

Harry S. Truman

I have a great faith in people, whatever their race, or religion or locale of living. They value freedom above all else, and no conqueror or dictator has ever held them down for long.

Harry S. Truman, the man from Missouri who became the thirty-third President of the United States, remains at eighty-four the brisk, bouncy everyman whom almost every man has come to admire. Jaunty and direct, courageous and controversial, the former farm boy, county judge and field artillery captain stunned America and the free world when his rigorous whistle-stop campaign returned him handily to the White House in 1948. A U.S. senator since 1934 and Vice President since 1944, Truman ascended to the Presidency on the sudden death of Franklin D. Roosevelt in April, 1945.

Without college or professional training, "Give 'em hell, Harry" was the ordinary public servant who became an extraordinary President. Of average age, antecedents and ability when he entered the wartime White House, he swiftly demonstrated a triumph of virtues which made him the champion of democracy in a divided world. His decisiveness (Hiroshima and Korea), his vision (the Marshall Plan and Truman Doctrine), his courage (the firing of MacArthur and 1948 victory at the polls) helped him leave an imprint of greatness on the Presidency and the American people. As his friend Jonathan Daniels said of him, "Truman is both the product and embodiment of the American faith . . . and he expresses that faith in the language of his countrymen."

Born, brought up and educated in Missouri, Truman still maintains his home and office in Independence. In 1919, after service in France with the 55th Army Division, he married the former Bess Wallace; their daughter, Margaret (now Mrs. Clifton Daniel), lives in New York City. His famous nature walks and his pithy outbursts on public issues keep him regularly in the news, while his enthusiastic interest in such enterprises as the Truman Library, American Bible Society and Harry S. Truman Center for the Advancement of Peace shows his unflagging faith in freedom's fulfillment. A lifelong Baptist and Master Mason, Truman is the author of *Years of Decision* and *Years of Trial and Hope.*

(The Christian credo of former President Truman was prepared by the author from the former President's pertinent speeches, statements and interviews.)

Freedom's Fulfillment

I was talking to a young man the other day, believe it or not an educated young man, and I told him that he should read the twentieth chapter of Exodus because it would do him some good. That Bible passage, you will recall, is the famous one where Moses amid thunder and lightning on quaking Mount Sinai spoke to the Lord and received the Ten Commandments. Well, the young man looked at me quizzically and said, "What is Exodus?" What would become of the United States if all of our young people were as ignorant of God's words as that "educated" young man! I think every youngster should be told by his mother and father to read one book of the Bible each month until he gets all the way to Revelation. It won't do him any harm, as I can attest from the inspiration and guidelines gained from my own Bible-reading youth.

The fundamental basis of the good life—and of good government too—is that great Judaic-Christian textbook, the Bible, and it started with Moses on Mount Sinai. In St. Matthew's Gospel alone where in chapters five to seven Jesus' Sermon on the Mount is recorded, there is wisdom and inspiration for a lifetime. All Americans should read these sublime verses again and again because there is a tragic difference between a people with a moral code and a people without one. You may recall in John Bunyan's *Pilgrim's Progress*, there was a certain fellow who was always looking down and hoping to find a treasure, when all he had to do was look up and there it was! So, in the Holy Bible, is our moral treasure and God-given birthright.

I never give up hope that young people will someday accept more readily the experience of the past as a starting point and go on to enlarge the scope of human achievement. In general I am never more reassured than when I talk to college boys and girls and see how eager they are to know the past. Most of my own ideas on how the world runs I obtained very early in life from the Bible, the King James version of the Old and New Testaments. The Bible is, among other things, one of the greatest documents of history. Every trouble that humanity is heir to is set out in the Bible. And the remedy is there, too, if you know where to find it. I read the Bible at least a dozen times, and maybe more, before I was fifteen years old. The Bible must be read over and over again to get the full meaning out of it. The same is true of the Constitution of the United States. And the moral code contained in the Old and New Testaments is needed by all mankind. If civilization is to continue, the majority of the people of the world must have a moral code by which to live and for which to live. The moral code set forth in the Bible is unequaled.

I have been a voluntary member of the Baptist Church since I was eighteen years old. How highly individualistic my people were and how self-reliant and independent they were in their personal views is illustrated by a story told me by my uncle when I was eighteen. I was named for my uncle (my mother's brother) whose name was Harrison Young. Although a good Baptist, he did not attend church regularly. I told my uncle that I was going to the field to get an armful of green corn so that we could have corn pudding. He asked me if I knew the record number of ears of corn a man had ever eaten at one sitting. When I told him I did not know, he told me the story about a pal of his who won the record on a bet by eating thirteen roasting ears. This fellow contracted a severe stomach ache and had to send for the doctor. The doctor worked over him the rest of the night, and in the morning told him that he had better send for the preacher and do a little praying. The man was in such pain that he sent for the parson. The parson prayed for him, and recommended that he also pray for himself; but the stricken man told the preacher he was not a praying man and did not think he could do it. However, as the excruciating pain continued, the man decided to make an attempt. He got down on his knees in the old-fashioned revival manner, and this was his petition to the Almighty: "Oh, Lord, I am in great pain and misery. I have eaten thirteen roasting ears of corn and I don't seem to be able to take care of them. I am praying to you for help. And, Lord, I am not like those howling church members in the 'Amen' corner. If you will just relieve me of seven of those ears of corn, I'll try to handle the other six by myself."

I have had to meet and deal with many people and events, all of which has given me an opportunity to take a long look at life. Young students, who come to see me at the Library in Independence, often ask me whether we have changed much morally and spiritually since the beginnings of civilization. I tell them that, as I see it, the human animal has not changed much. He has to be guided in the proper direction under a moral code, and then there must be some machinery to make him live within that moral code. A man cannot have character unless he lives within a fundamental system of morals that creates character. There are many moral and religious codes in the world and most of them are similar. In my opinion, the moral code of the Christian religion is about as good as there is. The Mohammedans have a code based closely on Christian precepts, and the Buddhists, Hindus and Confucians have moral codes that are excellent. I have been asked whether the failure of Christianity is not partly responsible for the growing spread of Communism in the world. I cannot agree that Christianity has been a failure. But ruthless men have been able to impose Communism on helpless people because of the absence of Christianity and the lack of a code that upholds the freedom and dignity of the individual. No nation has ever adopted Communism by the choice of a people in a free election; on the other hand, we have progressed a long way toward civilization and religious tolerance and we have set a good example in this country.

While there are disturbing things taking place in many parts of the world, I continue to be optimistic about the future. It is only fair to say that I am an optimist by disposition, but my confidence in the future is based more on my reading of history, on my religion and the evolution of man's works. I have never seen pessimists make anything work, or contribute anything of lasting value. It takes idealists to make the world work, because eventually some of the ideas they develop are put into practice to help mankind. One idea that has always seemed to me worth trying is to bring about the active cooperation of the leaders and followers of the great religious faiths of the world. If such a common religious and moral front would be organized, a vital force for the advancement of peace could be harnessed. Minor, and even major, differences in how we worship God strike me as being of relatively little importance in the face of an aggressive foe threatening to destroy all freedom of worship, freedom of expression and other individual liberties.

There has been a lot of talk lately about the burdens of the Presidency. Decisions that the President has to make often affect the live of tens of millions of people around the world, but that does not mean that they should take longer to make. Some men can make decisions and some cannot. Some men fret and delay under criticism. I used to have a saying that applies here, and I note that some people have picked it up: "If you cannot stand the heat, get out of the kitchen!"

The most dangerous course a President can follow in a time of crisis is to defer making decisions until they are forced on him, and thereupon become inevitable decisions. Events then get out of hand and take control of the President, and he is compelled to overcome situations which he should have prevented. When a President finds himself in that position, he is no longer a leader but an improviser who is driven to action out of expediency or weakness. Not only must a President be fully informed but he must be constantly alert to what lies ahead. And he can see ahead only if he has a sense of history, a habit of religion and understands the times he lives in.

Thus, I believe to acquire extra spiritual perception is really very necessary if you are interested in improving your life. I have found that reading the New Testament for about five minutes a day, year in and year out, underlining whatever seems important for further or future study, soon adds up to spiritual understanding. God communicates with us as we read His Holy Scripture through the medium of the Holy Spirit. It works a little like this: As we read the Bible or some religious book or even the daily papers, we will come to some passage that seems to contain a message meant for us. Some call that intuition, and the more sensitive our consciences become through Bible study the better we understand the advantages of God's moral and spiritual life. Righteousness is rightness with God. The letter of His law seems to have more authority when His Spirit is there to guide us. Sin may be anything that tends to separate us from God. The love of luxury or of money can, if it becomes possessive enough, separate us from Him. Some hidden defect in our character that our best friend would not mention could serve to keep us from a fuller appreciation of all His blessings and especially His baptism of the Holy Spirit. We might go through life without realizing what is wrong with us until someday we happen to read of someone else with the same fault and realize that it is we all along who have had the beam in our own eye and were blind to our faults. I wonder how many people do not quite reach full spiritual enjoyments or blessings of this life through too much pride and ego or not enough humility and love.

Not all of us are suited to become priests or ministers or missionaries, but we can all live like Christians should and by our very actions speak for Christ. We can be seen going to church regularly and be witnesses for the truth, honesty, morality and generosity without even uttering a word. Actions often speak louder than words where Christianity is concerned. Dr. Schweitzer's example of Christian love in action is worth more than all the speeches about Christianity he could have made in a lifetime. Christ wants us to lead a crusade for a better world where the common man may learn and practice Christian or unselfish love and where all hate and fear will gradually recede from the earth. What finer objectives could anyone have in life than to work for and with Christ to bring in His kingdom here on earth!

Kipchoge Keino

———————◆———————

As a runner, I am training hard to win my races. But, win or lose, I know God is guiding me and has a plan for my life.

Kipchoge H. Keino, twenty-eight, a skinny, born-again Christian from Kenya, emerged in the mid-1960s as the best runner Africa ever produced. He is the first African ever to run a mile in under four minutes. He is the world record holder at 3000 and 5000 meters. A purely natural athlete with practically no formal instruction, he likes to jump into the lead at the start of each race, try to hold it all the way and to sprint to victory with a hat-tossing last lap.

In his professional career, Keino is a member of the Kenya, East Africa, police department where he serves as a subinspector. He also teaches gymnastics, basketball and volleyball at the Police College in Kiganjo. One month out of every year he receives a leave of absence in order to compete in major track meets in Europe and the United States. Keino, who has run the mile in 3:54.2, has won both the mile and two-mile events in New York and Los Angeles Invitational meets.

In the 1968 Olympic Games in Mexico City, Keino copped the coveted Gold Medal in the 1500-meter and the silver medal in the 5000-meter run. As captain of Kenya's Olympic team, he was given an unprecedented hero's welcome on returning to Nairobi. Of him and his Olympic teammates, President Jomo Kenyatta said: "They won because they had unity. They had the heart for success when they left Kenya for Mexico."

Running the Race Eternal

Police work is my chosen vocation, long-distance running is my joyful avocation and faith in the ever-living Lord gives me the strength to pursue both with equal vigor. If answers to your questions should prove interesting to either track fans or fellow Christians, I shall be glad to answer them.

QUESTION: When did you first start running?

KEINO: As long as I can remember I have enjoyed running. I remember as a child I used to run with my father around our farm in the Nandi hills. However, it wasn't until I started school that I took running seriously. Here, I usually ran the 220 or 440 yards. I became interested in long-distance running during the last year of my schooling.

QUESTION: Where were you born and what is your occupation?

KEINO: I was born in the Nandi district of Kenya, East Africa. While my tribe, which is Kalenjin, is noted for raising and herding cattle, I have more or less broken away from this and have joined the Kenya police where I am a subinspector.

QUESTION: When was the most exciting moment in your competitive running?

KEINO: It was during the Olympic Games at Tokyo [1964]. This I regard as a turning point in my running career, for my near record winning performance in the 5000 meters gave me a new inspiration to put more effort and see if I could rise higher and achieve my objective one day.

QUESTION: You talk of achieving your objective in running. What do you mean?

KEINO: I mean I trained so that one day I might win the Olympic Gold Medal either in the 1500-meter, 3000-meter or 5000-meter runs. As you know I have just achieved that goal in the 1968 Games in Mexico City.

QUESTION: What do you consider your most unusual race?

KEINO: I guess that was when I raced an ostrich! Some sportsphotographers arranged it as a joke! It was fun though. Of course the ostrich won—I didn't have a chance.

QUESTION: Many sportsmen feel you are a "natural" runner. They say this is your heritage. What do they mean and do you agree?

KEINO: They say this because my people have a fine physique and are built for running because of their lean bodies and long limbs. Certain people claim that this, plus the high altitude in which I live *plus* my forebears' ability to travel long distances over barren land by foot is the contributing factor to my running skill. However, while some of this may be true, I do not consider myself a "natural."

QUESTION: If you are not a "natural," to what do you contribute your success in running?

KEINO: To be successful in anything requires a determination to work hard. I must constantly keep fit and have a determination to win. Personally, I attribute my success to training (I run six miles every day), courage, and prayer. I am a Christian and therefore depend a great deal on prayer. Before each race I pray asking the Lord to help me do my best.

QUESTION: How did you become a Christian?

KEINO: My father-in-law used to read the Bible to me. He often explained difficult passages to me and many times we would discuss the Word of God until late at night. The Bible convinced me of my need for salvation.

Verses from the Bible showed me how to be saved. Such as John 3:16: "God so loved the world, that he gave his only begotten Son, that whosoever believeth in him should not perish, but have everlasting life"; and Romans 10:9-10: "If thou shalt confess with thy mouth the Lord Jesus, and shalt believe in thine heart that God hath raised him from the dead, thou shalt be saved. For with the heart man believeth unto righteousness; and with the mouth confession is made unto salvation." I asked Jesus to forgive me my sins and confessed Him as my Saviour.

I would certainly recommend the Christian life for everyone! As a runner, I am training hard to win my races. But, win or lose, I know God is guiding me and has a plan for my life.

Fulton J. Sheen

When you try to make everything clear by reason, you somehow only succeed in making everything confusion. Once you introduce a single mystery, everything else becomes clear in the light of that one mystery.

The Most Reverend Fulton J. Sheen, one of America's most renowned Catholic churchmen, is respected for his rare scholarship, dynamic oratory and ability to draw noted converts into the Roman Catholic Church. The author of sixty books, many of them best sellers, he has lectured extensively throughout the world and gained fame in the United States as a radio and television speaker. From 1950 until his 1967 appointment as Bishop of Rochester, New York, he served the Church as national director of the Pontifical Society for the Propagation of the Faith.

Bishop Sheen was born in El Paso, Illinois, in 1895, and ordained to the priesthood in St. Mary's Cathedral, Peoria, in 1919. Following his ordination, he studied at the Catholic University of America in Washington, D.C., Louvain University in Belgium, and at the Collegio Angelico in Rome. Father Sheen taught dogmatic theology in Westminster Seminary, London, before joining the faculty of the Catholic University of America where he was professor of philosophy for twenty-three years. In 1951, His Holiness Pope Pius XII named him Titular Bishop of Caesariana and Auxiliary to Francis Cardinal Spellman of New York.

Bishop Sheen holds that there is no settled path to God, but rather that each soul finds its way individually. In reference to the West's world-wide conflict with totalitarianism, Bishop Sheen's vigilant anti-Communist campaign on behalf of freedom has always been conducted in the spirit of a priest who hates sin but loves the sinner. Among his most popular books are *Peace of Soul, The Seven Virtues, Go to Heaven, Communism and the Conscience of the West, Life of Christ* and *The Power of Love.*

The Romance of Orthodoxy

Faith is the acceptance of a truth on the authority of God revealing.

Before faith, one makes an investigation by reason. Just as no businessman would extend you credit without reason for doing so, neither are you expected to put faith in anyone without a reason. Why should you put faith in Christ?

Your reason investigates the miracles He worked, the prophecies which preannounced Him and the consonance of His teaching with your reason. These constitute the preambles of faith, from which you form a judgment of credibility: "This truth, that Christ is the Son of God, is worthy of belief." Passing to the practical order, you add: "I must believe it."

From then on, you give your assent: "I believe He is the Son of God, and this being so, whatever He reveals, I will accept as God's truth." You would not believe unless you saw that you must believe. Faith, therefore, never is blind. Since your reason is dependent on uncreated reason or divine truth, it follows that your reason should bow down to what God reveals. You believe now, not because of the arguments; they were only a necessary preliminary. You believe because God said it. The torch now burns by its own brilliance.

The nature of the act of faith was revealed by our Lord's attitude toward the unbelieving Pharisees. They had seen miracles worked and prophecies fulfilled. They were not lacking in motives for belief. But they still refused to believe. Our Lord took a little child in His midst and said: "Amen I say to you, whosoever shall not receive the kingdom of God as a little child, shall not enter into it."

By this He meant that the act of faith has more in common with the trusting belief of a child in his mother, than with the assent of a critic. The child believes what the mother tells him because she said it. His belief is an unaffected and trusting homage of love to his mother. You cannot argue, or study, or reason, or hypnotize, or whip yourself, into faith. Faith is a gift of God. When anyone instructs you in Christian doctrine, he does not give you faith. He is only a spiritual agriculturist, tilling the soil of your soul, uprooting a few weeds and breaking up the clods of egotism. It is God who drops the seed. "For by grace you are saved through faith, and that not of yourselves, for it is the gift of God" (Ephesians 2:8).

If faith were a will to believe, you could produce your own faith by an act of the will. All you can do is dispose yourself for its reception from the hands of God. As a dry stick is better disposed for burning than a wet stick, so a humble man is better disposed for faith than a know-it-all. In either case, as the fire which burns must come from outside the stick, so your faith must come from outside yourself, namely, from God.

When you try to make everything clear by reason, you somehow only succeed in making everything confusion. Once you introduce a single mystery, everything else becomes clear in the light of that one mystery. The sun is the "mystery" in the universe; it is so bright you cannot look at it; you cannot "see" it. But in the light of it, everything else becomes clear. So with faith.

Faith is unique and vital. There are not many faiths. There is only one faith: "One Lord, one faith, one baptism" (Ephesians 4:5). Yet every religion in the world contains some reflection of one eternal truth. Every philosophy, every world religion, every sect contains an arc of the perfect round of the natural and revealed truth. Confucianism has the fraction of fellowship; Indian asceticism has the fraction of self-abnegation; each human sect has an aspect of Christ's truth.

That is why, in approaching those who have not the faith, one should not begin by pointing out their errors, but rather by indicating the fraction of truth they have in common with the fullness of Truth. Instead of saying to the Confucian: "You are wrong in ignoring the fatherhood of God," one should say: "You are right in emphasizing brotherhood, but to make your brotherhood perfect, you need the fatherhood of God and the sonship of Christ, and the vivifying unity of the Holy Spirit."

The great beauty of the Catholic faith is its sense of proportion, or balance, or should we say, its humor. It does not handle the problem of death to the exclusion of sin, nor the problem of sin to the exclusion of human freedom, nor the social use of property to the exclusion of personal right, nor the reality of the body and sex to the exclusion of the soul and its function, nor the reality of matter to the forgetfulness of the Spirit. It never allows one doctrine to go to your head, like wine in an empty stomach. It keeps its balance, for truth is a precarious thing.

It is easy to be a Communist in this century, as it was easy to be a liberal in the nineteenth. It is easy to be a materialist today, as it was easy to be an idealist in the nineteenth century. But to keep one's head in the midst of all these changing moods and fancies, so that one is right, not when the world is right, but right when the world is wrong, is the thrill of a tightrope walker, the thrill of the romance of orthodoxy.

But the acceptance of the fullness of the truth will have the unfortunate quality of making you hated by the world. That is what our Lord said would happen to those who accept His truth. "If you had not been of the world, the world would love its own: but because you are not of the world, but I have chosen you out of the world, therefore the world hateth you. Remember my word that I said to you: The servant is not greater than his master. If they have persecuted me, they will also persecute you: if they have kept my word, they will keep yours also" (John 15:19-20).

Hence I believe that if the grace of God did not give me the fullness of truth, and I were looking for it, I would begin my search by looking through the world for a church that did not get along with the evil in the world! If that church were accused of countless lies, hated because it refused to compromise, ridiculed because it refused to fit the times and not all time, I would suspect that since it was hated by what is evil in the world, it therefore was good and holy; and if it is good and holy, it must be divine. And I would sit down by its fountains and begin to drink the waters of everlasting life.

With Paul I could then say in the strength of a great faith: "I am sure that neither death, nor life, nor angels, nor principalities, nor powers, nor things present, nor things to come, nor might, nor height, nor depth, nor any other creature, shall be able to separate us from the love of God, which is in Christ Jesus our Lord" (Romans 8:38-39).

Robert M. Hutchins

*The biggest enemy of human progress is mental in-
dolence. As Aristotle said, "Learning is accompanied by
pain." Too many people won't go through that pain.*

An internationally eminent educator with a reputation as a "national
intellectual resource" and as "a man one hundred years ahead of his
time," Dr. Robert M. Hutchins of Santa Barbara, California, is president
of the Fund for the Republic, Inc., and the Center for the Study of
Democratic Institutions. Once the *enfant terrible* of U.S. education and
at age thirty the tradition-smashing president of the University of
Chicago, America's elegant "Mr. Chips" still stirs irresistible rustles in
the groves of Academe even while drawing the world's pundits, philosophers and government leaders into creative assembly at his successive
Pacem in Terris conferences in New York City and Geneva. He also
serves as chairman of the board of editors of *Encyclopaedia Britannica*
and as a director of Encyclopaedia Films.

Now sixty-eight and possessing a name and fame synonymous with
the Center's searching discussions, critical inquiry and education for
democracy, Dr. Hutchins' main activity remains at the Center (fondly
labeled "America's Thinking Establishment") and its sophisticated illumination of the institutions and issues affecting freedom and justice among
men. The Center's studies, Dr. Hutchins says, "are chiefly directed at
discovering whether and how a free and just society may be maintained
under the strikingly new political, social, economic and technological
condition of the second half of the twentieth century." The two
successive *Pacem in Terris* convocations brilliantly demonstrated the
Hutchins blend of vision and practicality: based on Pope John XXIII's
momentous papal document and backed by the Center's intellectual and
financial resources, the two international assemblies became "summits for
peace" and attracted hundreds of the world's religious, diplomatic and
cultural dignitaries in man's most vital quest—peace.

Dr. Hutchins' dedication to the compelling causes of peace, freedom
and the educated man derive directly from his family tradition. The
son and grandson of Presbyterian ministers, he graduated magna cum
laude from Yale in 1925 and two years later was appointed dean of the
Yale Law School. In 1929 he was named president of the University of
Chicago, where in twenty-two action-packed years he revolutionized

the University's character and curricula and introduced such innovations as the Great Books studies for which he is world-renowned. An officer of the Legion of Honor and the recipient of honorary degrees from leading universities in the U.S. and Europe, Dr. Hutchins is the author of *The Conflict in Education, No Friendly Voice, The Higher Education in America,* and *Freedom, Education and the Fund.*

The Religion of Freedom

I was born in Brooklyn in the usual way sixty-eight years ago and brought up in a way that was not unusual for persons born at that time. We had morning prayers with a Bible-reading every day. We went to church twice on Sunday. The result of the first is that I was amazed when in a class I was teaching I found a senior at the University of Chicago who had never heard of Joshua. The result of the second is that it is very hard for me to go to church now and that I find myself singing, humming, or moaning third-rate hymns like "Blest Be the Tie That Binds" while shaving, while waiting on the platform to make a speech, or in other moments of abstraction or crisis.

We had at that time many advantages that have been denied to college students in recent years, but that may be restored to their successors. We had no radios, and for all practical purposes no automobiles, no movies and no slick-paper magazines. We had to entertain ourselves. We could not by turning a small knob or paying a small fee get somebody else to do it for us. It never occurred to us that unless we could go somewhere or do something our lives were empty. We had nowhere to go, and no way to get there. Our recreations were limited to two: reading and physical exercise. The first meant reading anything you could lay your hands on. The second meant playing tennis.

You will notice that the circumstances under which I was brought up gave me some knowledge of one great book, the Bible, and the habit of reading. The habit of physical exercise I was fortunately forced to abandon at an early date. You will notice, too, that the educational system had nothing to do with any of these accomplishments or habits. I do not remember that I ever thought about being educated at all. I thought of getting through school. This, as I recall it, was a business of passing examinations and meeting requirements, all of which were meaningless to me but presumably had some meaning to those who had me in their power. I have no doubt that the Latin and Greek I studied did me good. All I can say is that I was not aware of it at the time. Nor did I have any idea of the particular kind of good it was intended to do me. Since I had got the habit of reading at home, I was perfectly willing to read anything anybody gave me. Apart from a few plays of Shakespeare nobody gave me anything good to read until I was a sophomore in college. Then I was allowed to examine the grammar and philology of the *Apology* of Socrates in a Greek course. And since I had had an unusual amount of German, I was permitted to study *Faust!*

Why since those early school days with its discovery of the Bible, Shakespeare and the Great Books have I directed my lifework to the interrelated cause of education and freedom? I suppose because of the tradition in which I was raised. My father's family was descended from a long line of Connecticut doctors and ministers; my mother's was a long line of sea captains from Maine. My childhood was nourished by the stories of their independence—my maternal grandfather went to sea in a sailing ship at the age of eleven and was on the voyage for four years—and I began to think at an early date that the ideal American was the perpendicular man. These ancestors of mine were all stubborn, and some of them were vain. Their notion of success did not seem to involve material goods as much as it did holding on to their own convictions in the face of external pressure. I remember that when I was about fourteen my father received for Christmas a portrait of a friend of his who had amassed a great deal of money and power by concentrating on doing so, and who looked it. My father put the photograph on the piano and said, "I will put this here to remind us of the things we are fighting against." I have sometimes thought that if I were to write my autobiography I would call it *The Picture on the Piano*.

Then there was Oberlin. My minister father became a professor there when I was eight, and I lived there until I went into the army at eighteen. In that stationary age Oberlin was a Puritan island in the Middle West. Nothing like it has been seen since; for the automobile and prosperity have changed the Oberlin of that day, perhaps for the better. The motto of the college was "Learning and Labor." Poverty, work, service, and what the president, Henry Churchill King, called Rational Living were the ideals that were held before us. But the principal one was nonconformity. The legacy the college left to every Oberlin man or woman of that day was the nonconformist conscience. Oberlin was the first college to admit women and the first to admit Negroes.

The great episode in the history of the college was the Wellington Raid, an occasion on which the faculty and students had gone to a neighboring town and rescued a fugitive slave. We were proud to remember that Oberlin had been a station on the Underground Railroad and to point out to one another the buildings, then still standing, that had been used for the purpose. We seriously believed that the greatest thing in the world was to lay down your life for your principles, and we considered that the Oberlin missionaries killed in the Boxer Rebellion, who were memorialized by the Martyrs' Arch in the center of the campus, had shown us how to die.

At home and in the college I lived in an atmosphere of discussion. It was not an accident that the leading extracurricular activity of the college was debating. There were no fraternities; their place was taken by the literary societies. We were not merely free to talk about everything; we were required to. You were entitled to your own opinion, but only if you were willing to submit it to examination and to change it if it could not survive rational scrutiny.

Neither the army, in which I conducted a successful private war against all attempts to make a soldier of me, nor Yale, then a stronghold of conformity, nor a lifetime devoted to money-raising and other forms of compromise, has been able to wholly eradicate the attitudes formed by these early influences. I still cherish the view that the independent individual is the heart of society, that his independence is his most precious attribute, and that discussion is the essence of democracy. It is hard for me to concern myself with the material prosperity of my country or with that of the individuals who compose it, because I was brought up to believe that prosperity and power were secondary, perhaps even dangerous, goals. Adjustment as the aim of education strikes me as a contradiction in terms. The Bill of Rights, instead of being a set of ancient prescriptions that do not affect me because I do not run a newspaper, do not belong to an unpopular church, and do not have to plead the Fifth Amendment, is a statement of the way in which I must demand that the government conduct itself toward all its citizens all the time. The press appears to me as a means of purveying accurate information and as a forum for discussion, or at least as a place in which honest opinions are honestly set forth. Academic institutions are bodies of men pursuing the truth, discussing it with one another, and criticizing the environment with the utmost freedom: it is for this reason that they exist.

This, of course, is not the way things are, but the way they ought to be. I do not assume that all or many of them can be changed. I would remind you of the words variously attributed to William the Silent and Charles the Bold; I have quoted them over and over: "It is not necessary to hope in order to undertake, nor to succeed in order to persevere."

The effort to bring about changes of the kind I have described requires a simple—perhaps too simple—faith in the rationality of man, in democracy, and in freedom. This faith leads one of the faithful to try to do what he can to develop and train the reason, to struggle for a more perfect democracy, and to fight on every front for freedom.

The most striking change in education in the last half-century is its intellectual and moral degradation. It is hardly too much to say that the first two years of college now consist of work that was formerly done in high school. Much high school and college work is too trivial to be done anywhere; it is composed of recent inventions that are thought to have some utility in adjusting the young to their environment or in keeping them harmlessly occupied until they are old enough to go out into the world. When efforts to justify these developments have proved fruitless, their proponents have taken refuge in the allegation that large numbers have made these developments inevitable. What else can you do when you have so many students to deal with?

The moral degradation of education is evident in the current supremacy of public relations. In many colleges and universities the public relations man is either the president or the man who tells the president what to do. I concede the value of a public relations program aimed at interpreting an educational policy that has been reached and can be justified on educational grounds. I see nothing but moral degradation in an educational program that has been reached and can only be justified on public relations grounds.

Size, numbers, quantity—in these terms we, in America, are inclined to think of all our undertakings, and it is natural that the educational system should be appraised in the same way. Numbers of students, amounts of money, the size of departments, appear both to the faculty and the public as the only intelligible criteria of success.

By the time I became the president of the University of Chicago, in 1929, I was full of questions; but I did not try very hard to answer them until I was forced to. That happened when the Great Depression hit us. The income of the University began to slide off so fast that our estimates had to be revised downward every day. The remedy proposed was a flat percentage reduction in our expenditures. This did not seem very intelligent to me; for anybody could see that all of our expenditures were not equally important. But what was the standard of importance? If the maintenance of buildings and grounds was not as important as the salaries of the faculty, why not? Why was the library more important than the gymnasium? It was clear that we would have to abandon a good many courses, but which ones?

My education as an administrator began when at the age of thirty-two I opened Aristotle's *Ethics* for the first time and read, "In practical matters the end is the first principle." I was shocked to realize that in the ten years I had been in universities I had never seriously asked myself what they were for. I had taken them for granted, had assumed that the aims they proclaimed were valid, and had attempted to administer them in terms of those aims. About the only idea I had of the University of Chicago when I went there was that it was great. It was my business to make it greater. The Depression seemed to postpone any immediate hope of making it greater in ways that I understood: I could not expect to make it richer; it was more likely that I would take it into bankruptcy. What was a great university anyway?

I had to admit that the University of Chicago, and all other universities and colleges, were unintelligible to me. On the level to which I was accustomed, the level of obtaining popular support, unintelligibility seemed to me a handicap. How could the people be expected to be enthusiastic about what they could not understand? We all knew that educational institutions were not country clubs and that the records of their football teams were not an infallible index of educational excellence. But the noneducational activities of educational institutions were the ones, and perhaps the only ones, that the public could comprehend. They were almost the only ones that I could comprehend myself.

It was fortunate that, meanwhile, Mortimer Adler had dragged me, much against my will, into teaching the Great Books with him. I had read Shakespeare and Goethe, and that was about all. Plato, Aristotle, Augustine, and Aquinas, and the other books to which these led, notably those of Jacques Maritain, as well as the discussions about them that I got into with John Nef, Robert Redfield, Beardsley Ruml, Richard McKeon, Clarence Faust, and Edward Levi illuminated for me the principles I had accepted at home and at Oberlin. So did my extracurricular activities. Talks with Scott Buchanan and Stringfellow Barr about the reorganization of St. John's College; the meetings of the Commission on the Freedom of the Press, which included Archibald MacLeish, Reinhold Niebuhr, and George Shuster; the sessions about publishing Great Books with William Benton, Alexander Meiklejohn, and Mark Van Doren; and the conferences of the Committee to Frame a World Constitution, in which many of the men I have named took part, raised the same fundamental issues.

I was a classic example of the young man brought up to good habits who could not understand why he or anybody else should have them until his own experience forced him to try to find out. Perhaps it was stubbornness or the inability to learn that led me to conclude that my early training was sound. At any rate, it seems to me that a lifetime of experience and reflection has supplied me with the reasons for defending the faith in which I was brought up.

That faith, I say again, was faith in the independent mind. Its educational consequences were belief in free inquiry and discussion. Its political consequences were belief in democracy, but only in a democracy in which the minority, even a minority of one, could continue to differ and to be heard. Those who desire to conform but are prohibited or hindered from doing so by intolerance and prejudice must be aided; the nonconformist conscience must not be stifled. Hence my interest in the Fund for the Republic.

The opportunity to establish the Fund arose because the trustees of the Ford Foundation, with which I became associated in 1951, had in the previous year announced that among its other objects the Foundation would support activities directed toward the elimination of restrictions on freedom of thought, inquiry and expression in the United States. In its early days the Foundation established several independent corporations to carry out programs that were too large and complicated for the Foundation to manage itself. W. H. Ferry, then public relations counsel to the Foundation, and I worked out the plan for the Fund for the Republic as an independent corporation to receive funds from the Foundation for work on civil liberties. After a year and a half of discussion, the Fund was incorporated and given a sum that was expected to last about five years. When the Fund lost its president, I was glad to accept an invitation to succeed him, because the Fund combined two interests that I had had all my life; education and freedom.

The first grant of the Fund was to the Committee of the American Bar Association on National Security and Individual Rights. That Committee decided to study congressional investigations. Because of the public ignorance of and indifference to the Bill of Rights, it was possible to make people believe that anybody who studied congressional investigations was undermining the national security. Such a conclusion is of course irrational. My simple faith in the nationality of man compels me to regard such lapses as temporary.

One point still baffles me. A remarkable characteristic of our epoch is the use of one's attitude toward Communism and Communists as the index, touchstone, or test of one's patriotism. An enormous amount of popular, and hence effective (or it would not be popular), political argument runs this way: I am very frightened of Communism; you are not as frightened as I am; therefore, you are not as patriotic as I am. Of course, in both cases, if you are not as patriotic as I am you are not a good American. Apparently patriotism and Americanism are made proportional to one's fright of, or opposition to, Communism.

In both cases the degree of preoccupation with Communism is very important. The assumption is that, in order to show yourself properly frightened of Communism, you must think of nothing else. This appeared in the legislative inquiries into the University of

Chicago, where the committees seemed to feel that unlesss I dropped everything and spent all my time trying to find subversive influences at work among the faculty and the students I was slightly treasonable. The fact that no charges had ever been made that any reasonable man could take seriously was, for the committees, irrelevant.

At a large meeting at which I spoke recently it was suggested that my address on the Bill of Rights would be much improved if it said that the Fund for the Republic was set up to fight Communism by defending and advancing the principles of the Declaration of Independence, the Constitution, and the Bill of Rights. This would mean that if there were no Communists in the world, there would be no need for the Fund, and presumably no need for the Bill of Rights when it was adopted. Admitting that Communism is most important and a most important threat to civil liberties, I believe it is still possible to say that your primary interest is in something else, like education or the general defense of civil liberties, without laying yourself open to the charge of un-Americanism.

Due process and the equal protection of the laws are the basis of our society. If I insist that every person accused of crime must be given a fair trial, that accusation is not proof, and that the presumption of innocence extends to every man accused of anything, I do not expect to be called a criminal or a pro-criminal or anti-anti-criminal. One would suppose that the best way to display one's Americanism would be to insist on justice under the law. To insist on it only for those who are sure to get it anyway does not seem a profitable expenditure of energy. I should have supposed that the test of one's Americanism would have been whether one was prepared to insist on justice under law for the scurviest and most unpopular persons around. They are the ones who need it. And if they don't get it, we may be certain that, if events run riot, eventually nobody will get it.

The education that should be given in our schools, colleges, and universities is that which would prepare every member of our society to play his part as a citizen of a free, democratic society. This basic education is necessary for everybody, for the suffrage is universal. But that is not the only reason. Everybody is entitled to liberal education, not only for the benefit of the community, but also for his own. The end of life is happiness. This does not mean contentment, cheerfulness, or self-satisfaction. It means, in the old phrase, activity in accordance with virtue, or the fullest development of one's highest powers. A society composed of such persons, such persons composing such a society—these are the objects of education, freedom, and the Fund.

Chiang Kai-shek

If you can renovate yourself, do so from day to day.
Only the reborn can retain their new personality.

Generalissimo Chiang Kai-shek, world symbol of a free democratic China since before World War II, today directs the destinies of Nationalist China from his island fortress of Taiwan (Formosa). Now in his twentieth year of exile from the mainland, the erect eighty-one-year-old statesman is president of an island nation of twelve million people and commands a modern army of six hundred thousand men. He believes that the belligerent Peiping regime must be destroyed before it builds a stockpile of nuclear weapons—and unleashes World War III.

Born of Buddhist parents in 1887 in the farming province of Chekiang, Chiang was largely brought up by his mother, a woman of exceptional character and devotion. His early career aspirations were strengthened by his schooling at the Paoting Military Academy near Peiping and later by his studying military science at the Shinbo Goyko in Tokyo. The most eventful occurrence of his three years in Japan was his meeting with Dr. Sun Yat-sen, later the leader of the successful Chinese revolt which overthrew the Manchu regime.

Studious, brave and by 1911 a fervent revolutionary, the young soldier's life now entered the mainstream of China's twentieth-century history. Through a series of interrelated military and political campaigns—the bloody overthrow of the 267-year-old Ch'ing dynasty, the North Expedition and the capture of Nanking, the establishment of the first democracy in Asia and the counter-thrusts of the Red Chinese, the warning against Japan's Manchurian invasion—the trim, poised generalissimo unified all China and by 1927 emerged as Dr. Sun's inevitable successor. During the early 1930s he became commander-in-chief of China's armies and first president of the new Nationalist government.

The architect of modern republican China, Chiang moved as one of the Big Four during World War II and his varied strategy contributions in the field and at the conference table helped bring Japan to her knees. His New Life Movement, aimed at reviving the ancient virtues, stressed propriety, justice, integrity and conscientiousness. In 1947, with the glacial advance of Communist armies overrunning China, he salvaged a measure of the government's economic and military assets and established a Free China in the island citadel of Taiwan. Here, encouraged by his beauteous wife, Madame Mayling Soong Chiang, and the steadfast support of the U.S.A., the dynamic generalissimo still pursues his vigilant purpose of recapturing and rebuilding the mainland.

The Unvanquished Spirit

Against a natural mountainous backdrop of China's remote Chekiang Province and against the sterner invisible background of her Confucian ethics, I was born into a poor, yet traditional, family of farmer-scholars in the gateway town of Chekow. The date was October 31, 1887, during a decade when China suffered military defeats at the hands of both France and Japan, and even then the whispered laments of my elders were beginning to rise against the misrule of the Manchus. Thus, very early as a boy brought up in an atmosphere of national humiliation, I came to understand that Western technology and Western education would be essential if China was to regain her power and prestige.

Although today I am a Christian, my mother was a devout Buddhist. She was a strict vegetarian and never omitted daily worship, becoming increasingly fervent as the years went by. Frequently she lectured me on the Buddhist sutras, discoursing on such noble texts as "All beings seek happiness, so let your compassion extend itself to all," or "Let a man overcome anger by love, evil by good, greed by liberality and lies by truth." "All that I pray for you," she once said, "is that you should love your country, practice the Buddhist virtues of benevolence, fortitude and meditation and preserve the good name of your ancestors, who were men of reputation."

Even while learning to love the mountain trails and fish-filled streams near our home, I was never allowed to shirk the burden of work. In fact, when I was a little boy, I was required by my parents and teachers to do many tasks such as sweeping and mopping the floor, cooking rice and preparing food in general, and even washing dishes. If I carelessly dropped a few grains of rice, or failed to fasten my clothing properly, I was severely taken to task. Then, suddenly my father died. Now, deprived of any protection after the death of her husband, my mother was exposed to the most ruthless exploitation by neighboring ruffians and the local gentry. The efforts she made in fighting against the intrigues of these family intruders certainly endowed her child, brought up in such an environment, with an indomitable spirit to fight for justice. I felt throughout my childhood that my mother and I were fighting a helpless lone war. We were alone in a desert, no available or possible assistance could we look forward to. But our determination was never shaken, nor hope abandoned.

Such an environment inevitably molded the shape of my personality. There is constantly a smoldering fire burning inside me, although I am reticent in giving vent to my emotions. Throughout my life, I have always been surrounded and sometimes overpowered by enemies; but I know how to endure. This is one of the peculiar characteristics of one who has learned to work, study, sacrifice and rely in the end on God's guidance.

And yet, in the long view of what was ahead of me, a life of hardship was an almost ideal upbringing. In my youthful wanderings, I often sat by limpid streams and watched schools of fish fighting their way upstream like soldiers advancing against a hostile force. In the same way, I concluded, men have to fight against the odds of life, often repulsed but never despairing. Religion was for me, even as a boy, a source of deep strength for the struggles of life.

So it continued as I became a man—my high-school years at Fenglu and Liangching, my military training at Paoting Academy, my first trip to Japan in 1907 and my first momentous meeting with Dr. Sun Yat-sen, who was to become my mentor and friend and father of the revolution to overthrow the decadent Manchu regime. I soon joined his secret Kuomintang movement, and began preparing myself consciously and unconsciously for my role in the long-simmering revolution.

It was during the next two turbulent decades—checkered with military campaigns, against the Manchu war lords and Communist conspirators alike—that I began to study Christianity. I was encouraged in this by a beautiful, American-educated young lady, Mayling Soong, who in 1927 became my bride and who in war and peace to this very day shares my morning and evening prayers and reading of the Bible. Since my baptism in Nanking in 1928 by the Reverend Kiang Chen Chun, my Christian faith has become such a heartening personal experience that not even the most urgent state business is permitted to interrupt my prayer periods.

Without faith we are constantly in danger of being overwhelmed by adversities. With faith we unite ourselves with the deep stream of the Eternal's purpose and meaning, and are thereby enabled to accomplish the impossible.

China's epic defiance of Japanese domination between 1937 and 1945 is a striking instance of the efficacy of faith. When Japan hurled its military machine upon us in 1937, opinion in the outside world gave China little more than a few weeks of possible resistance. But the unshaken faith of my wife and my loyal coworkers galvanized China to achieve the unbelievable. The miracle of Chinese resistance was prolonged for eight years, four of them unaided and alone, and in the end, it was Japan that failed.

Faith points out to us that the one irretrievable attitude for men and for nations is the attitude of passivity and fatalism. If we accept defeat we become frustrated. Then we are indeed lost. But if we refuse to accept defeat by pressing onward in the face of external setbacks, then we develop an inner integrated wholeness of character which is invincible.

Thus, in the present awful struggle of my country with the evil forces of Communism, the Christian attitude is not—as some Christians have mistakenly believed—one of submission and expedient compromise. One cannot compromise with evil and remain unsullied. In China today there are countless instances of unpublicized Christian martyrdom at the hands of Communism. From the blood of such martyrdom will spring the seeds of the reborn China which will arise in the future.

Christian faith means that we must and can fight for our principles even at the risk of temporary defeat, and perhaps death. There can be no opportunistic bargaining, anytime, anywhere, between right and wrong. Only this indomitable determination of man to make the supreme sacrifice for the substance of his faith has kept Christian right alive in this world through tortuous nights of human history. And, because there are men and women ready to live and die for their convictions, the victories of Communism will prove transient and ineffectual.

On March 29, 1911, seventy-two courageous young patriots staged an uprising in Canton by attacking the Manchu troops and proclaiming Dr. Sun Yat-sen's three Principles of the People as the basis of a democratic government. Although this first uprising failed and the seventy-two lads died a gallant death, their martyrdom watered the seeds of revolution which did succeed in October of that year. During the past half-century, national independence, democratic freedom and social and economic well-being of the Chinese people have become the universal common goals of mankind. The purpose of our national revolution is the implementation of the three Principles of the People. First we overthrew the despotic monarchy and established our republic of democracy! Next we won victory in our war of resistance against Japanese aggression in fulfillment of the principle of nationalism! Today, we are fighting Communism to ensure the successful realization of the principle of people's well-being and of our national cause of recovery and reconstruction.

There has always been an Infinite Creator, Eternal Lord of the everlasting universe—Almighty God—who glorifies truth, upholds justice and leads his followers to final victory. Therefore, to the bona fide faithful in the depth of despair and hopelessness after numerous futile struggles, the truth of God will be made known right then and there. In religion, we call this "the grace of God"; and this is the secret source of that sufficiency always available to God's followers. This has been my personal experience in years of revolutionary war, in which several times I had to face the danger of death. I have often said that whenever the forces of darkness and evil are at their worst, the best opportunity for our revolutionary victory—for the revival of our people, and the reconstruction of our nation—is closest at hand.

This truth stands out in bolder relief today than ever before. Today, we Chinese at home and abroad are a nation of more than 700,000,000 people. In terms of armed forces alone we have more than 600,000 men on Taiwan. This figure, 600,000, is nearly ten thousand times the total number of the martyrs, namely seventy-two, who by their utmost sincerity aroused the nation into action to end despotic rule and found the Republic of China. This anti-Communist manpower is the reincarnation of the undaunted spirit of these very martyrs, and is the inheritor to their spirit of sacrifice for carrying on the struggle for the salvation of our nation and people.

We thank God and Jesus that we have not disappointed our

revolutionary martyrs, nor will we disappoint our fellow Christians and compatriots who are now suffering on the Chinese mainland. We will abide by the will of God and Spirit of Jesus so as to bring solace to the souls of Dr. Sun Yat-sen and the revolutionary martyrs now in heaven. Let me repeat: whenever the forces of darkness and evil are at their worst, the opportunity for our revolutionary victory— for the revival of our people, for the reconstruction of our nation, and for the germination of a new life—is also at its best and closest at hand. Fellow Christians! the darkness and fetidness of the Communist regime on the mainland today warrant a bright, pure, renovated China for us tomorrow.

Eleanor Searle Whitney

Be a channel God can use. Speak for Him with a holy boldness.

A great American lady who has become a global crusader for Christ, Eleanor Searle Whitney belongs to that rare genus—the millionaire missionary who "goes and tells God's Word." A former concert singer, winner of fashion awards and wife of Cornelius Vanderbilt Whitney, comely best-dressed Eleanor Whitney still maintains her place in New York society, philanthropy and the arts. But, since 1957 when she attended Billy Graham's summer crusade in New York City, she has committed her life entirely to Jesus Christ and strives by her concerts, lectures and Bible-study classes to advance the knowledge of Christianity and its application in daily living.

"Something happened in my life twelve years ago," she says, "for I became a Christian that God can use seven days a week." Today, using her own resources and burning with a reformer's fire, Mrs. Whitney spends ten months of the year traveling in the United States and abroad speaking and singing in churches, colleges and universities, Catholic priories and convents, Protestant missions and leprosariums as well as before service clubs, cultural and civic groups. She consistently emphasizes the importance of a personal encounter with the grace of God, the application of Christ's teachings in one's personal life and business activities, and a deeper understanding of God's Word through Bible-discussion groups and more active participation in one's own church.

Mrs. Whitney's activities include membership on seven boards of directors including the Salvation Army, American Bible Society, Functional Fashions for Handicapped, Travelers Aid Society of New York, and the International Council for Christian Leadership, an interdenominational lay movement active in thirty-seven countries. She also is a member of the National Federation of Music Clubs and the National Council of the Metropolitan Opera and a founder member of the National Society of Arts and Letters, and she frequently serves on the Billy Graham Evangelistic Crusade Teams and Campus Crusade for Christ.

Born and brought up in a five-generation Lutheran family in Plymouth, Ohio, Eleanor Searle was educated at Methodist Florida Southern College and Columbia University, holds an honorary Doctor of Music degree, and studied singing with private coaches and tutors. She was a successful concert oratorio and opera soloist until her marriage to Mr. Whitney in 1941. Named repeatedly to America's best-dressed and best-hatted lists, Mrs. Whitney frequently models at charity balls and fashion shows. A confirmed world traveler and patron of the arts, chic Christ-led Eleanor Whitney has visited the Holy Land five times, criss-crossed Europe, Asia, Africa and the U.S. many times—all to become like the woman in the Bible: "She hath done what she could." She gives God the glory and says, "Only by the working of the Holy Spirit in me could any of these things occur."

Salvation for the Up-and-Inners

Since 1957—that was the year my life was transformed at the Billy Graham Crusade in New York—I have had only one major purpose: to share what Jesus Christ means to me and to tell others what I believe He can mean to them—to be a witness. A witness in court is allowed to testify only about what he knows through personal experience, about something that he saw or heard or felt. I try to do this in life in various ways, by singing, by lecturing, by private conversations and by public crusades for Christ. I try to be like the woman in the Bible whom Jesus told, "Go and tell."

Love of God must find its expression in service to mankind. Today the love of Jesus Christ and the peace and joy that He brings are the greatest things in my life. I feel a tremendous urge to share that love and peace and joy with others; I try, as it were, to do missionary work among all classes and especially the rich, to bring God's Word to what I call "the up-and-inners" as well as to the "down-and-outers." Compared to the joy of serving the Christ I love, the world has nothing of value to offer me.

When I was a busy socialite as Mrs. Cornelius Vanderbilt Whitney, I thought I was a Christian but I was an "ethical do-gooder." I never spoke about Jesus to my friends and thought of people who did as "far out" or "fanatics." It was not until I went forward in secret at the Billy Graham Crusade to commit my life to Christ that I became a Christian whom God can use seven days a week. Since 1957 I have tried to live one step at a time, as the Lord leads me. Sometimes, for example, I find it impossible to accept a speaking or singing invitation even though I may want to do so. I have learned that this is one way in which God reveals His will—provided, of course, that we are willing to accept it and do not rebel against it. The Bible tells us that the Apostle Paul tried on one occasion to go into Bithynia, but was prevented by the Holy Spirit. St. Paul, accepting the leading, then saw a vision in which a Macedonian said to him, "Come over into Macedonia and help us." I have found that when God wants me to accept an invitation or assignment, acceptance always becomes possible.

For many years I have had everything the world could offer. I had homes, apartments, fishing lodges, shooting camps, stables of horses, yachts and a private airplane. I thought I had no need. The French physicist Pascal said, in describing the longing of humanity, "In every heart there is a God-shaped vacuum that cannot be filled with man-created things. It can be filled only by a relationship to God, as revealed through Jesus Christ."

A year after my waking up and becoming a "Christian God can use," my world fell apart, and when I was deeply disappointed in my husband of seventeen years and was forced to have a divorce, much of my worldly wealth disappeared, but today I have God's wealth, and this is available to all. That is what a Christian is, someone who has invited Christ's Holy Spirit to live within them, someone within whom God dwells and who has all of the riches of heaven now and forever.

Christianity, you see, is not a series of negations. Christianity is claiming what is available to us, having all of God's abundant joy and radiance and love and happiness in your life—letting it show and letting it radiate through you now and forever. If somebody says he is a great Christian and he looks morose and unhappy, you might ask him why he doesn't look as though he is claiming God's joy. No, Christianity is the most joyful relationship we can have. But I didn't know this twelve years ago.

During Billy Graham's New York Crusade, our Episcopal rector encouraged us to attend the Crusade many times and took carloads of friends. Often I wanted to go forward and pray that God would take over my life, but I couldn't get up in front of my friends and make a silly goose of myself and walk down that aisle. No, sir! Every time I would start a little voice would say, "You don't have to do that, you *are* a Christian. You are a twenty-year Episcopalian and you are a five-generation Lutheran. You are a Christian." Oh, the devil uses such subtleties: "You are too intelligent, you have too much pride, you have too much ego to let anyone know you love Jesus Christ."

I hope these verses in Romans 1:16–17 will be engraved upon your heart. "For I am not ashamed of the gospel of Christ: for it (the gospel only) is the power of God unto salvation to every one that believeth; to the Jew first, and also to the Greek. For therein is the righteousness of God revealed from faith to faith: as it is written, The just shall live by faith." You see, I was timid and ashamed to let anyone know that I loved God for I truly did and prayed daily. You see, I was Mrs. Nicodemus as depicted in the third chapter of the Gospel of John when Jesus was talking to that great leader of the Jews. After he came to Jesus alone at night when no one would see him, Nicodemus really wanted to know how he could be sure of eternal life. He was doing all the correct ritualistic things, and Jesus told him those acts did not suffice but that he must be born again of the spirit or he would never see the Father in heaven.

Recently, the president of one of our great universities said, "The finest fruits of higher education should culminate in the ability to speak the Word of God and Jesus Christ without embarrassment or restraint." In reality, I didn't know enough to talk things over with God. It doesn't matter where we do this—with a minister, with a friend, with a teacher, with your parents, children or alone with God. The important thing is to ask Christ to come and live in you with his Holy Spirit; then turn your life to Him. Jesus said in Revelation 3:20: "Behold, I stand at the door, and knock: if any man hear my voice, and open the door, I will come in to him, and will sup with him, and he with me."

When we ask Christ into our hearts, that is when we become new spiritual babies; and when we become awake as Christians, then God can use us. I found after I had gone forward at the Crusade that three friends of mine had done the same thing. Well, we four little baby Christians started a Bible binge. "What won't they think of next for kicks?" And yet today, twelve years later, we have twelve Bible classes that meet every week in our homes and two in churches. We suggest daily quiet times with God when we study His word and pray. One of the greatest parts of prayer is listening to what God is saying to you. It isn't "gimme, gimme, gimme," or "help me, help me, help me," but it is "God, to whom do you want me to talk today for you? Guide me, Lord. Where shall I go? What decision shall I make in my factory or business?"

It is so easy in life to have the wrong set of values, to look for happiness in the wrong places. We say, "Oh, if I had a new boy friend, if I had a new girl friend, if I had a new wig, a new fur coat, a new house, a new car, then everything would be fine." "If only I had position, power, money." Well, what about Marilyn Monroe? What about Ernest Hemingway? The only way to have inner peace, abundant joy and God's riches is to claim them, if He is *your* *Father* and you know you're His child, let Him use your life. "But as many as received him, to them gave he power to become the sons of God, even to them that believe on his name" (John 1:12).

There are only three decisions in your whole life that are important. The third one is the career you choose. The second one is the mate you marry. Do you ever pray for the mate you are going to marry? Maybe you know the one and maybe you don't. Pray that God will keep that person close to Him. Pray that yours will be a godly mate. Think of your life as a triangle with God at the top of the triangle and you and your mate forming the other two angles. The closer each of you grows to God in learning and in prayer and in understanding and in working for Him, the closer you grow to each other. Couples that pray together, stay together.

But the first and most important decision is what you will do with Jesus Christ. Will you accept Him or reject Him?

Now, it doesn't mean that if you say, "God help me, I'm yours," that everything will be rosy and that you will have no problems. As I said, it was only a year after I made my commitment to Christ that my "status" social life collapsed, I divorced my husband, then a few years later my stepdaughter, who had been like my own daughter for twenty years, died of leukemia. If I had not had my new-found Christian faith, I would have become a candidate for the minister's shoulder, the alcohol bottle, the psychiatrist's couch, the sleeping pills, any crutch to hold me up when everything else was falling apart around me. This would have happened if I had not known that "all things work together for good to those who love the Lord and are called according to His purpose," and if I had not had the prayers of my Christian friends and the power of Christ. "Let not your heart be troubled neither let it be afraid; I will never leave you or forsake you!"

My message is always the same. I urge people to examine the claims of Christ and accept him as Lord and Master; to acquire a deeper understanding of God's love for us, a deeper understanding of His Word, and then apply it in our personal lives, in our family activities and in our business enterprises. We hear a great deal in these days about the importance of keeping our country free, but in the words of the Psalmist, "Except the Lord keep the city, the watchman stays awake in vain" (Psalms 127:1). Unless the United States remains "a nation under God," it will not remain free. Freedom and love cannot be legislated. Let each of us have a return to personal righteousness by asking God's forgiveness and let His love flow through us to our fellow man.

Woman's role, now as always, is to teach her children of God, to teach them the love of Christ so that they will make Him the Lord of their lives, for children get their first impression of God from their parents, and especially from their mothers. Do our children know how we stand with God? Do we read the Bible with them and pray with them? Do we take them to worship services? When Christ rose from the dead, he didn't send for Pontius Pilate. He didn't go to see the king, president or the mayor—or what corresponded to these officials in Jerusalem. He revealed Himself first to a woman. He spoke to Mary—who had been cleansed and changed and forgiven through His love—and He gave her a great message to give the world: "Go and tell!"

Douglas MacArthur

Duty, Honor, Country—these hallowed words reverently dictate what we ought to be, what we can be, what we will be.

General of the Army Douglas MacArthur, an American hero in our highest tradition, served as commander-in-chief of all Allied powers in the Pacific Theater and was the architect of victory against the Japanese forces in World War II. Following the collapse of Japan in 1945, he directed the successful peacetime occupation of that country and commanded United Nations troops in the defense of South Korea. He became chairman of the board of the Sperry Rand Corporation soon after his retirement from the Army in 1951. Until his recent death, General MacArthur lived quietly in New York City as secure in the hearts of his countrymen as he is in history's pages as one of America's greatest hero soldiers.

General MacArthur was born in Little Rock, Arkansas, in 1880. Following his graduation from West Point in 1903, he began the military career that has had few equals in history: first lieutenant in the Philippines; captain in the Panama Canal Zone; brigadier general in France in World War I; superintendent of the U. S. Military Academy; Army chief of staff in the 1930s when, despite the Depression, he saved and modernized the skeleton army; military adviser to the Philippine government prior to the outbreak of World War II. In July, 1941, as conditions in the Orient became critical, President Roosevelt appointed him comanding general, U. S. Army Forces in the Far East.

Under MacArthur's leadership, the stubborn defense of Bataan by American-Filipino forces upset the Japanese timetable of conquest and gained the Allies valuable time for the defense of Australia. From April, 1942, on—with insufficient forces and inadequate armor—General MacArthur planned and mounted the great offensives which drove the Japanese back upon their home islands. By July, 1945, he had completed his recapture of the Philippines and made good his famous promise, "I shall return." After his retirement as supreme commander, General and Mrs. MacArthur lent their immense prestige to many worthy church and charity causes even as they provided continuing "images of magnificence" for the entire free world.

(The Christian credo of General MacArthur was prepared by the author from his pertinent speeches, statements and interviews.)

Three Hallowed Words

On September 2, 1945, just following the surrender of the Japanese nation after four cruel years of war's agony and destruction, I broadcast a message to the American people from the battleship *Missouri* lying in Tokyo Bay. Before the massed representatives of the Allied powers, the Japanese delegates Shigemitsu and Umedzu had just signed the instrument of surrender; four hundred American B-29s and fifteen hundred carrier-based aircraft had flown over the warships in a final aerial salute. The ceremony was over, and I withdrew to broadcast to my fellow countrymen as follows:

"Today the guns are silent. A great tragedy has ended. A great victory has been won. The entire world is quietly at peace. The holy mission has been completed. And in reporting to you, the people, I speak for the thousands of silent lips, forever stilled among the jungles and on the beaches and in the deep waters of the Pacific which marked the way. . . .

"As I look back on the long, tortuous trail from those grim days of Bataan and Corregidor, when an entire world lived in fear; when democracy was on the defensive everywhere; when modern civilization trembled in the balance, I thank a merciful God that He has given us the faith, the courage and the power from which to mold victory. We have known the bitterness of defeat and the exultation of triumph, and from both we have learned there can be no turning back. We must go forward to preserve in peace what we have won in war.

"Men since the beginning of time have sought peace. Various methods through the ages have been attempted to devise an international process to prevent or settle disputes between nations. Military alliances, balances of power, leagues of nations, all in turn failed, leaving the only path to be by way of the crucible of war. The utter destructiveness of war now blocks out this alternative. We have had our last chance. If we do not devise some greater or more equitable system, our Armageddon will be at our door. The problem basically is theological and involves a spiritual recrudescence and improvement of human character that will synchronize with the almost matchless advances in science, art, literature, and all the material and cultural developments of the past two thousand years.

"It must be of the spirit, if we are to save the flesh."

In the same spirit four years before, when I left Bataan for Australia to mount the Allied counterattack against the advancing Japanese, I cabled the pastor of the Little Rock, Arkansas, Episcopal Church where I had been baptized: "At the altar where I first joined the sanctuary of God, I ask that you seek divine guidance for me in the great struggle that looms ahead." Or again on the bloody beaches of Leyte Gulf—after our forces had landed to re-establish the government of the Philippines—I spoke to the assembled troops as follows: "By the grace of Almighty God, our forces stand again on Philippine soil—soil consecrated in the blood of our two peoples. The hour of your redemption is here. Your patriots have demonstrated an unswerving and resolute devotion to the principles of freedom. . . . Let no heart be faint. Let every arm be steeled. The guidance of divine God points the way. Follow in His name to the Holy Grail of righteous victory!"

Occasionally, after such momentous events, I have been asked by friends and critics alike how as a military commander I could be so religious or why I invoked God's blessing before and after battle. Invariably, I have replied essentially as follows: "In war when a commander becomes so bereft of reason and perspective that he fails to understand the dependence of arms on divine guidance, he no longer deserves victory." The truth is that ever since my upbringing in a sincere Christian home and my regular church and Sunday-school attendance as a boy, I have considered myself religious. At home or abroad, in peace or war—and, as Milton tells us, "Peace has its victories no less renowned than war"—I have worshiped in church whenever possible, I have prayed in private whenever alone.

For sixty years, practical everyday Christianity has been most meaningful for me in the traditional motto of West Point—"Duty, Honor, Country"—the code of conduct and chivalry of those who guard this beloved land. These three hallowed words reverently dictate—not only to the West Point Corps, but to all loyal Americans—what we ought to be, what we can be, what we will be. They are moral rallying points: to build courage when courage seems to fail; to regain faith when there seems to be little cause for faith; to create hope when hope becomes forlorn.

During a recent valedictory visit to West Point, as I listened to those songs of the glee club, in memory's eye I could see those staggering columns of the First World War, bending under soggy packs, on many a weary march from dripping dusk to drizzling dawn, slogging ankle-deep through the mire of shell-pocked roads, to form grimly for the attack, blue-lipped, covered with sludge and mud, chilled by the wind and rain; driving home to their objective, and, for many, to the judgment seat of God. I do not know the dignity of their birth but I do know the glory of their death. They died unquestioning, uncomplaining, with faith in their hearts, and on their lips the hope that we would go on to victory. Always for them—Duty, Honor, Country; always their blood and sweat and tears as we sought the way and the light and the truth.

And twenty years after, on the other side of the globe, again the filth of murky foxholes, the stench of ghostly trenches, the slime of dripping dugouts; those boiling suns of relentless heat, those torrential rains of devastating storms; the loneliness and utter desolation of jungle trails, the bitterness of long separation from those they loved and cherished, the deadly pestilence of tropical disease, the horror of stricken areas of war; their resolute and determined defense, their swift and sure attack, their indomitable purpose, their complete and decisive victory—always victory. Always through the bloody haze of their last reverberating shot, the vision of gaunt, ghastly men reverently following your password of Duty, Honor, Country.

The code which those words perpetuate embraces the highest moral laws and will stand the test of any ethics or philosophies ever promulgated for the uplift of mankind. Its requirements are for the things that are right, and its restraints are from the things that are wrong. The soldier, above all other men, is required to practice the greatest act of religious training—sacrifice. In battle and in the face of danger and death, he discloses those divine attributes which his Maker gave when he created man in His own image. No physical courage and no brute instinct can take the place of the divine help which alone can sustain him. However horrible the incidents of war may be, the soldier who is called upon to offer and to give his life for his country, is the noblest development of mankind.

We now face a new world—a world of change. The thrust into

outer space of the satellite, spheres and missiles marked the beginning of another epoch in the long story of mankind—the chapter of the space age. In the five or more billions of years the scientists tell us it has taken to form the earth, in the three or more billion years of development of the human race, there has never been a greater, a more abrupt or staggering evolution. We deal now not with things of this world alone, but with the illimitable distances and as yet unfathomed mysteries of the universe. We are reaching out for a new and boundless frontier. We speak in strange terms: of harnessing the cosmic energy; of making winds and tides work for us; of creating unheard-of synthetic materials to supplement or even replace our own standard basics; of purifying sea water for our drink; of mining ocean floors for new fields of wealth and food; of disease preventatives to expand life into the hundreds of years; of controlling the weather for a more equitable distribution of heat and cold, of rain and shine; of spaceships to the moon; of the primary target in war, no longer limited to the armed forces of an enemy, but instead to include his civil populations; of ultimate conflict between a united human race and the sinister forces of some other planetary galaxy; of such dreams and fantasies as to make life the most exciting of all time.

Years ago, in measuring my hopes for my son and in thinking the long, long thoughts of faith in God, I put on paper what has become known as "A Father's Prayer." Today for my grown boy—and for me—it is still the creed of Christ:

"Build me a son, O Lord, who will be strong enough to know when he is weak and brave enough to face himself when he is afraid; one who will be proud and unbending in honest defeat, but humble and gentle in victory. Build me a son whose wishes will not replace his actions—a son who will know Thee, and that to know himself is the foundation stone of knowledge. Send him, I pray, not in the path of ease and comfort but the stress and spur of difficulties and challenge; here let him learn to stand up in the storm, here let him learn compassion for those who fail.

"Build me a son whose heart will be clear, whose goal will be high; a son who will master himself before he seeks to master others; one who will learn to laugh, yet never forget how to weep; one who will reach into the future, yet never forget the past, and after all these things are his, this I pray, enough sense of humor that he may always be serious yet never take himself too seriously. Give him humility so that he may always remember the simplicity of true greatness, the open mind of true wisdom, the meekness of true strength; then I, his father, will dare to whisper, 'I have not lived in vain.'"

Rudolf Ray

The secret is hidden deep within our hearts. Art is living faith, not merely intellectual grasp. Art is religion.

World citizen, universal man, intimate friend of such international dignitaries as India's scholarly former president, S. Radhakrishnan, England's eminent critic Sir Herbert Read, and Japan's leading Buddhist Daisetz Suzuki, seventy-five-year-old Rudolf Ray bestrides the divided East-West world of art like a colossus. As a Vienna-born painter who is also a philosopher, this pink-cheeked, peripatetic "soul" painter reflects the spiritual wisdom of the East as fully as he does the technical prowess of the West. As a world traveler who has worked in Paris, studied in India and now lives in Mexico, Rudolf Ray today emerges as an inspired interpreter who sees beyond dualities into life's essential oneness and who captures on colorful canvases the invisible being of man and nature.

Like Plato in philosophy, Wagner in music and Shakespeare in poetry, Ray is a seer. Over the years he has brilliantly painted the objective reality of people and things in five continents; but, more important, in hundreds of immense oils lit with a supernatural aura, he goes beyond form and figure to reveal the inner essence, universal truth, Goethe's "thing-in-itself." Today, with his highly praised work hanging in homes and galleries from New Delhi to New York, Ray the philosopher-artist unifies model and environment, religion and art, East and West by painting what *Time* magazine calls "portraits of the soul."

Ray took up serious painting in 1920 after having studied medicine, philosophy and law at the University of Vienna. National acclaim first came to him in 1933 when publication of his first book, *Super Realism in Portraits*, led to his first one-man show of two hundred paintings in a Vienna gallery. Work, travel and subsequent exhibitions of his art took him over the next three decades to Paris, London, New York, Washington, Bombay, and Mexico City, where he now makes his home. Recently Dr. F. S. C. Northrup, Stirling Professor of Philosophy at Yale University, wrote of his art: "Rudolf Ray, born and raised in the technological society of the West, has discovered the art of the all-embracing formlessness of the non-technological East. The scientific, philosophical, legal and aesthetic insight necessary to reconcile and preserve both types of civilization appears therefore to be at hand."

The Language of the Soul

More than a decade ago I painted a series of portraits which are called "Images of the Self" and which when exhibited from Bombay to New York evoked either stinging rejection or singing adulation by the critics. The artistic problem was not difficult to fathom: (1) the eight unorthodox paintings were an attempt to show forth the progressive *inner* experiences of the Zen Buddhist scholar Suzuki; (2) the unorthodox, yet sympathetic, style demanded that as an art creation all eight build as a unity from personal or waking consciousness to the impersonal or transcendental wisdom; (3) these "Pictures of the Soul," as one critic called them, represented my attempt to translate the particularistic present into the Eternal Now and thus intuit the essence of universal man for all to see. In this view, art becomes a revelation of the infinite, a union of the profoundly-sensed particular and the all-embracing continuum.

My knowledge or approach as a painter has nothing of the mental or rationalistic in itself. It is *seeing* directly and intuitively the concrete, the substantial, the Real in all things and the path that leads to that Reality. This path is not Eastern or Western; it belongs to no race. The only authority is within the soul itself. The summit of Reality can be realized only within the individual.

So it is that the Suzuki series expresses both my philosophy of life and my "landscapes of the soul." Please remember that I painted a "concrete" portrait of Suzuki, not an imaginary vision or abstract aberration. Coomaroswamy in his *Traditional Conceptions of Ideal Portraiture* points out "the distinction between the appearance of a man on the one hand and on the other the interior image of the very man, invisible to the physical eye but accessible to the eye of contemplation . . . and in the realization of the whole transcendent person by means of the transformative constitution of all its parts. It is then a question of ideal portraiture in the likeness of 'a mystical body.'"

The Suzuki portraits thus demonstrate all the elements of my painting and my philosophy—and both end in transcendence. Transcendence, yet penetration; oneness, yet personal uniqueness. The rationale is mystical experience.

It is not surprising to me that I have found confirmation of my approach in the most important Indian books of wisdom, such as the Upanishads and the Bhagavad-Gita. It is not surprising that an Eastern sage such as Suzuki should give this insight to me as a painter since he is a man of similar qualities to the sages who created these writings. In the Mandukya Upanishad is the famous theory of four stages of consciousness: (1) waking or outwardly cognitive; (2) dreaming or inwardly cognitive; (3) deep sleep, or unconsciousness; (4) samadhi or the only real, impersonal consciousness. The Gita goes on to say that the impersonal is not the whole truth unless *linked with the individual cosmic spiritual reality*. My paintings embrace this span of experience from the working stage to the real state to what the Gita calls Supreme Reality, where the self is no more.

By a process of abstraction, therefore, I transcend the layers of body, mind and intellect in my work and reach the Universal Self. Gradually one sinks into the measureless being that is without limitation and determination. Here the universal and the unique, the absolute self and the absolute particular, are one. The secret is hidden deep in our hearts. Art thus becomes living faith, not merely intellectual grasp. Art is true religion. Art is, above all, synthesis. Space and soul are as inseparable as infinity and eternity. Where space and soul are inseparable, there is freedom. Where creation is a necessity, there is beauty and wisdom. Never has the desire for synthesis been stronger than today. Art reflects this desire, this longing, this religious aspiration.

I believe that I have developed a new approach to art, through which painting is not only an emotional and aesthetic experience but can also have important implications for psychology, philosophy, religion and science. I am also convinced that a new form of art which will help us to understand not only ourselves but also the desperate age in which we live, is greatly needed today. Neither facts nor logic, not even language, will help us to understand and accept the people of the world, particularly those who differ from us.

I feel that I as a painter have an important contribution to make in helping to solve some of the pressing conflicts of our time.

During my work in India, it became clear to me how important it is "to reach sources of inspiration that do not belong to our time and civilization, but are archetypal and universal." This art form is based on belief that art is being. That being is preceded by cognition which, transcending all limitations of space, time and mental structure, arrives at the formless, which is the image of infinite molding the finite. This is a return to the transformed beginning, a regeneration, a new creation which never was before and yet relates from whence I started. The human seed never perishes. Immortality is the destiny of man.

Eugene Carson Blake

*It never was possible to be a Christian all by yourself—
your Christianity is always in relationship with another
human being.*

The Reverend Dr. Eugene Carson Blake, former chief executive officer of the United Presbyterian Church and now general secretary of the World Council of Churches, is often acclaimed as America's "Mr. Protestant." Big, burly and broad-smiling, Dr. Blake rates the accolade for several reasons: he was an early leader in the church's crusade for human rights, he headed the fifty-million-member National Council of Churches from 1954 to 1957, he became Protestantism's celebrated unifier when in 1960 he proposed a plan of church union embracing the Methodist Church, the Protestant Episcopal Church, the United Church of Christ and the United Presbyterian Church. Now extending his progressive work and word to the world scene, Dr. Blake organized and directed the Fourth Assembly of the World Council of Churches and its 234 Protestant, Anglican and Orthodox denominations in Uppsala, Sweden, in the summer of 1968.

With offices in New York and Geneva, Switzerland, and with World Council of Churches assignments taking him to all parts of the globe, Dr. Blake is a Christian soldier who travels fifty thousand miles a year. He serves as chairman of the National Council's Commission on Religion and Race. He is a delegate to the periodic conventions of the World Council of Churches and the World Presbyterian Alliance. Every Christmas he preaches to U.S. servicemen scattered from Greenland to Korea; only recently he became the first U.S. Protestant leader to make a courtesy call on Pope Paul VI and, in closing the cordial thirty-minute visit, they repeated the Lord's Prayer together.

Dr. Blake, a graduate of Princeton Theological Seminary and New College, Edinburgh, has received honorary degrees from eighteen universities and colleges. An indefatigable teacher, preacher and radio-TV panelist, he is the recipient of the Catholic Interracial Council Award and the B'nai B'rith Democratic Legacy Award for "inspired leadership in the fight for human rights." He is married to the former Valina Gillespie, and they make their home in New Canaan, Connecticut, and Geneva, Switzerland.

The Race Set Before Us

For many years now most American ministers, priests and rabbis have said all the right things about civil rights. For years my own Presbyterian denomination—and, indeed, the National Council of Churches—have issued official pronouncements calling for "a non-segregated church in a nonsegregated society." But, at this critical time in the life of our nation, we have achieved neither a nonsegregated church nor a nonsegregated society. And, because the course is long and the hour late, we might recall with Thomas Jefferson: "Indeed, I tremble for my country when I reflect that God is just."

It is partly because the churches of America have failed to put their own house in order that more than a century after the Emancipation Proclamation, 177 years after the adoption of the Constitution and 175 years after the adoption of the Bill of Rights, the United States of America still faces a racial crisis. Most of us come late to this revolutionary struggle for the establishment of freedom, justice and equality for our Negro brothers. Most of us come late to the nation's moral battleground, but I pray that we come at last in the reconciling spirit with which the humble Lincoln once replied to a delegation of arrogant churchmen, "Never say God is on our side, rather pray that we may be found on God's side."

When ordered not to preach publicly about Jesus, Peter and the Apostles answered, "We must obey God rather than men." In that spirit several years ago, I was arrested in Baltimore, Maryland, for having with other ministers and laymen, Negro and white, broken deliberately the trespass law of that state. The occasion was a demonstration organized by the Congress on Racial Equality (CORE) designed to protest the standing indignity offered the large Negro community by a private amusement park which regularly advertised that it was open to the public (it even appears in Rand McNally maps) and just as regularly has refused admittance to all dark-skinned Negroes.

One of the most distinguished Presbyterians of Baltimore, Furman Templeton, an elder, the director of Baltimore's Urban League, was with me. He is a Negro. We approached the gate of the amusement park together. The guard stopped us, saying that we could not enter. I protested. The guard said that I could go in, but Mr. Templeton could not. I protested again. The trespass law was read to us. We were asked to leave the private property. We refused, continuing our protest, and were arrested. Scores of others were arrested too, including six Roman Catholic priests, a Jewish rabbi, a dozen Protestant ministers and many young people of both races. I was there as acting chairman of the Commission on Religion and Race of the National Council of Churches. Three others went with me from New York, representing the National Council of Churches, including Bishop Corrigan of the Protestant Episcopal Church. The question is: Is this kind of action right, or is it wrong?

So we must be entirely clear that law is not God. It has always from the first been a basic Christian conviction that there are times when a Christian ought to break law, any law. Let us look at a New Testament precedent. As Christians, Peter and the Apostles believed that they must not obey any order, however legal, which would stop them from making their witness to the Lord Jesus Christ. They said, "We must obey God rather than men."

I do not believe that any of you would argue in general that it is never right to break a law. What about Christians or Jews under Hitler? What about the Boston Tea Party? What about the whole series of arrests in the New Testament when Christians regularly refused to obey some laws even when they were taught through the Apostle Paul that "the powers that be are ordained of God"? Thus, in my opinion, the present-day effort by American Negroes to win equality in voting, in education, in job opportunity and advancement, in housing, and in public facilities (even amusement parks) has as much to do with witnessing to Jesus Christ, as acts of Christian heroism in the first century.

The 1963 march on Washington and the 1965 march on Montgomery marked the peak of moral and spiritual determination of the American people, white and Negro, to make the nation face up to revolutionary change in race relations. Since then the strains of battle have threatened the unity of our movement. We have allowed ourselves to be divided about such questions as the legality of demonstrations. We have been beaten in battles for ending *de facto* segregation of education in our Northern cities. Our unity is threatened, and our will is weakened because we forget the firm basis of morality upon which the cause is based. We who profess faith in the God who spoke through the prophets of Israel, and we who believe that that same God was revealed in Jesus Christ, are united in the belief that by creation all mankind is one family. The prophet Malachi speaks for us all as he asks, "Have we not all one father? Has not one God created us? Why then are we faithless to one another . . . ?"

The crisis of the nation is no more severe than the crisis in our churches and synagogues. How can any of us ministers, priests or rabbis stand safely eloquent behind our pulpits, reflecting the moral confusions of American culture in our tactful balanced prose when God is thundering at *His* people, calling them to repent and to be saved? Never in the life of the nation have the churches and synagogues through their best leadership been so fully united on any moral issue confronting the American people. But such intellectual unity will reveal the weakness and irrelevance of our pulpits, unless from them we speak and in the world we act to persuade our people to commit themselves to the new pattern of justice and freedom that must be established.

All Americans should remind themselves now of the unargued, and I believe, unarguable, morality upon which civil rights legislation and civil rights action is based. In our several traditions, the Judaeo-Christian convictions about God and man are one in asserting: (1) That God made man in His image, which is to say that man is not merely an animal of a complicated sort but is in essence a spiritual being. His worth is not in his vigor, weight or cleverness but in his origin. Because man, every man, is created by God, he must be treated, despite his sin, as a potential son of God, by covenant between God and man. (2) Right relations among men is based upon a personal concern for each one which we believe is not only our concern but that of God *Himself*. (3) The most important ethical considerations, and perhaps the only ones, are directly related to the effect of our actions upon the life and well-being of other men—all other men.

Years ago I read an amazing biography, *Saints, Sinners and Beechers*. It was the story of one of the most interesting families that ever lived in one house: Lyman Beecher, the father, a great man in his own right. Henry Ward Beecher, the most famous preacher of his day. Harriet Beecher Stowe, who wrote *Uncle Tom's Cabin*. And all the rest were talented beyond the common run of men and women too.

As a minister, I was most attracted to Thomas K. Beecher who for almost fifty years was minister of a Congregational church in Elmira, New York. He was about the first minister to start an institutional church anywhere—he developed recreation programs under church auspices for the boys and girls of the community. Thomas Beecher had a queer streak in him that I think was the queerness of genius.

When he was called by the Elmira congregation to be their minister, he wrote in reply a long letter in which there were five questions, numbered 1 to 5. He suggested that they could answer by telegram yes or no by number. If they were all yes, he indicated they could expect him on the following Sunday morning. These were his questions:

1. Will you pay me $1500 a year? Yes–No.
2. Will you allow $40 for moving? Yes–No.
3. Do you understand that neither you nor I must make promises to keep this relation of pastor and people beyond one month? That we owe each other nothing except to love one another? Yes–No.
4. My exclusive aim is to help men as individuals to be Christians. No church prosperity dazzles, no poverty or adversity will trouble me. Do you remember this? Yes–No.
5. Do you fully remember that I don't think much good can be done by a preacher's preaching? It must be by Christians working that good is done if at all. My choice is to work with my hands and do good on a small scale. Do you remember this? Yes–No.

The telegram came with five yeses, and the great pastorate began. It is that last point of that amazing letter that I want us to remember. *"It must be by Christians working that good is done if at all."*

This last year has been marked, I believe, by signs that Christians all over America are realizing that there is a contest on and that you must run in this race if you are a follower of Jesus Christ. Applause from a seat in the grandstand is not enough. Certainly in the effort to establish a new pattern of race relations in this nation, it is clear that the ministers and young people who have acted, marched, demonstrated, been jailed, been beaten, and a number been killed, have been a mark of the renewal of the Christian church and deserve credit for the beginning of progress that has been made.

I like the comment of the mother superior of a Chicago convent who, when asked to give permission for some of her nuns to demonstrate in Chicago's streets, said, "I have seen pictures over these years of nuns playing jazz instruments, running out base hits, coaching basketball teams—I don't see any reason why there shouldn't be some pictures of nuns acting as Christians as well!"

There are other signs of the renewal of the church of Jesus Christ in the actions of its members. Worship begins to be recognized as distorted if it is but a good performance by choir and preacher.

Perhaps the greatest challenge to the church in this decade is for ministers and people to recapture a connection between what happens in church on Sunday morning and what happens in our homes, our schools, on our streets, and in the nation. We must learn again that worship is work for all the Christian people and that all our work must be given to God if it is to have real meaning. "It must be by Christians working that good is done if at all."

These next months and years are critical for the nation and world and for the church of Jesus Christ in both the nation and world. Last year the churches were enabled to participate effectively in the political effort to pass the civil rights legislation. This year our task is to return to a more normal type of church activity. Our task is conversion, preaching and living for decisions to act as followers of Jesus Christ. To love rather than to hate. To serve others rather than to serve our greed. To live by faith in God, rather than to live by fear, or in confusion. To build a new nation in freedom and justice, rather than to criticize from a comfortable seat in the grandstand or pews.

For the Apostle Paul reserved the spectators' seats for those whose race was over and their victory won. And it is to us that his word is spoken: "Run with endurance the race that is set before us, looking to Jesus, the author and finisher of our faith."

Haile Selassie

*Our admiration for the Creator's handiwork, which in-
cludes the human race, should not be limited to those
things which He has provided us with for our daily
needs, but should include all that is good, human and
beautiful.*

High in the African hill country rises a kingdom old when Europe
was young—Ethiopia. Resplendent as the kingdom's modern ruler reigns
a black-bearded, seventy-six-year-old successor to the dynasty established
by King Solomon and the Queen of Sheba—His Imperial Majesty
Haile Selassie. Today, as sovereign of one of the world's oldest independent countries, the Ethiopian Emperor not only governs a land
of twenty-five million people but also helps lead an emerging Black
Africa in its struggle toward statehood and freedom.

The career of Emperor Haile Selassie, who ascended Ethiopia's
dynastic throne in 1930 at age thirty-eight, has been noteworthy in
two interrelated ways: (1) his internal achievements in the fields of
education, industry and agriculture, and (2) his external diplomatic
ventures which led Ethiopia to become a charter member of both the
League of Nations and the United Nations and which today makes
him a respected leader of the Organization of African Unity. One of the
most spectacular events of his thirty-eight-year reign took place shortly
after his coronation when he decreed the nation's first written constitution in three thousand years. Under a succession of five-year plans, the
Ethiopian people have seen their standard of living steadily strengthened,
their social and cultural services increased and their resources of oil,
minerals, chemicals, coffee and livestock properly utilized for the first
time.

The Lion of Judah first attracted world acclaim when he boldly
opposed Fascist Italy's unprovoked invasion of Ethiopia in 1935. Brave
in his leadership of troops at the battlefront, eloquent in his plea for the
integrity of small nations before the League of Nations, Haile Selassie
lived to return in triumph to the capital, Addis Ababa, in 1941 and to
see the principles for which he fought become moral pump lines in
international politics. Following the end of World War II, he began in
earnest the cultural and industrial renaissance of Ethiopia and kindred
Black African countries; notable first fruits of his farsighted programs

have been the socioeconomic five-year plans, the establishment of Haile Selassie University and the convocation of several African summit conferences.

An ardent, God-fearing Christian and the benevolent ruler of an ancient people, the Emperor's enlightened policies have earned him the respect of the entire civilized world. As the U.N.'s late secretary general Dag Hammarskjold said to him on the occasion of a state visit to United Nations headquarters: "Your Majesty stands in the perspective of the history of our time as a symbolic landmark, a prophetic figure on the path of man's struggle to achieve international peace and security through concerted international action."

God's Handiwork and African Liberation

All Ethiopians are the bearers of a long, rich and glorious heritage which has come down to them over the centuries as the fruits of the unswerving idealism, discipline and sacrifice of their forefathers. As one of the oldest countries of the world and as the senior independent nation of the African continent, Ethiopia has a long, uninterrupted history dating back before the Christian Era. And when one considers that Ethiopia embraced Christianity in the fourth century, it is obvious that its rich religious culture is also founded on a very ancient basis.

As the inheritor and exemplar of that sublime culture, His Imperial Majesty has proudly lived by Christian tenets since his youth and earnestly opens and closes each day with his favorite Christian prayers. At the same time he knows that religion is personal and subjective, and so one of his first acts on ascending the Ethiopian throne thirty-eight years ago was to decree freedom of religion for all. Emperor Haile Selassie knows equally that the glories and advantages of freedom can never be purchased with the world's material wealth, but rather that freedom's price reflects the sacrifice of innumerable heroes living and dying for their country and its religion. Thus, to this day and even in the dark ages through which Ethiopia and other African nations had to pass, Ethiopia's name was well-known throughout the world because its heroic forefathers made God their shield and their defender.

It is this kind of heroic Christian leader that the living Emperor has tried to be during these difficult decades of the twentieth century. We may look to earthly power or search the pages of history for solutions and find none. The answer to our survival, he believes, is to look into the depths of our own souls. Education, environment and experiences in life all may help. But it is in our religious faith and the moving experiences of the soul that we can become bigger persons than we are, larger in outlook and in spirit, on our way to being a new race of men who overcome petty prejudices and who pay allegiance not to nations but to mankind and to God.

In this modern day, when materialistic goals and selfish aims dominate the scene of human effort, this high ideal of self-sacrifice and selfless devotion to one's fellow men may appear too remote, its demands too severe. But man is not meant to live for himself alone; he exists with others and for others, and it is this sense of social consciousness which distinguishes him from all other beings. And this goal can and will be attained by those who realize their tremendous potential of spiritual strength in striving ceaselessly for the attainment of this high objective.

The living Emperor's preoccupations have not been concerned solely with the material welfare of his people. The development of the resources of intelligence which education draws forth from them —vital as it is—without moral inspiration and guidance, can never of itself work for the good of all. Man, who is by nature selfish, must learn that only in serving others can he reach the full stature or attain the noble destinies for which God created him. His Imperial Majesty has, therefore, spared no effort to encourage and sustain the church in its high mission of preserving and inculcating in youth those spiritual values and ideals which for centuries have guided the destinies of Ethiopians. It was, in consequence, with deep gratification that, during the past decade he has been able to bring about the full recognition of the Ethiopic Church as the national church of the empire—the church which, through centuries of struggle and martyrdom, has pursued its task of evangelism and education.

As man's capacity to improve his own lot has grown, so has his power to spread havoc and destruction correspondingly increased. The independent African states must assure that the growing weight of Africa is enlisted on the side of peace and justice to the end of avoiding a third holocaust which could well engulf the entire world and result in the total destruction of mankind. But dwarfing even man's material achievements in the twentieth century has been the emergence of peoples all over the world into freedom and independence. Today, for the first time, men everywhere to whom freedom and independence were, but a short time ago, only words, and for whom economic and political self-determination were no more than far-distant goals, have achieved the status of free men and are directing their efforts and energies to their own advancement. The Emperor is particularly gratified and proud that this development has been so marked and widespread on the great continent of Africa. Africa will no longer be the "unknown continent," for its human and material resources are beyond measure, and this great continent now stands on the verge of an economic, political and cultural development which, when realized, will be without parallel in history.

If man is to survive on this planet, the arms race which today clutches mankind in its unreasoning and inexorable grip must be halted, and it is to the United Nations that all nations, both large and small, must look as the medium to achieve this result. It is the task, rather the duty, of the smaller nations of the world to exert their utmost efforts to ensure that all possible measures are taken to this end. The living Emperor earnestly believes that the only sure way of achieving lasting peace is to place full confidence in and to apply the principles envisaged in the Charter of the United Nations and in the principle of collective security, thereby progressively reducing armaments, and to invest the amount thus saved in the fields of education, public health and religion so essential to the promotion of the welfare of humanity.

In summation of his Christian philosophy, Emperor Haile Selassie believes that he who would efface the sacred work of Almighty God, he who would abuse the mysteries of God's creation and discriminate between man and man, whom God created equal, on the basis of color, race or creed, calls down upon himself disaster and ruin. No one should forget that Africans differ from no other people in the world: they love those who love them, dislike those by whom they are disliked, and are jealous guardians of their freedom. This is the moment when the development of an attitude of sympathy and assistance for their legitimate aspirations can remedy and atone for the injustices perpetrated and the oppressions imposed in the past upon the lands and the peoples of Africa. So let all men and women never sacrifice love and compassion in their dealings with others for mere utility or temporary advantage. Our admiration for the Creator's handiwork, which includes the human race, should never be limited to those things which He has provided us with for our daily needs but should include all that is good, human and beautiful.

William W. Bradley

*As followers of Christ, we have chosen eternity, unpar-
alleled joy, a real feeling of vitality and victory.*

William W. "Bill" Bradley, one of the most heralded American athletes
of all time, received his Oxford Bachelor of Arts degree as a Rhodes
Scholar in June, 1967, and today has resumed his basketball career as a
star forward on the New York Knickerbockers. The personable, twenty-
five-year-old son of a Crystal City, Missouri, banker, Bradley signed a
four-year pact to play professionally with the Knicks at a reported figure
of $500,000. Upon completion of his sensational court career, he plans
to enter the U.S. diplomatic service.

While matriculating at Princeton University where he majored in
history, Bill Bradley made All-American basketball teams three years in
a row, led the Princeton Tigers to three Ivy League titles and in the
1964 Olympic Games at Tokyo starred as the youngest member of the
championship U.S. team. Long before he graduated with honors in
June, 1965, he was acclaimed by sports writers, coaches and fans alike
as "the best college basketball player in the country." In 1966 the
Associated Press named him to the All-America, All-Time team, composed of the outstanding players of the last twenty years.

A one-time Sunday-school teacher and a devout Christian since his
high-school days, the six-foot-five-inch, two-hundred-pound Missourian
won almost every athletic honor college and country could bestow—
repeated All-American laurels from Associated Press, United Press,
Sporting News, and U. S. Basketball Coaches, Most Valuable Player
Award in the 1965 NCAA Championship Tournament (in which
Princeton lost only to Michigan and Bradley set a new NCAA record of
177 points for a five-game tourney), 1965 Player of the Year by the
U. S. Basketball Writers, and from his alma mater the Harold W. Dodds
Achievement Award, the William W. Roper Trophy, and the Class of
1901 Medal, the latter given to the undergraduate who has done the
most for Princeton.

First drafted by the New York Knickerbockers in 1965, Bradley chose
Oxford University after winning a coveted Rhodes Scholarship for two
years of study in England. In addition to his liberal-arts studies, the
modest midwesterner kept in gangling-gazelle trim by playing occasional

weekend games at the university and as a "guest" forward on the Simmerthal championship five of Milan, Italy. Bradley's philosophy of winning, grounded in a deep evangelical Christianity and membership in Crystal City's Grace Presbyterian Church, has been expressed by him as follows: "You must develop self-discipline that makes you practice in one spot until you make twenty-five consecutive baskets; a self-discipline not to go to bed until you finish a difficult term paper; a self-discipline that makes you get up at 9:00 A.M. on Sunday and go to church instead of sleeping in."

The Big Victory

Several years ago during a Princeton summer vacation I worked in Washington, D.C. The nation's capital was a new town for me, and for quite a while I didn't have any close friends, didn't know where to go, didn't even find a church that satisfied me. Then one Sunday morning, in a God-guided way I guess, I attended a lesser-known Washington church and found it to be the most warm-hearted, Christ-spirited parish I had ever entered. Rather lonely and living away from my home in Crystal City, Missouri, for the first time during vacation, I found this church and its minister and people a real blessing. My long lonely summer turned into an exciting adventure.

Since my high-school days I have repeatedly discovered that fellowship with Christ makes life a challenge, a responsibility, a constant reaching out to new experience. Certainly, in this Washington interval, I entered eagerly into the fellowship of the Church of the Lord and was not disappointed. Indeed, I was filled to overflowing, as moved as I was at sixteen when I first experienced Christ during a Fellowship of Christian Athletes Conference at Lake Geneva, Wisconsin. It was then, under the inspiration of such sport stars as James Jeffrey, Frank Tarkenton and Don McClaren, that I came away saying, "I want to believe. I want to know and serve God."

In Washington I learned again that God's love and wisdom helps each of us with our problems whatever they may be. As followers of Christ we have chosen eternity, unparalleled joy, a real feeling of vitality and victory. We have chosen the never-dying rule on earth—God's kingdom. We are playing for the one team that will never lose—God's team.

It's a remarkable thing how relevant, how real and vital Jesus Christ is today. He is right here in my room at Oxford; He is in your room; He is in rooms in America, in England, in every nation. We cannot see Him but he lives. And blessed is he that believes without seeing Christ. He lives in your life; He lives in mine. We cannot afford to push Him out!

It's not easy to just become a Christian, however. So many want to become a Christian on their own terms. They may say: "I want Him to come into my life, and he can occupy all the rooms but one; I want the study for myself." Or some will give up becoming a follower of Christ because it is hard, and they won't be convinced until God shows them through a "bolt of lightning" or "burning bush" that He is real. That was my problem when I was searching for Christ.

For example, I went around during high school searching for the one big experience that would show me God is real. I thought I had to have a vision of some kind before I could believe. This went on for a year and a half. During this time I guess I thought I was pretty good, and though I appeared confident I was worried that I hadn't had that big experience. It just hadn't come! Then I enrolled in Princeton University. I had broken my foot and that year I didn't think I was going to play basketball very well. I was worried about my studies and it was the first time that I was away from home for any length of time.

After Christmas vacation at the university I took an oral exam and I did miserably. I walked back to my room and flopped on the bed. I didn't know where to turn. I thought I'd call home, but that was twelve hundred miles away. I considered talking to my friends, but would they really be concerned? I thought of turning to the Bible, but where would I look? I finally thought of a record I had from the FCA summer conference of the year before and as I listened to it I heard a man speak whom I've always idolized—Bob Pettit. I heard him say: "We are not trying for the state championship, nor are we playing for the national championship. We are playing but for one thing—the victory of Christ in the hearts of men."

Here I was worried about my studies, my basketball, about everything, and had been neglecting the one thing which counts the most. I never did receive that bolt of lightning, but I knew at that moment when I heard those words roll off that record that I was a Christian. I had been giving my life to the wrong goals. I knew then that I wanted to give my life to God and His service. I had been waiting for the outside light and all the time it was inside.

So Bob Pettit's words struck home. Suddenly I was able to see that I had failed to give Christ His rightful place in my life. I was physically, mentally and spiritually bankrupt. The regular disciplines of prayer and meditation and Bible-reading that are necessary for Christian growth had been buried in a file with some other items labeled "Things I know I should do."

My next step was obvious to me. Beside my bed, on my knees, I asked God to forgive me for being so foolish as to think I could run my life or accomplish anything meaningful without Him. I asked Him to take over and guide me in all my actions. There must have been many other things I talked over with God that day, but I can't begin to remember all I said. What I do know is that from that day forward things have been different. I don't mean that suddenly all my difficulties disappeared. Christ did not promise that, but He did promise to give us strength to handle any problem in life.

As I began to study the Bible, some of His promises became clearer to me. Verses that I had read many times before without understanding now came alive with new meaning. Instead of reading the Bible out of a sense of duty, I suddenly found it a new kind of adventure which I actually enjoyed.

Because this experience, which had its beginning four years ago, means so much to me, I tell my story wherever I think others may identify with my predicament. Following the Olympic Games in Tokyo—where I played basketball for the U.S. team—I told it to some university students in Hong Kong; I have told it at Oxford. Since they also are interested in basketball, I drew some parallels I had discovered between the sport and Christianity.

Because I want to be in top-notch condition to play my best, I do not smoke or drink. I have to practice regularly. I must work hard for a good mental attitude. During a game there must be no distractions

—just total concentration on basketball. Christianity has similar disciplines. Like basketball, where there is no such thing as a born athlete, there is no such thing as a natural Christian. It takes work. It requires a devotion to Christ above anything else. This is the cost of being one of His disciples. You can't go halfway. Being a Christian is an "all or nothing" proposition. And Jesus told us what He thought about tepid followers when He said, "Because thou art lukewarm, and neither cold nor hot, I will spew thee out of my mouth."

I find wide application in this verse for it tells me that lukewarm dedication to any endeavor is not enough to succeed. This is just one of the truths I have discovered in the Bible, the greatest source of wisdom and really the book of life.

Life at magnificent old Oxford, where I studied philosophy, history and economics, was almost ideal for the constant enrichment of one's mind and spirit. While there, I also played basketball, especially during long vacations when I flew to Milan to play on the Italian championship team, Simmerthal, for their European Cup games. Through these stirring games, as well as through the ever more stirring game of life, I try to keep in mind a stanza from one of my favorite poems:

> Show me the way not to fortune and fame,
> Not how to win laurels and praise for my name;
> But show me the way to know the great story
> That Thine is the Kingdom and the Power and the Glory.

A. Ronald Heaver

In ourselves, we fail. In Christ, we triumph.

In England's "green and pleasant land," A. Ronald Heaver has steadily grown as one of the world's postwar protagonists of renaissance, regeneration and renewal. A former Royal Air Force fighter pilot and former magazine editor, this saintly sixty-nine-year-old Englishman today serves as president of the Avalon Group which has amongst its aims the perpetuation of the Glastonbury tradition of King Arthur and Joseph of Arimathea and the spiritual ideal which this tradition represents.

Alfred Ronald Heaver was born in London on February 10, 1900. Educated at Felsted School, Essex, he enlisted in the Royal Naval Air Service during World War I. After passing through the Royal Naval College at Greenwich, he saw active service in France with a crack fighter squadron popularly known as "the anti-Richthofen circus." His long journalistic career included editing such British magazines as *The National Message* and *The Monthly Science Review*, and for forty years he made his influence felt as a controversial propagandist awakening Englishmen to their spiritual, social and political responsibilities. In World War II, although handicapped by leg-crippling paralysis, he volunteered to "carry dispatches" for the Chief of Air Staff from the Air Ministry in London to Mid-East R. A. F. Headquarters in Egypt and Palestine.

Possessed of a dynamic faith in God and belief in the divinity of Christ, coupled with what he describes as "a vision inspiring people to press toward their divinely determined destinies," Ron Heaver is of that brave translunary breed who feel the urge to do something about it. A member of many public movements in the past, including societies espousing the cause of Anglo-American friendship, he also for twenty-five years was an executive of the Garden Tomb (Jerusalem) Association which has secured in perpetuity trusteeship of the true sites of Christ's Crucifixion and Resurrection. In 1958, when forming the Avalon Group, he wrote a manifesto entitled "Impasse and the Way Out" as spearhead of the public campaign calling for a National Day of Prayer to be celebrated as an official act of state.

The following aphorisms are characteristic of the pungent quality of Heaver's style of writing: "The state was made for man, not man for the state." "Man cannot live by bread alone, but it is equally certain he cannot live at all without it." "Because every man is entitled to his own opinion, this does not mean that every man's opinion is of equal value." "Men were born to practice the art of living, not spend their lives earning the right to live." "Many are the colors in the spectrum of the light of truth, yet the light is one." His published works include *The English People, The Divine Cure for World Depression, The Economic System of the Kingdom of God* and *The Great War of Ignorance.*

The Inward Vision

Faith and spiritual experience have played a dominant part in my life chiefly because from my earliest days spiritual perception has been natural to me. Asked at seven what I wanted to be when I grew up, my spontaneous reply was: "All I know is that I was born for a purpose." There was nothing consciously egotistical about this affirmation, which on the contrary was a simple straightforward description of the strong sense of faith in an unfolding purpose inwardly felt.

Born in London, I was sent at the age of ten to a preparatory school at Taunton in Somerset where on half-holidays I liked to climb a certain hill and sitting alone gaze at Glastonbury Tor some fifteen miles away. Such philosophical questions as "Why am I here in this world?" or "Why is there anything at all?" used to engage my solitary contemplations. It baffled me that everyone seemed to take the world for granted and there seemed to be no one who shared my own sense of the wonder of existence. Fortunately there was nothing morbid in such introspection; in fact I recall my astonishment on being accused of "always being so happy," as if the radiance which naturally comes from experiencing the glow of spiritual consciousness was a crime!

That distant view of a green hill across the flats of Sedgemoor held a magnetic attraction and irresistible fascination for my youthful mind although a decade was to pass before I began to learn from books about the founding of the first Christian church in all the world by Joseph of Arimathea in Avalon. Nor could I then foresee at that time the way in which a vital part of my task in life was destined to be intimately concerned with the Garden of Joseph of Arimathea in Palestine, occupying as it does a site adjoining that other and more famous "green hill far away" outside the city wall of Jerusalem.

Meanwhile, the early grounding in religious faith received had been a blend of the best from opposite viewpoints represented respectively by the Nonconformist as well as the National Church of England liturgical teaching. To this day my natural inclination is to adopt an interdenominational rather than sectarian outlook on religious questions. Indeed, the answers of orthodoxy never seemed to provide satisfactory solutions to the problems which beset my questing spirit. Those childhood meditations on Falcon Hill, however, had endowed me with a deep abiding sense of direct communion with God which grew ever stronger throughout the ordeals and trials of two world wars.

At sixteen, one brother having been killed in the Battle of the Somme and another wounded, I succeeded in "wangling myself" under age into the R.N.A.S., in preference to waiting two years to get called up. Taking to the air as if it were my native element, I made my first solo flight successfully after only three and one-quarter hours of dual instruction. Flying "Camels" in France my squadron formed part of the first mobile wing of the R.A.F., and contained such famous ace fighter pilots as Bishop, Ball, Maddock and McCudden.

Finally, in a dogfight with "the Richthofen circus" in which the odds were seven to one against us, my plane was shot down over Arras and crashed within the enemy lines. Used as a ground target for fourteen machine guns I should have been "a sieve," but miraculously emerged from the wreckage unscathed except for one leg which was badly sprained. This was before the days of parachutes, and paralysis as a consequence of the shock to my spine was to develop later. Subsequent experiences as a prisoner of war, first in occupied territories, then in southern Germany, gave me a unique insight into human nature seen at its best and worst. It was enlightening to see how the varying temperaments of British, French, Italian, Portuguese and Russian prisoners reacted to the same stress of suffering and rigors of privation.

After repatriation came demobilization in 1919. When walking across the Westminster Bridge over the Thames one day, I found myself exclaiming: "All this is new. I have never seen life through these eyes before." It was not until some weeks later that the familiar words "He that is in Christ Jesus is a new creature. Old things have passed away, all things have become new," revealed themselves in full light so that the realization dawned suddenly that this was the transformation which had actually happened to me. Such indeed was the sequence in which spiritual experiences invariably occurred. First I would receive the experience itself, the necessary confirmation following afterward.

On May 3, 1926, the national daily press in Britain came out with the headlines "Last night paralysis swept over the country." This was a reference to the general strike. At the same moment in time I was also completely paralyzed, the doctors giving me only forty-eight hours to live. Surviving this crisis, I faced a crisis of confidence when Sir Farquhar Buzzard, the king's physician, announced bluntly that I would never walk again. My rejection of this verdict with the remark that in my experience it was always the unexpected that happened, prompted the eminent specialist to give vent to the vehement contradiction: "Your experience! What is *your* experience? I have had years of experience of these things and I tell you, nothing of the sort."

The biblical assurance that those who wait upon the Lord shall renew their strength and "mount up with wings like eagles" was a sheet anchor to me at this time. But under orthodox treatment I made no progress at all. It was not until I abandoned orthodox treatment entirely that progress moved fast toward recovery. In two years I was driving a car and by 1930 had traveled alone through France to Barcelona and back just to prove that I really had regained personal independence. The intervening period of enforced immobility had brought with it the compensation of enabling me to indulge in the inclination to think deeply. I had been able throughout also to maintain a weekly commentary upon world events which prompted the headmaster of Harrow to describe its author as "the man with a million eyes."

Nine years following paralysis, I was elected suddenly to a position as chief executive of a world federation, taking over at the age of thirty-five from two outstanding leaders who in their mid-seventies died unexpectedly within a few months of each other. It was also during this time that the impression kept on impinging itself insistently on my mind that I really must go to see for myself this sacred site in Jerusalem with which I had been associated for so long, namely, the Garden of Joseph of Arimathea surrounding the tomb of our Lord. As usual the decision to do anything of this kind always seemed beset with seemingly insurmountable difficulties. However, in an all-night silent vigil at Glastonbury my resolution was confirmed and on return to London I booked my passage on the Cunard liner *Laconia* due to sail from Southampton for Haifa almost immediately.

On returning from this memorable visit, I found that Lord Lee of Fareham, a former Civil Lord of the Admiralty who had given "Chequers" to the nation as a private residence for prime ministers, had made an appointment to see me at my office. His opening remark, "I have just seen the Garden Tomb in Jerusalem. It has the most powerful aura of any place on earth I have ever contacted," made a profound impression on my mind coming as it did from a man of such renowned practical attainments. It then transpired that we had both reached an identical conclusion about the urgent necessity for taking steps to protect from desecration the site of Golgotha adjoining the tomb known locally as "Gordon's Calvary" since the site was originally discovered by the famous General Gordon when making the first geographical survey of Palestine for the Turkish government. I returned by air to Jerusalem intending to stay three days, but remained on the spot negotiating through a maze of legal and technical obstacles for eleven months. At long last I was able to report, "Objective attained; the impossible achieved," although I was not to know then that another decade would pass before all the relevant documents would finally be signed and sealed.

In August, 1939, two weeks before war was declared, by sending telegrams to His Majesty the King, the Prime Minister and the Archbishop of Canterbury, I took the initiative in launching my first campaign for a National Day of Prayer which culminated ultimately nine months later at the time of the crisis of Dunkirk. This campaign conducted in face of official opposition from the churches was accompanied by the slogan "We must mobilize the spiritual resources of the Nation," and was promoted through the journal of which I was editor and which then enjoyed the second largest circulation of any religious weekly in Great Britain.

It was round about this period of turmoil that Sir Waldron

Smithers, M.P., parliamentary secretary to Prime Ministers Baldwin and Chamberlain, confided in a mutual friend his opinion: "Heaver is not a man but a force," a view which served to demonstrate that the power operative in my life had indeed been the power of faith since otherwise this influence would not have won recognition from others as manifesting the quality of an impersonal force.

My wartime staff were responsible for the air raid protection of the office block from Nos. 1 to 10, Buckingham Gate, opposite the side entrance to Buckingham Palace, and including the Imperial College of Defense headquarters and also the head office of the Duchy of Cornwall Estates. From this position in the heart of London many crises occurred which presented stern tests of faith during the Blitz.

Once in a famous London club I found myself face to face suddenly with a group of refugees from occupied countries expressing acute alarm at the fate of Britain then standing alone under the threat of imminent invasion. A distinguished Belgian professor confronted me with the spirited challenge: "Do not tell us that Britain has faith. France had faith; Belgium and Holland had faith; Poland had faith, but their faith did not save them. Why should you think that your faith is better than our faith? It is not sufficient for you to say you have faith. Do not give us your faith but give us your reasons for faith in ultimate victory!"

Dead silence followed this outburst and I was conscious of a sea of eyes tormented by an agony of apprehension looking at me imploringly. It was a dramatic incident but one which proved to be an example of the way in which spiritual experience alone enabled me to give a reason for the faith which was in me, without premeditation, spontaneously and effectively, at the drop of a hat.

Further confirmation that the power of faith can go on working long after the operating cause, if forgotten, was evidenced when meeting a prominent Arab physician unexpectedly in Jerusalem. "Ah, I remember you," said Dr. Freij. "All through the darkest days of this war when defeat seemed imminent I would remind my friends of the Englishman I had met in 1934 who foretold then that all of these things would happen. Because of what you said I was able to convey to them the absolute certainty that by steadfast faith in God the cause of freedom would triumph over tyranny." The doctor then concluded: "Your predictions may not have always been correct in every detail but they were right often enough to establish your reputation as a twentieth-century prophet."

It was under the continuing shadow of the thermonuclear stalemate that the Avalon Group came into being. As an organism rather than an organization this group is dedicated to the task of perpetuating the Arimathean and Arthurian traditions embodying as they do all that the symbol of the Holy Grail inwardly and truly represents. A long-term aim of the Avalon Group is to work for the realization of the vision of William Blake who spoke of building "Jerusalem in England's green and pleasant land," a vision which we interpret as meaning the manifestation on earth of the conditions of the plane of divine perfection, made possible as a consequence of the coming regeneration of the whole creation.

In 1959 the decision was made to leave London and live instead in the heart of the Avalon countryside of Somerset. Again God's guidance directed the steps necessary for discovering an appointed place exactly midway between Glastonbury and Camelot, the geographical centers of the Arimathean and Arthurian traditions respectively. Here a Sanctuary of Avalon was created, dedicated to the power of the Divine Name and set apart for prayer and silent meditation.

My living faith embraces the conviction that the English-speaking peoples acting together in unity have a unique role to play in the service of mankind which no other people can play: a destiny to fulfill which no other people can fulfill. This is a vision which enables us to stand as firm as a rock in a tumultuous world as we see continually with greater clarity the past alive in the present, pressing on toward a divinely-determined destiny in the future.

Archbishop Iakovos

We need to learn to appreciate one another and become less centered in our little castes and traditions. We will secure unity, not through uniformity, but through mutual love, trust and respect.

Archbishop Iakovos, the tall bearded Primate of the Greek Orthodox Church of North and South America, towers today as an authoritative champion of the ecumenical movement for Christian unity as well as the leading spokesman for Greek Orthodoxy in the United States. As exarch in America of the Ecumenical Patriarchate in Istanbul, he exercises ecclesiastical jurisdiction over two million communicants in the rapidly expanding Orthodox churches in North and South America. As a president of the World Council of Churches, he is an instrumental influence in the increasingly important role that Greek Orthodoxy has gained in world Christendom.

Archbishop Iakovos, who is an American citizen with his headquarters in New York City, was born Demetrios A. Coucouzes in 1911 on the Turkish island of Imbros. Ordained a priest in Boston, Massachusetts, in 1940, he served during the next fifteen years as preacher or dean at Greek Orthodox cathedrals in Boston, New York, and St. Louis, Missouri. Elected Bishop of Melita and ecumenical representative to the World Council of Churches in 1955, he became his Church's chief liaison officer in central and western Europe. On April 1, 1959, he was enthroned as head of the Greek Orthodox Archdiocese of North and South America at New York's Holy Trinity Cathedral.

In his eight years of denominational leadership, Archbishop Iakovos, whose Greek name means "James," has encouraged a phenomenal growth within the Greek Orthodox fold and brought a new cohesion into its scattered ranks. A powerful preacher, respected theologian and world traveler, the Harvard-educated prelate initiated the organization of a Standing Conference of Canonical Orthodox Bishops in the Americas and has pressed steadily toward unifying the dozen separate nationally-originated branches of Orthodoxy in the Western Hemisphere. As the chief international diplomat for the senior Patriarch, Athenagoras I of Constantinople, he moves impressively through a communion of nearly two hundred and fifty million Christians and emerges more and more today as a pivotal leader in bringing the two-thousand-year-old Eastern faith into the mainstream of world affairs.

An Ecumenical Witness

"Behold, I make all things new." I know of no other scriptural passage that sounds more promising, more joyful or more triumphant. It reminds me of another equally beautiful passage, the third verse of the first chapter of Genesis, which says, "And God said: Let there be light: and there was light." Both passages mark the beginning of a creation: the one already completed, and one about to start.

For, the ecumenical movement among all Christian churches is, in essence, the beginning of a new creation. I cannot imagine a new creation that could be molded outside the ecumenical movement. Behold its radiance; it has penetrated the soul and filled the hearts of all with hope! Behold its beauty; it has restored the sweet expression of an expectant smile upon the lips and in the eyes of every Christian! Behold its unique newness! It has refreshed the air of the interfaith encounter, dispersed the dust of self-righteousness, and renewed our faith, hope and love for one another.

It is not the modern ecumenical movement itself, however, that has brought the newness in which we breathe and live. It is He who guides us into the truth. It is the Holy Spirit, the Paraclete, that substituted discomfort with comfort, spiritual anguish with consolation, despair with a new perspective. It is the same spirit of God which moved upon the face of the waters just before the beginning of the first creation.

Who can deny that we are standing at the threshold of a new era? Who can argue against the signs of the times which point with such clarity to the new epoch? Who can refuse to heed the pronouncement of God: "Behold, I make all things new"? Who can shut his eyes or insist that churches are not being led forward and toward reunification by the invisible arm of Him, who made both the far-off and the nigh one, and crumbled the middle wall of partition?

"Behold," says He, "I make all things new." Behold around you and within you, and you will find for yourselves, how true this is.

Prejudices and religious bigotry have vanished long ago. Provocations and mutual accusations are lessening. Monopoly of truth or excessive scripturalism and traditionalism have definitely come under the control of Christian consciousness. Excommunications against one another are a past experience. Understanding has replaced misjudgment, and genuine respect for one's belief and practices characterizes our present attitudes. Common prayer is recommended now as being more in accord with true and genuine Christianity rather than prayer behind walls of partition. Embracing one another is thought of as an act of obedience to Him, who embraced the sinners and the just alike, as His brothers.

Behold, we live in the eve of a new creation! All we must do is pray in humility so that this new creation which will unite us, one with another, unify our church and make all mankind the household of God, may in no way be hindered by human sin and frailty or by suspicious ways and mistrust which are already being implanted by the adversary, within the hearts and minds of the weak. Let us prove that "the fruit of the Spirit is in all goodness and righteousness and truth." And yet evils and error, murder and strife still stain the countenance of evolving mankind.

In the spring of 1965, for example, after the brave Unitarian Universalist minister James Reeb had given his life in the struggle for basic human rights at Selma, Alabama, I took part in a special memorial service for him in New York City. I did this because I believed that it was an appropriate occasion not only to dedicate myself as well and our Greek Orthodox communicants to the noble cause for which he died, but also in order to show our willingness to continue this fight against prejudice, bias and persecution. For our Greek Orthodox Church and our people fully understand from our heritage and our tradition such sacrificial involvements. Our Church has never hesitated to fight, when it felt it must, for the rights of mankind; and many of our churchmen have been in the forefront of these battles time and time again.

The great poet John Milton said in the closing lines of *Samson Agonistes:*

> All is best, though oft we doubt
> What the unsearchable dispose
> Of Highest Wisdom brings about.

I would like to believe that these words have deep relevance to the meaning of the tragic and violent death of the Reverend James Reeb. The ways of God are not always revealed to us, but certainly His choice of this dedicated minister to be the victim of racial hatred and the hero of this struggle to gain unalienable constitutional rights for those American brethren of ours who are denied them, and to die, so to speak, on this battlefield for human dignity and equality, was not accidental or haphazard.

Let us seek out in this tragedy a divine lesson for all of us. The Reverend Mr. Reeb felt he could not be outside the arena of this bitter struggle—and we too must feel that we cannot. Let his martyrdom be an inspiration and a reminder to us that there are times when we must risk everything, including life itself, for those basic American ideals of freedom, justice and equality, without which this land cannot survive.

We live in the year 1969, one thousand nine hundred and sixty-nine years after Christ's birth, and yet we do not seem to realize how grave is our responsibility to attest to our professed faith in Christ and to live together in love according to His commandments. Our age is called the space age. And rightfully so. We are about to explore and conquer space. Yet there is another space—an unexplored and vast space, of far more imminent concern—separating Christian hearts, that must be conquered for Christ's and for our own sake. We owe it to Christ, and to ourselves. The whole world, Christians and non-Christians, are waiting for this great day that God has made for us and from which we are still far away.

Unity is too sacred a word to be taken irreverently or lightly. It is as sacred as prayer. And it is as dangerous as prayer. Prayer and unity are not empty words; both are a kind of commitment: a serious commitment to God. When we pray to God and call Him our Father, we must act as His children; otherwise we are committing a double sin and evoking the wrath of God upon us. So it is with unity. Only those united with Christ, and only those willing to live "unity," are entitled to talk about it.

Instead of having a united Christianity, busy, dedicated to serving human want and distress, we have state-supported welfare to come to the aid and assistance of all those in need. We all shed tears over present-day immorality and low ethical standards. We even prophesy the end of the world and are content to shake our finger from the pulpit, and point out the source of the ills of our times. We grumble and growl over the small omissions of divine law, while "we ourselves omit the weightier matters of the law, judgment, mercy and faith." As far as our relations to Christ are concerned, we act no differently from the women who stood afar off, beholding a part. But unlike the soldiers, we have tried to rend the seamless robe of the Lord—and then we cast "arguments" and "pseudo documents" to prove—that *ours* is the Christ, and ours is the *church*.

The present world crisis provides us with more than illustrations, demonstrating the duty of Christians toward Christ and the church. The robe of Christ is without seam and so is the church. The robe of Christ belongs to Him and to no one else. The robe of Christ is woven from the top throughout. It is our obligation to respect it and to keep this robe stainless, without blemish or wrinkle or any such thing.

The Greek Orthodox Church—the mother of all Slavic churches, and sister of the ancient churches of Antioch, Jerusalem, Alexandria, and Rome—mourns over the continued existence of *dis*unity, caused only by *human vanity*. We find the seeds of this disunity even in apostolic times. The Holy Scriptures refer to cardinal and mortal sins; but I find no cardinal or mortal sin greater than our disunity—an act of treason and betrayal of Christ, and of our very soul. If we must be tortured by remorse, the greatest of all should be that we failed Christ in a most lamentable way. If we actually recognized this, we would not be worried about unity, for it would become more than obvious that Christ is our *bond* of unity—or, as St. Paul says, "Christ is our peace, who hath made *both one*, and hath broken down the middle wall of partition between us." It is apparent, therefore, that instead of talking of church unity we should talk about unity or *reunion with Christ*, for it is in Him that we, as Christians, "live and move and have our being."

What, therefore, shall we do? How should we understand unity? How shall we act from now on about it?

I will try to answer these three questions as follows:

1. We must repent and ask the compassion and the forgiveness of our Lord, because we have tried to make Him our possession—instead of making ourselves possessed by Him.

2. We must understand unity as an organic unity between man

and Christ and try, therefore, to incorporate ourselves into the life and body of Jesus. He is the vine and we are the branches. If a man abide not in Him, he is cast forth as a branch, and is withered. It is only this unity that can lead into church unity.

3. If we are truly concerned with unity, we must learn to love it; it is the most difficult art; to be compassionate, understanding, tolerant, brotherly. We have much to gain from such an approach to unity. Unity can result from such an attitude. Humility, obedience and prayer are the only elements that can enhance church relations. Living together and praying together without any walls of partition raised, either by racial or religious prejudices, is the only way that can lead surely to unity, for unity in its last analysis is the work of God, not of man.

Unity will, by no means, sever our relations with our own particular tradition; on the contrary, it can fortify our common tradition, which emanates from the Holy Spirit. We need to learn to appreciate one another and become less centered in our little castes and traditions. We will secure unity, not through uniformity, but through mutual love, trust and respect.

Let us, therefore, pray and live with the image of a united church, sheltered under the saving Cross and guided by its Founder, our Lord and Saviour Jesus Christ.

Aldous Huxley

*"Though He slay me, yet will I trust Him." This is
the utterance of someone who is totally aware.*

Aldous Huxley, the world-famous author of a number of brilliantly
satirical novels exposing the empty pretenses of modern life, died while
this book was in the final stages of preparation. His work lives after him
in such titles as *Crome Yellow, Point Counter Point. After Many a
Summer Dies the Swan, Ape and Essence* and *Island.* He was also an
eminent philosophical essayist whose books *The Perennial Philosophy,
Ends and Means* and *The Doors of Perception* probe the divine ground
of all existence. One of his most important books, *Brave New World,*
pictured the society of the future dominated by science and inhabited by
mentally and morally shattered human beings.

Born in England in 1894, Aldous Huxley was the grandson of the
great scientist, Thomas H. Huxley. His father, Leonard, was a well-
known writer and editor and his mother was the niece of Matthew
Arnold; Sir Julian Huxley is his eminent humanist-biologist brother.
Educated at Eton and Oxford, young Huxley was forced to learn
Braille and undergo a long struggle to correct a serious eye defect. After
working on several publications in England, he went to Italy in 1923,
moved to southern France in 1930, traveled through Central America in
1934, and finally settled in southern California where he wrote a
number of distinguished screen plays.

Unsatisfied by his creative accomplishments and the wide range of his
intellectual powers, Aldous Huxley delved deep into the world of
Vedanta and spiritual experience. In recent years he won recognition
and respect as a proponent of the healing, unifying power of what he
calls "the divine Reality substantial to the world of things and lives and
minds."

Married in 1919, he had one son, Matthew. Following the death of
his first wife, Mr. Huxley was married a second time, to Laura Archer
in 1956. Mrs. Huxley is herself a noted modern author whose latest
best-selling work is *You Are Not the Target.*

In Search of the
Final End of Man

Men have put forth enormous efforts to make their world a better place to live in. But, except in regard to gadgets, plumbing and hygiene, their success has been pathetically small. "Hell," as the proverb has it, "is paved with good intentions." And so long as we go on trying to realize our ideals by bad or merely inappropriate means, our good intentions will come to the same bad ends. In this consists the tragedy and the irony of history.

Probably the primary example of the utilization of absurdly inadequate means toward an end—man's Final End, according to the theologians of the great historical faiths—is the attempt to achieve solely by knowledge, and its prerequisite, language, what can only be realized through understanding. Language made possible the accumulation of knowledge and the broadcasting of information. It was language that permitted the expression of religious insights, the formulation of ethical ideals, the codification of laws. It was language, in a word, that turned us into human beings and gave birth to civilization.

Yet St. Paul said that we ought to "serve in the newness of the spirit, and not in the oldness of the letter." For "the letter killeth, but the spirit giveth life." In other words, "Gray is all theory, green life's golden tree."

Too much theorizing is fatal to the soul. Too many lectures will cause the green tree to wither, and will turn its golden fruits to dust. Life flows back into us when we turn from the stale oldness of theological notions to the newness of spiritual experience; when we exchange the learned astronomers' proofs and figures for nocturnal silence and the stars.

Perhaps because knowledge and pseudo knowledge are common enough commodities to be taken for granted, and understanding is very nearly as rare and highly prized as emeralds, most men cherish the comfortable delusion that knowledge and pseudo knowledge are understanding. This is one of the most prevailing and most dangerous of all intellectual sins. Knowledge is acquired when we succeed in fitting a new experience into the system of concepts based upon our old experiences. Understanding comes when we liberate ourselves from the old and so make possible a direct, unmediated contact with the new, the mystery, moment by moment, of our existence.

Genuine revelation is simply the record of the immediate experience of those who are pure enough in heart and poor enough in spirit to be able to see God. The saints and sages of all religions make fundamentally the same report about the nature of Ultimate Reality. As the Hindu formula, "That art thou," affirms the oneness of Atman, the imminent, eternal Self, and Brahman, the absolute Principle of all existence, so the last end of every human being is to discover the fact for himself, to find out who he really is.

These masters of the spiritual life define Truth as understanding. Hence, according to Emerson, it is clear that "truth must be lived and there is nothing to argue about in this teaching; any arguing is sure to go against the intent of it." Understanding is not inherited, nor can it be laboriously acquired. It is something which, when circumstances are favorable, comes to us, so to say, of its own accord. All of us are knowers, all the time; it is only occasionally and in spite of ourselves that we directly understand the mystery of given reality.

William Law, like Emerson, knew enough not to try to argue understanding into existence. "Away, then, with the fictions and workings of discursive reason, either for or against Christianity! They are only the wanton spirit of the mind, whilst ignorant of God and insensible of its own nature and condition. . . . For neither God, nor heaven, nor hell, nor the devil, nor the flesh, can be any other way knowable in you or by you, but by their own existence and manifestation in you. And any pretended knowledge of any of those things, beyond and without this self-evident sensibility of their birth within you, is only such knowledge of them as the blind man hath of the light that has never entered into him."

If reality is to be understood in its fullness, as it is given moment by moment, there must be an awareness which is not limited, either deliberately by piety or concentration, or involuntarily by mere thoughtlessness and the force of habit. Understanding comes when we are totally aware—aware to the limits of our mental and physical potentialities. This, of course, is a very ancient doctrine. "Know thyself" is a piece of advice which is as old as civilization, and probably a great deal older. In practice, it is a call to total awareness, which is a primary, choiceless, impartial response to the present situation as a whole. Be totally aware of what you do and think and of the persons with whom you are in relationship, the events which prompt you at every moment of your existence. Be aware impartially, realistically, without judging, without reacting in terms of remembered words to your present cognitive reactions. If you do this, knowledge and pseudo knowledge will be relegated to their proper place, and you will have understanding—in other words, you will be in direct contact with reality at every instant.

Better still, you will discover what Carl Rogers calls your "delicate and sensitive tenderness towards others." And you will discover not only your tenderness, but also the cosmic tenderness, the fundamental all-rightness of the universe—in spite of death, in spite of suffering.

"Though He slay me, yet will I trust Him." This is the utterance of someone who is totally aware. And another such utterance is, "God is love." From the standpoint of common sense, the first is the raving of a lunatic, the second flies in the face of all experience and is obviously untrue. But common sense is not based on total awareness; it is a product of convention, of organized memories of other people's words, of personal experiences limited by passion and value judgments ("Judge not, that ye be not judged"), of hallowed notions and naked self-interest.

Total awareness opens the way to understanding, and when any given situation is understood, the nature of all reality is made manifest, and the nonsensical utterances of the mystics are seen to be true, or at least as nearly true as it is possible for a verbal expression of the ineffable to be. (As in Eckhart's "To gauge the soul we must gauge it with God, for the ground of God and the ground of the Soul are one and the same.") For when there is understanding, there is an experienced fusion of the End with the Means, of the Wisdom which is the timeless realization of Suchness with the Compassion which is Wisdom in action.

Of all the worn, smudged, dog-eared words in our vocabulary, "love" is surely the grubbiest. Bawled from a million pulpits, lasciviously crooned through hundreds of millions of loud-speakers, it has become an outrage to good taste and decent feeling, an obscenity which one hesitates to pronounce. And yet it has to be pronounced, for after all, Love is the last word.

Eleanor Roosevelt

O Lord, make me an instrument of Thy peace.

Universally acclaimed as "the first lady of the world," Mrs. Franklin D. Roosevelt died at seventy-eight not long after being interviewed for this volume. She is included because she lives on in the hearts of millions of admirers and because her influence as diplomat, author, and gentle world leader has been brightened, not dimmed, by death. Gradually, since the passing of her husband, President Roosevelt, in 1945, she had become not only "the most admired woman in the world," but the symbol of all the awakened women everywhere working to achieve a joy-wreathed world of peace.

To the gracious manner born, Eleanor Roosevelt grew up in the Oyster Bay branch of the Roosevelt family, watched her Uncle Theodore become governor of New York, Secretary of the Navy, and finally Republican President of the United States. When she married another Roosevelt—a cousin from the Hyde Park branch—her sheltered life as Mrs. Franklin D. Roosevelt became channeled into the almost identically turbulent course followed by her "Uncle Teddy." During her thirteen crowded years in the White House, she brought to the first-lady role a new dimension of humanitarian activity for the succor of all.

With her uncle's "Square Deal" and her husband's "New Deal" days finally behind her, Mrs. Roosevelt proceeded to broaden her own distinguished career. She became U.S. delegate to the United Nations, chairman of its Human Rights Commission, and one of the authors of the epochal Universal Declaration of Human Rights—an experience she called "one of the most wonderful, important, and worth while of my life." She traveled ceaselessly, from Lebanon to India to Japan, wrote her column "My Day" and such books as *This I Remember* and *On My Own*, and never withdrew her working support of the Democratic party. When her great soul passed from earth, she left not only four sons and a daughter and a singular legacy of love in action, but also "a name to shine on the entablatures of truth forever."

Faith, Hope, and Charity, These Three

Greatness in life may lie in different fields. To me it is a proof of life's nobility and prodigal gifts that so many people from so many countries, cultures, and centuries have contributed so much to man's upward progress. And yet, in evaluating what men and what power have had the greatest influence on history we must name the religious as the first and final cause. Indeed, when I was once asked to list the five men who had done the most to shape the world's thinking, I named Christ, Confucius, Mohammed, Buddha, and Plato.

Although denominations mean little to me, I have been a church-going Episcopalian all my life. If we pattern our lives on the life of Christ—and sincerely try to follow His creed of compassion and love as expressed in the Sermon on the Mount—we will find that sectarianism means less and less. Jesus was Jewish and yet He founded the Christian religion. To me, the way your personal religion makes you live is the only thing that really matters.

Life is meant to be lived as fully and as helpfully as possible. In addition to prayer and congregational worship, I have found the Holy Bible a remarkably wise and beautiful book and reading a few verses every day a helpful habit. My favorite verses are in First Corinthians, chapter thirteen, which starts: "Though I speak with the tongues of men and of angels, and have not charity, I am become as sounding brass or a tinkling cymbal," . . . and which ends so beautifully, "Now abideth faith, hope, charity, these three; but the greatest of these is charity."

Today, religious skeptics frequently charge that Christianity has failed, even as political isolationists carp that the United Nations has failed. I do not think Christianity has failed, because Christianity is something that is accepted or rejected by the individual; even when one accepts it he may not live up to it all the time or even part of the time. Whether you believe as a Protestant, Catholic or Jew, Hindu, Buddhist or Moslem, it is the fruits of your belief as evidenced in your daily life that are of concern to your fellow human beings. If you believe in God, you naturally think that the Supreme Being will judge you both by your acts and by your intentions, taking into account your temptations and sometimes giving you credit for your victories.

So with the churches, so with the United Nations. The U.N. is only an instrument, a piece of man-made machinery whereby imperfect human beings strive for greater perfection here on earth. Thus, I believe in Christianity and in the United Nations, which I consider to be a working expression of Christianity in the world. That is why, when President Harry Truman requested me to be a delegate to the organizing meeting of the United Nations in San Francisco, I accepted for one reason: I believed the United Nations to be the greatest hope for a peaceful world. My husband often expressed his bright hopes for the new peace organization, and somehow I felt a personal responsibility.

Since that day in 1945 when I accepted Mr. Truman's invitation, I have had no reason to change my mind. Indeed, I believe more completely in it today than I did in January, 1946, when I met the delegates in London and was assigned to Committee Three. It was while serving on this committee, concerned with humanitarian, educational, and cultural problems of mankind, that I began to see the inner workings of the U.N. Later, working on the Human Rights Commission in an effort to write a Charter of Human Rights, I learned how the Soviets operate and the need for forceful, patient dealings with them.

Why is this work so personal to me? Well, it seems to me that the only really organized work for peace today is being done through the United Nations. This is the only instrument we have with which to work, the only instrument whose purpose it is to keep peace in the world, the only instrument which can create an atmosphere in which peace may grow. We *must* use all the knowledge we possess—all the avenues for seeking agreement and international understanding—not only for our own good, but for the good of all human beings.

A moral and materialistic struggle now engulfs our planet. We might even call it a bloodless war, which is now going on between

Communism and democracy. The war for Communism, both in an economic way and an ideological way, is led by the Soviet Union; the cause of the free, democratic-believing world is led by us. Now, if we are going to lead people we have to understand them: what their conditions are, what they care about and believe in, what their religion is, what their customs and habits are.

In this regard, it is time we Americans took a good look at ourselves and our shortcomings, remembering how we established a land of freedom and democracy, remembering what we believed in when we did it. The only thing that really causes me worry is that I don't think our people are aware we have been challenged; that this great struggle is going on; and it is critical whether our way of life and our hard-won freedoms are to survive. Thus, in this continuing struggle it is most essential for Americans to learn to understand people of other lands.

We wonder, for example, why having given so much help, we do not have friends. It is fantastic, really, what we have given—billions of dollars' worth of aid. But what we have failed to do is send the right administrators of this aid—men who understand the people they are giving it to. We are apt to say, "Oh, are you still doing it that old-fashioned way? This is the way we do it in America!" and already we have made our first mistake. No under-developed country can make the leap of a thousand years into a highly organized society like ours. All peoples want to do things a little better, see themselves move ahead, apply their moral and spiritual values in their own way. Also, as we get to know them, we are more apt to forgive their trespasses. For instance, I adopted a plan during my U.N. years of inviting small groups of delegates for a social meeting. It was here I found that much more under-standing was possible, that you really could get to know people and what they believed. I must confess there was one exception—the Russians.

When I visited Russia several years ago, I had one persistent, frightening thought: that we might continue to be apathetic and complacent in the face of this gigantic challenge that is the Soviet Union. I can never believe any government preserved by fear can stand permanently against a system based on love, trust, and co-operation among its people. Our system, based on love and trust, removes fear so all are free to think and express their ideas, to work

and worship as they choose. In the past, we have never failed
to meet any challenge or threat which confronted us. In the future,
I am confident we will master this too, but we must use the full
resources of our faith in order to prevail.

Lester B. Pearson

It is not always within our power to command success. But we can deserve it. That to me is the power of the religious life.

The Right Honorable Lester B. Pearson, one of Canada's men of the century, served until 1968 as that country's fourteenth prime minister. Statesman, soldier, diplomat, teacher, author and peacemaker, "Mike" Pearson has been active in almost every area of Canadian action and achievement since he joined the Department of External Affairs in 1928. His long public career as ambassador, deputy minister and Opposition leader reached its zenith in the fall of 1963 when the Liberal party he helped rebuild was returned to power and he was named prime minister.

Born in Newtonbrook, Ontario, in 1897, Mr. Pearson is the second son of a long line of Methodist ministers. He was educated at the University of Toronto and Oxford University, and served as a flying officer overseas in the First World War. His exceptional governmental career over nearly four decades has included such influential roles as Canadian delegate to the League of Nations, ambassador to the United States, adviser at the U. N. Charter Conference in San Francisco, chairman of the North Atlantic Council of NATO and chief of nine successive Canadian delegations to the United Nations. Mr. Pearson was elected president of the U. N. General Assembly in 1952.

Lester Pearson's signal combination of parsonage upbringing, personal idealism and public accomplishment resulted in the National Conference of Christians and Jews selecting him for its 1963 World Brotherhood Award. The recipient of twenty-seven honorary degrees, he is the author of *Democracy in World Politics* and *Diplomacy in the Nuclear Age*. As Canada's most distinguished son, he attained the ultimate in international recognition when in 1957 he received the Nobel Peace Prize. The citation read: "It is given not to the political leader or the Secretary of State as such, but to the man because of his personal qualities, his powerful initiative, strength and perseverance displayed in attempting to prevent or limit war operations and restore peace."

Idealism in Action

In April, 1963, as head of the resurgent Liberal party, I was elected Canada's fourteenth prime minister. When I telephoned my parents in Halifax to give them the good news—my father, the Reverend Edwin Pearson, was a Methodist minister like his father before him—my mother listened quietly for a minute and then spoke: "Well, Lester, thank God you're a minister at last— even though you're not a real one!"

It was in such an ardent Christian household that my two brothers and I learned the hard lessons of faith and idealism. Our minister's home, as we lived in many parts of southern Ontario from Toronto to Hamilton, was rich in everything but money. Companionship with Dad was especially close as we not only felt his inspiration in church and home, but also on the baseball field where he played an impressive center field on the local team— a most unlikely role for a Canadian Methodist minister circa 1900! Both at prayer and at the plate, we learned something of the necessity of looking deep within ourselves for the qualities of courage, zeal and the competitive spirit which are the strength of every man and woman.

Then, as now, the Bible occupied a central place in my life and thought. Although the Bible is such a great source of beauty, strength and inspiration that you find your "favorite" passage changing as you grow older, you learn that there is comfort and promise to help you through all the changing circumstances of life. This is what I have found and, as a result, I have particularly liked various passages at different times: many of the Psalms, Paul's First Epistle to the Corinthians; the Beatitudes and the Sermon on the Mount from St. Matthew.

I have retained particular affection for Isaiah 40:31: "But they that wait upon the Lord shall renew their strength; they shall mount up with wings as eagles; they shall run, and not be weary; and they shall walk, and not faint." For these particular times, however, in view of the problems facing us as Canadians and as world citizens, I would say that my present favorite is Psalms 133:1: "How blessed it is for brethren to dwell together in unity."

Today, more than ever, as individuals it is our duty to stand firm on the Christian principles which have been taught in our churches and which, in themselves, have the key to the solutions of every kind of problem—personal, social and political. We should apply these principles of faith, love and understanding, not merely in opposing something wrong, but with zeal in crusading for the things we love. It is not always within our power to command success. But we can do more! We can deserve it! That to me is the power of the religious life.

During my lifetime, greater and more spectacular progress has been made in the physical sciences than in many centuries that preceded it. As a result, the man who lived in 1505 would have felt more at home in 1905 than one who died sixty years ago if he came back to life today.

A great gulf, however, has been opened between man's material advance and his social and moral progress—a gulf in which he may one day be lost if it is not closed or narrowed. Man has conquered outer space. He has not conquered himself. If he had, we would not be worrying today as much as we are about the destructive possibilities of scientific achievements. In short, moral sense and physical power are out of proportion. This imbalance may well be the basic source of the conflicts of our time; of the dislocations of this "terrible twentieth century."

All of my adult life has been spent amidst these dislocations; in an atmosphere of international conflict; of fear, and insecurity. As a soldier, I survived World War I when most of my comrades did not. As a civilian during the Second World War, I was exposed to danger in circumstances which removed any distinction between the man in and the man out of uniform. And I have lived since— as we all have—in a period of cold war, during which we have ensured by our achievements in the science and technology of destruction, that a third act in this tragedy of war will result in the peace of extinction.

I have, therefore, had compelling reason, and some opportunity, to think about peace and religion; to ponder over our failures since 1914 to establish them in our lives; and to shudder at the possible consequences if we continue to fail. I remember particularly one poignant illustration of the futility and tragedy of war. It was concerned, not with the blood and sacrifice of battles from 1914 to 1918, but with civilian destruction in London in 1941 during its ordeal by bombing.

It was a quiet Sunday morning after a shattering night of fire and death. I was walking past the smoking ruins of houses that had been bombed and burned during the night. The day before they had been a neat row of humble, red brick, workmen's dwellings. They were now rubble except for the front wall of one building, which may have been some kind of community club, and on which there was a plaque that read "Sacred to the memory of the men of Alice Street who died for peace during the Great War, 1914-18." The children and grandchildren of those men of Alice Street had now in their turn been sacrificed in the Greater War, 1939-45. For peace? There are times when it does not seem so.

True, there has been more talk of peace since 1945 than, I should think, at any other time in history. At least we hear more and read more about it, because man's words, for good or ill, can now so easily reach the millions. Very often the words are good and even inspiring; the embodiment of our hopes and our prayers for peace. But while we all pray for peace we do not always, as free citizens, support the policies that make for peace; or reject those which do not. We want our own kind of peace, brought about in our own way.

The choice, however, is as clear now for nations as it was once for the individual: peace or extinction.

The desire for—and the attainment of—peace requires more than prayer, important as that is. It requires an enlightened moral policy on the part of nations and an enlightened moral policy on the part of individuals. My years of service in representing Canada at the United Nations and at various international conferences convince me there is now real hope for peace—because millions of people care and because millions of people are working for this difficult, often dangerous, goal.

For example, when I was awarded the Nobel Peace Prize, I was inundated with letters and cables from all parts of the world. In Canada alone in the first week, I received more than two thousand messages of congratulations and good wishes on receiving this award. They have come from children at school and from an old friend of ninety-eight years of age; from persons in the highest places and from those who work and live as plain, ordinary people. The President of the United States of America addressed me as "Dear Mike" and a newly arrived laborer from a refugee camp as "Excellency." One envelope that intrigued me was addressed to: "L. B. Pearson, Peacemaker, Late United Nations, New York."

Wherever these messages came from—and however addressed—there was in them all a deep longing for peace in the world, one made more intense by the realization of what the alternative could now mean.

Perhaps never before has this yearning been more intense or widespread—and so mixed with anxiety. Here are a few, but typical, excerpts. "I am just an ordinary wife and mother who looks at her children and is afraid." "We were refugees from a Nazi concentration camp, but our boys are now Canadian doctors and we want to serve this country that has brought us peace." "Please do keep on trying to help nations get along with each other."

In the long struggle of men and nations to get along with one another, where are we now? What would the Unknown Soldier—either of the First or Second World War—think today if he could come back and live again in our troubled world? Certainly, he would find the most startling changes, the most dazzling scientific feats in earth, sea and air, the most amazing progress in everything except man himself, his soul and his conduct. He would, perhaps, find it incomprehensible that, after having gone down twice in ghastly world holocausts, mankind again is floundering on the brink of a third.

He would find less sense of peace and security in the world than in any peacetime since 1918. The fear that grips the world today has, of course, been made more intense by the realization that total war now means total destruction. It is focused on space satellites and intercontinental missiles, or rather on their manufacture and use by men under the orders of a government whose purposes we distrust.

Our first and feverish reaction to these developments is merely to speed up and improve our own facilities for defense and destruction and deterrence. This is important, even essential, in the circumstances of today. Important also is the strengthening of the unity, the partnership, of the free nations. But these things are not enough. If they are the only response to today's challenge, the Unknown Soldier can be sure that he will one day be joined by the rest of us, victims of a failure and a fury far greater than anything in recorded history.

When I talk or write like this someone always, and rightly, asks what has gone wrong and what can we do about it. There are those who feel like giving up and falling back on the normal animal reactions to danger—flight or hide or run away. The other day I received a letter from a friend who, exposed to the turbulence and violence of life in the Middle East, and momentarily overcome by despondency, expressed his longing for "escape from a world of unbelievable fraud, falsehood and hatred and passions that know no bounds; where there are no answers, where the chemicals of disaster surround us and no man can prevail."

He added, "It's like the Oklahoma farmer in John Steinbeck's *Grapes of Wrath* who took down his gun from the wall when the bank foreclosed the mortgage and asked, 'Who can I shoot?'" The "who can I shoot" reaction is understandable, but futile and danger-ous. Men in all ages have faced situations which seemed quite as menacing as our, for history is a record of terror as well as triumph. But throughout the ages there have always been the wise, the good, and the strong who have been able to find in themselves the re-sources to face and defeat that terror.

Today, both as an international citizen and as the former leader of a great peace-loving country, I remain a practical idealist or true realist. For, the true realist is a man who sees through to things both as they are and as they can be. In every situation there is the possibility of improvement; in every life the hidden capacity for something better. True realism involves a dual vision—both sight and insight.

The size of contemporary problems is apt to make them appear overwhelming; the fundamentals relate rather to questions of values or proportion. Quantity itself is relative. It is one of the character-istics of life, for societies as well as individuals, that the consequence of success in grappling with problems is often the obligation to meet and master greater ones. We are forever climbing the ever-mounting slope.

Although man is indeed the measure of all other things, there is also a measure for him, for the individual human being, against which he can be tested. That measure is to be found in values that, while fully human, are at the same time both universal and absolute; that are, in short, moral and spiritual.

On a Canadian grave in France there is an epitaph which I believe captures what is sought by all men of good will. It is on the headstone over the grave of a Canadian boy who won the Victoria Cross and who was buried in the first of far too many war cemeteries. Whether he was English-speaking or French-speaking I do not know; some of both races lie in all those cemeteries side by side. The biblical epitaph on the grave of this particular young World War II lad, which was chosen by his Canadian mother, reads: "How blessed it is for brethren to dwell together in unity." It is for all of us today to seek that unity too.

Maurice Chevalier

Work and love! These have been from the beginning the two great forces of my life.

A youthful sprite at eighty and a legend in his own lifetime, silver-haired Maurice Chevalier has been the balladeering *bon vivant* of two continents for more than half a century. Now entering his 68th year as an entertainer, Chevalier's influence as a singing star of stage, screen, cabarets, concert halls, records, radio, and television, has been incalculable. Today his in-person one-man shows, both in Europe and America, have made him one of the most sensational attractions on the international concert stage.

Born and raised in Paris, the young Chevalier's singing career took a vaulting leap ahead when he was seventeen years old and discovered by the cabaret queen, Mistinguette. Where before he had played the nightclub circuit as "Le Petit Chevalier," he now took his familiar tuxedo and straw hat to the Folies Bergère and joined Mistinguette's show-stopping act; swiftly they became the toast of Paris. Wounded and imprisoned on the Western Front during World War I, he returned to show business in 1920, starred in revues in Paris and London, and soon began his meteoric career in French musical films.

Crossing the Atlantic for the first time in 1929 and starting still another phase of his career, "Marvelous Maurice" made his American movie bow in *Innocents in Paris* and immediately topped this success with a starring role in the Ernst Lubitsch film *The Love Parade*. His more recent U.S. cinema triumphs have included *Gigi*, *Pepe*, *Can-Can* and *Count Your Blessings*, while he brightened American home screens in such TV spectaculars as *The World of Lerner and Lowe* and *The Maurice Chevalier Story*. When in Paris, where he now lives with his second wife, Mons, Chevalier resides at Marnes La Coquette, an art-filled treasure house which is considered one of France's most magnificent private homes.

The Religion of Love

Like many of my fellow Frenchmen, I was born and brought up a Catholic and undoubtedly will die one . . . I hope with the blessings of the Church. But again, like many of my countrymen, I have not been as interested in the familiar routines of religion such as church membership, attendance and committees as I have been in trying to live my Christianity in the big, bright, tinseled world of show business. Of the many personal and professional reasons for this, perhaps the most revealing is that my father's sudden death in Paris in 1898 forced me to become the family breadwinner at age ten and, when the next year my brother Paul and I joined the circus as acrobats, my vagabonding career as a showman had begun. Thus, after sixty-eight years as a balladeering *bon vivant* in Europe and America, I can say that my inward Christianity has meant more to me than any outward "churchianity."

During the big moments of life—the so-called turning points of one's career—I have always felt the nearness of God, my prayerful need for His guidance, and a firm belief that things were working out according to higher wisdom. So it was that, when I was singing at the Paris Eldorado Club at age seventeen, I was seen by the legendary nightclub queen, Mistinguette, invited to join her act, and together at the Folies Bergère we became the "rage of Paris." So it was when I was wounded and captured by the Germans in World War I, or when I made my American movie debut in 1929 in *Innocents in Paris*, or when I sat out the Nazi occupation of Paris in World War II without performing for them once! It is in times like these, as Pascal says, that God is felt more in the heart than in the church or cloister.

I have always been something of a mystic and my world travels, especially those today in high-flying jets, give me ample time for Bible-reading, meditation and prayer. I sleep little in airplanes. When the night surrounds me and reading becomes a trial, I flick off the light and sit in silent awareness of the smallness of humans and the vastness of the universe. Then I think of time and of God and of the chain which links everything and governs all that befalls us.

Work and love. These had been from the beginning the two great forces of my life. The first was strong and vital still, and happiness was surging in me because of it. The second is only memory now, but I will be forever grateful that love has touched me, for it has given me perhaps its greatest gift: it has left me richer than it found me.

If you have not loved at all, it's pretty sad because you have had nothing. But with love even when its pain brings suffering you become richer, because it leaves its mark in your heart and in your way of living after that. It can teach you to be more humble, to be less pretentious and to understand more deeply. And in love, just as in work, to learn truly you must try to go through failures in the best possible way. I think that what makes people great is not to have only moments of success—it is also to have moments of failure and to survive them in as beautiful a way as you can.

But there is more to the wealth of love than that. For me at least, it has left a tender and separate souvenir from each of the women with whom I have shared it. And though fate has not chosen to bestow on me the gift of that marvelous love with one woman for a whole lifetime, I have nonetheless been blessed; for though love has gone now, its rewards will be with me always.

Friendship, I believe, must be part of an enduring marriage. If you can have a woman that you like in your arms and at the same time a woman that you like to have in your heart, then you're very rich. When you have both the physical happiness and the spiritual happiness, a good friend to run to for understanding and response, then you're truly blessed. There is a hazard in every affair, I agree, but every day is a risk of some kind from birth to death. Surely it is better to live dangerously and be truly alive than to act so prudently and only half exist? Yes, exactly as I cannot justify retirement from the stage, so I cannot vindicate a kind of retiring from life.

Now that I am approaching eighty-one, you ask about retirement? Impossible. Would the tranquillity of a house and garden fill my days, or do I need the excitement, the challenge and the reward of my metier to keep me alive, completely alive? I know the answer. So long as I am physically able to walk out on stage and sing and dance and clown I must do it. The time for such musings and recollections is brief, for soon there comes a knock on the door and friends are there to say farewell for this season and to query you about the next. And the past is set aside to make way for the crowding future. Even after more than half a century of it . . . you can't simply stand still. You either quit entirely, or you must keep going forward.

Always in my heart there will be the desire and the need to return to the stage, to stand alone before a theater full of living, breathing people with the footlights blazing in my eyes and to sing and dance and hear the beautiful sounds of laughter and applause roaring up from the audience. For me it is a kind of nourishment . . . especially when there is someone to enjoy it with you, someone who really cares.

Eighty candles, eight decades of living, I keep asking myself, aren't you a little bit depressed that so much life has already gone by? To which I can honestly reply No, for what I cannot change never makes me unhappy, never has. If I do my best and I cannot change it, then I have to accept it and not get upset because it is stronger than I. I had to learn for myself: there is no cure for life but to live more; there is no remedy for love but to love more. Perhaps, from loving a beautiful woman, you learn to love all men and women. From loving all humanity, you learn to love God.

David Sarnoff

Whatever man conceives in his heart and mind can become a reality.

Brigadier General David Sarnoff, chairman of the board of the Radio Corporation of America, is recognized throughout the world as a pioneer in the development of radio, television, and the electronics industry. Inventor, educator, executive, organizer of the National Broadcasting Company, General Sarnoff long ago earned the broadcasting industry's tribute as "Father of American Television."

Under his unswerving leadership in championing both black-and-white and color TV, R.C.A. introduced the first postwar receiver in 1946 and to date has manufactured 24 million home sets. Against sturdy odds, he also championed all-electronic, fully compatible color television to the end that color programming now fills virtually all network hours. The result: millions of Americans today share his great dream of mass communication, and television is a reality for millions of human beings everywhere on earth.

Born in 1891 near Minsk, Russia, young Sarnoff was brought to this country in 1900 by his parents. Fascinated as a youth by the new means of communication, "wireless," he landed a job as an office boy and then an operator with the Marconi Wireless Telegraph Company of America. In 1919 when the Radio Corporation of America was formed at the request of the government, it acquired the Marconi Company, and Sarnoff became commercial manager. In 1926 he organized N.B.C. "to provide the best radio programs available for broadcasting in the United States." In addition to his scientific and industrial activities, General Sarnoff has achieved international recognition for his efforts in military communications, especially during World War II. As government consultant, he has served on several special presidential commissions. General and Mrs. Sarnoff, who live in New York City, have three sons and nine grandchildren.

Invisible to Infinite

It was my good fortune to have been born about the same time the electron was discovered, shortly before the turn of the century. By a similar and equally happy accident of fate, at age fifteen I was drawn into the newly emerging art, science and industry of radio, where I have found active occupation ever since. Thus, for the past sixty-two years, the electron has been my constant—and constantly challenging—companion.

In the course of my more than sixty years' relationship with electronics, I have seen it exchange the telegraph key for satellite television, and watched it grow from a means primarily of communications for ships at sea to a mighty influence over the destinies of mankind.

Through electronics, we can range from invisible to infinite; probe the inner secrets of the living cell, or those of Venus. We can, with the swiftness of light, transmit voice and images high in space above the Atlantic and cause them to reappear on the television screens of an opposite continent. Space television reports the world's weather, and so helps predict it and perhaps ultimately control it.

Electronic "sentries" guard the nation's security in the far north. Electronic "eyes" supervise operations too remote, inaccessible or dangerous for human eyes to view. Electronic "brains" perform in seconds and in volumes calculations that normally would take man years to complete. Electronic "hands" outrace and outpace the finest human efforts, relieving much of mechanization's tedium. The electron has become the most versatile instrument ever placed in the hands of man, and the uses of this atomic sub-particle, the smallest bit of matter known to nature, have barely begun to be explored.

Having been so closely associated with the development and growth of electronics for well over half a century, it would be untrue to deny a deep sense of pride at man's accomplishments, and the vaulting progress of his sciences. Nevertheless, there also is a feeling of awe and humbleness, springing from a lifetime's association with science, at the awareness of powers beyond the capacities of mind or science even to comprehend.

Everywhere in science, we can behold the handiwork of a Supreme Architect of the Universe. The myriad suns of which our own resembles one grain in the Sahara sands, their majestic cycles—these cannot be regarded as mere accidents.

Nor can the harmony of their relationships and their effects upon life on this planet be measured by the human mentality. An intuition beyond reason informs us that these are the revelations of a Divine Intelligence.

It was Hans Christian Oersted, the Danish scientist who discovered the relationship between electricity and magnetism, who correctly said: "The Universe is a manifestation of an infinite reason, and the laws of nature are the thoughts of God."

Thus, as the horizons of science advance, and as our knowledge expands, we become more and not less humble, more reverent, not less. For science is presenting us with questions of ever-greater profundity to which it does not possess the answers.

To provide fulfillment on this earth for humanity, science alone is not enough. Man's yearning reaches past mere comfort or knowledge or power to seek dignity, beauty, truth and purpose in life. For these, there are no substitutes to take the place of our Judaeo-Christian precepts. If the role of science is to pave a path of progress for mankind, the role of religion is to guide it along true lines of morality and principle.

Today, science and religion meet on common ground, in a common effort to achieve a common need of world understanding, peace and harmony. Never were science and religion more compatible.

At a time of almost unlimited capacity for human advancement —or human destruction—it is perhaps our high destiny to rekindle an awareness of the divine attributes with which we are endowed, and to rededicate our responsibility for giving them expression.

We may yet be a generation which, hopefully, by taming its fears, its hungers and its terrible weapons, may serve to usher in an age of universal understanding and peace.

Wernher von Braun

Science is helping to put a face on God.

Dr. Wernher von Braun, Director of the George C. Marshall Space Flight Center in Huntsville, Alabama, is one of the world's leading rocket authorities and space scientists, whose pioneering achievements helped open the road for American astronauts to travel in space. Since the NASA Marshall Center was officially activated in July, 1960, the Saturn rocket program under the direction of Dr. von Braun, which is destined to provide giant launch vehicles for a manned lunar landing, has reached many significant milestones. The Saturn I series, for example, was launched successfully from Cape Kennedy ten out of ten times—a new record in the history of rocketry.

A world-renowned, German-born space scientist who is now an American citizen, Dr. von Braun came to the United States soon after the end of World War II to assist in the development of America's infant guided-missile program. From 1935 to 1945 the tall, burly rocketry engineer had gradually become the principal power in developing Germany's advanced guided rocket, the V-2 long-range missile and, as a joint enterprise of the German Army and Air Force, established the advanced experimental Rocket Center at Peenemünde. Thus, his enormous technical knowledge of rocket development was applied immediately at New Mexico's White Sands Proving Grounds and at Alabama's Redstone Arsenal, the two U.S. centers where such critical early rockets as Hermes II, or Redstone, or the later Jupiter, Juno and Pershing missiles were developed. His Juno rockets were also used for the first successful recovery of animals from space and the United States' first satellites around the earth and the sun.

With NASA's successful Gemini astronaut flights concluded and with the Apollo-Saturn V "moon shot" now scheduled for 1969, Dr. von Braun's work increases daily in significance. Recognition of this has resulted in his receiving sixteen honorary degrees and a score of scientific awards. Among the latter honors are the NASA Medal for Outstanding Leadership, the Gold Medal of the British Interplanetary Society, the Distinguished Federal Civilian Service Award, and the Dr. Robert H. Goddard Memorial Trophy. Dr. von Braun's published works include *Across the Space Frontier*, *First Men to the Moon* and contributions to *A Journey Through Space and the Atom*.

Science as Religious Activity

The two most powerful forces shaping our civilization today are science and religion. Through science man strives to learn more of the mysteries of creation. Through religion he seeks to know the Creator.

Neither operates independently. It is as difficult for me to understand a scientist who does not acknowledge the presence of a superior rationality behind the existence of the universe as it is to comprehend a theologian who would deny the advances of science. Far from being independent or opposing forces, science and religion are sisters. Both seek a better world. While science seeks control over the forces of nature around us, religion controls the forces of nature within us.

As we learn more and more about nature, we become more deeply impressed and humbled by its orderliness and unerring perfection. Our expanding knowledge of the laws of the universe has enabled us to send men out of their natural environment into the strange new environment of space and return them safely to earth.

Manned space flight is an amazing achievement. But it has opened for us thus far only a tiny door for viewing the awesome reaches of space. Our outlook through this peephole at the vast mysteries of the universe only confirms our belief in the certainty of its Creator. Finite man cannot comprehend an omnipresent, omniscient, omnipotent and infinite God. Any effort to visualize God, to reduce Him to our comprehension, to describe Him in our language, beggars His greatness.

I find it best through faith to accept God as an intelligent will, perfect in goodness, revealing Himself in the world of experience more fully down through the ages, as man's capacity for understanding grows. For spiritual comfort I find assurance in the concept of the fatherhood of God. For ethical guidance I rely on the corollary concept of the brotherhood of man.

Scientists now believe that in nature, matter cannot be destroyed without being converted into energy. Not even the tiniest particle can disappear without a trace. Nature does not know extinction—only transformation. Would God have less regard for His master-piece of creation, the human soul?

Immortality, to me, is the continuity of our spiritual existence after death. Since the dawn of history man has believed in im-mortality. This credo has been an essential element of many primitive cultures and it has been retained in the religions and philosophies of more enlightened ones.

Its meaning far transcends dialectic pronouncements by philoso-phers and theologians about what we can expect after our departure from this world. Since time immemorial the concept of immortality has exerted a profound influence on the lives of uncounted millions.

His soul is what distinguishes man from beast. An animal's actions are solely controlled by its basic urges such as hunger, fear, love, and need for shelter. These urges set upon the animal's glands and his response to the glandular impulses is entirely automatic. In an animal's make-up there is no room for freedom of the will, for searching curiosity, for freedom of doubt and conflict between urges and ethical standards. An animal does not know that mysterious little needle, called conscience, that tells us what is right and what is wrong. Only man has been burdened with the conflicts arising out of being an image of God cast into the form of an animal. And only man has been bestowed with a soul which enables him to cope with the eternal problems arising out of this conflict.

Today thousands of scientists all over the world are engaged in the greatest intellectual adventure ever undertaken by man: attempt-ing to understand the origin and functioning of a physical universe that is vast in space and time, complicated in detail, and awesome in its orderliness. Thus, to say that science's only purpose is trying to discover physical laws to increase man's control over the forces of nature is no longer an adequate explanation of science's goal; for, the concept of science itself has grown. The raw material of science is a set of experiences, observations, and measurements with which the scientist attempts to build a model of time, space, and matter. When new knowledge is discovered, the old model is not discarded;

it is simply changed according to the pattern of relationships which the scientist finds in this set of experiences.

By his willingness to change his model, or his concepts, the scientist is simply admitting that he makes no claim to possessing ultimate truth. His scientific laws are essentially descriptions of his observations. Scientific laws do not control reality, but merely try to explain it; therefore, the laws may be changed when new knowledge is revealed.

Scientific discoveries have come at an ever-increasing pace, for the truth is not static. For every new answer, a dozen new questions spring up. Science is facing wide-open frontiers in many fields; the atomic nucleus is becoming more and more enigmatic; the origin and structure of the universe are still shrouded in mystery; and the exact bodily functions of living organisms still evade complete understanding. The golden age of science is still ahead of us.

The scientist works in an atmosphere where doubt is an accepted way of life, and unnecessary authority rejected. Thomas Huxley has said of the scientist: "For him scepticism is the highest of duties; blind faith the unpardonable sin." The rise of science has been accompanied by a loss of tradition, which has been the mainstay of faith. Clashes between science and religion have therefore been frequent. And yet, it is one of the greatest tragedies of our times that science and religion have been cast as antagonists. To resolve the conflict, it has been tempting to adopt a policy of peaceful coexistence, and divide our experience into two parts, granting science control over one part, and permitting religion its authority in the other.

Let science investigate the physical world, while religion explains spiritual matters, this argument goes. When science gets to the end of its rope, let faith take over to account for the unexplainable. This is a fatal step. Two separate worlds for science and religion might work if no scientist were ever a Christian, and no Christian were ever a scientist. But science and religion do not operate in separate realms.

You cannot build a wall between science and religion. As science explains more of the intriguing mysteries of life and the universe, its realms expand into those areas which previously were either unknown or accepted solely by faith. Every experience we have—physical or spiritual—must fit together into a pattern that is credible and meaningful. Man is the observer of the universe, the experimenter, the searcher for truth, but he is not spectator alone. He is a participant in the continuing process of creation. He is the highest product of that creation. And he is directly affected as more and more of the wonders of that creation are unveiled.

Science and religion may be compared to two windows in a house, through which we may observe the world about us—or our neighbors. (And there are other windows, such as art, literature and history.) Whatever we observe through any of the windows in this allegorical house must fit into our model of the universe and our place in it. If it does not fit, we must revise our model, change our thinking, broaden our understanding of creation.

In our modern world many people seem to feel that our rapid advances in the field of science render such things as religious beliefs untimely or old-fashioned. They wonder why we should be satisfied in "believing" something, when science tells us that we "know" so many things. The simple answer to this contention is that we know many more mysteries of nature today than when the age of scientific enlightenment began. There is certainly no scientific reason why God cannot retain the same position in our modern world that He held before we began probing His creation with telescope and cyclotron.

While science is not a religion, it is a religious activity by its presuppositions, its method of working, and its search for truth. The Creator is revealed through His creation. As Charles A. Coulson says, "Science is helping to put a face on God." We should remember that science exists only because there are people, and its concepts exist only in the minds of men. Behind these concepts lies Reality —revealed to us only by the grace of God.

Each person receives a gift of life on this earth. A belief in the continuity of spiritual existence, after the comparative mere flick of three score and ten years of physical life here in the endless cycle of eternity, makes the action of each moment like an investment with far-reaching dividends. The knowledge that man can choose between good and evil should draw him closer to his Creator. Next, the realization should dawn that his survival here and hereafter depends on his adherence to the spiritual rather than the scientific.

Our decisions undeniably influence the course of future events.

Nature around us still harbors more unsolved than solved mysteries. But science has mastered enough of these forces to usher in a golden age for all mankind if this power is used for good—or to destroy us if evil triumphs. The ethical guidelines of religion are the bonds that can hold our civilization together. Without them man can never attain that cherished goal of lasting peace with himself, his God, and his fellow man.

Henry J. Kaiser

*The faiths that men and nations live by are at stake—
faith in God and worship, faith in achieving lasting peace,
faith in freedom and the sanctity of the individual. These
are the priceless values of the human spirit that we struggle
to keep alive today.*

Henry J. Kaiser, when he died in 1967, was the dean of America's
industrial statesmen and loomed larger than life as the greatest builder
in world history. More bridges, dams, highways, air stations, ships, steel,
aluminum, cement and even whole cities have been produced by his
proliferating industrial empire than were built by any other construction
genius who ever lived. And the end is not yet; upon the completion of
the Hawaiian Village Resort Center in Honolulu, Mr. Kaiser began the
development of an entirely new vacation city, Hawaii-Kai, which covers
six thousand acres on scenic Koko Head and which, when completed at a cost of $350,000,000 in 1970, will house sixty thousand
people.

Born the son of German immigrants in Sprout Brook, New York, on
May 9, 1882, young Kaiser started his business career at age thirteen
when he became a clerk and cash boy for a Utica dry goods store. In
1906 he and his bride moved to Spokane, Washington, where he worked
for a succession of hardware and construction firms before establishing
the Henry J. Kaiser Company, Ltd., in Vancouver, British Columbia,
in 1914. Fifteen years of highway, bridge and dam construction from
California to Cuba led to the shifting of Kaiser headquarters to Oakland,
California, and to such spectacular building assignments as the piers of
the San Francisco Bay Bridge, levees on the Mississippi River, and the
world's biggest dams—Hoover, Bonneville, Shasta, and Grand Coulee.

During World War II, Mr. Kaiser probably contributed more to our
massive industrial production than any other individual. He built the
Pacific Coast's first integrated iron and steel plant at Fontana and
erected the world's second largest cement factory at Permanente, California; his multiplying companies disgorged a steely avalanche of magne-
sium, aluminum, gypsum, aircraft parts and artillery shells to the war
fronts; seven Kaiser-built shipyards, averaging a ship a day, produced
1490 vessels including fifty aircraft carriers and one-third of all U.S.

merchant ships. For this stupendous achievement, Representative Wright Patman called him "the Magnificent American who is a model of inventiveness, ingenuity, integrity and drive . . . and who among America's great industrialists stands out as the ablest and noblest of them all."

As chairman of the board, Mr. Kaiser directed Kaiser Industries Corporation, the parent company, and sixty other Kaiser-managed companies turning out some three hundred different products in 173 plants and employing nearly eighty-seven thousand persons in thirty-one states and thirty foreign countries. From Jeeps to space missiles to one-fourth of the U.S. aluminum output, Kaiser companies rank among the production giants in such diversified fields as chemicals, coal, steel, cement, electronics, building materials, household products and community planning. All in all, the Kaiser industrial family has total assets of $2.5 billion with annual sales topping the $2 billion mark. With the passing of his father, Edgar Kaiser has now become executive director of one of the world's largest business empires.

The Happy Life

The great truths by which to live are simple. The Sermon on the Mount, the golden rule, the Ten Commandments are simple. A child can understand the plain words. But, for two thousand years of man's history, there has been nothing that so moved the hearts of men—nothing more right and true as a guide to human relations and a key to happy living—than these great truths. But to apply these sound principles in daily life—principles so simple and basic as to seem trite and, since seeming trite, to be neglected—can only work if we have the faith and courage to stick to them through thick and thin. Herein lies my philosophy of a happy and successful life. In a church in Rochester, New York, when I was sixteen years old, I was deeply impressed by a sermon entitled "The Beauty of Old Age." The lesson of that sermon was that when you come to the twilight of life, you can add up all the smiles and beautiful things of your whole lifetime and cherish the rich, satisfying memory of the smiles and sunshine you have given others, and the friendly smiles and sunshine that others have given you.

So, it seemed to me vital to start early in life accumulating smiles and meeting the world with a smile. Consequently, at the age of nineteen when I became an independent businessman in Lake Placid, New York, I placed over my store a sign the size of a billboard carrying just these words, "Meet the Man with a Smile." When there is a smile on your face and real happiness deep within yourself, the likelihood is that you have built your life upon a sound religious philosophy and the truest of human values. Now, sixty-five years later with my Hawaii development projects keeping me busier than ever on the other side of the world, I know that it is never too late in life to take a real account of yourself and to start accumulating smiles of happiness down through your future days and years.

There are those who never grow old in mind and spirit and interests. There are more and more persons finding that life can begin at forty, or at fifty, sixty, seventy—in fact that every day can bring a fresh beginning as long as they keep the zest for new discoveries, new ideas, new work, and renewed quests for achievement and happiness. How can each of us attain youthfulness in our latter years? By keeping young in our thinking, young in imagination, fresh in spirit, heart and soul. It can be accomplished.

It was my mother, Mary, a practical nurse, who first taught me some of the greatest values in life. The finest things she tried to impart during my school days in Utica, New York, were these: love of people . . . the importance of serving others . . . the joy of work . . . an intense devotion to this country (for she always was giving thanks to this Land of the Free for giving us such tremendous opportunities for the pursuit of human happiness) . . . and the truths of Christ's teachings, which can be of infinite value in shaping our daily lives.

Now, after reflection, it seems to me there are some simple, down-to-earth, provable and practical secrets of capturing the greatest values out of life—ways of making a greater success in your career and, at the same time, of achieving real happiness. The simple word "faith" sums up what I am convinced makes the difference between attaining or not attaining the greatest values in life. The fully-rounded faith has three interwoven parts:

1. Faith in yourself and your highest aspirations, which releases your creative inner powers and gives your daily life direction, adventure and meaning.

2. Faith in your fellow men, whom you love and serve.

3. Faith in God that answers the questions and longings of your soul—gives you help from the Highest Source—and sees the workings of the Creator in everything.

First, let's consider how faith can be a tremendous driving power throughout your practical daily living. *Faith gives you the courage to follow your dreams.* When you believe deeply that there is something worth while to do, you gain the spirit and energy to go out boldly in pursuit of new and greater goals.

I have experienced the proof of this, times beyond number. Like many another person, I had a dream of youth—to establish my own business, and I did in Lake Placid, New York, and in Florida. Yet I had faith that I could build a greater future if I were willing to pioneer in the adventure of crossing the continent and getting started in the West. There I picked out a merchant for whom I felt sure I could be of service, and, although he kept turning me down for a job, I went back thirteen times. Thirteen wasn't unlucky because on the thirteenth call, he hired me—as a laborer. It wasn't drudgery or defeat to start all over again at the bottom because faith in opportunities ahead made exciting fun out of each new task. And the dream came true that the Spokane job opened the way into what I wanted to do—become a builder.

I learned—and have kept on discovering since—that faith opens your eyes to new horizons of opportunity and generates the will to work and to keep yourself growing. It begins by trusting your hope and vision, for as Santayana wrote:

> Columbus found a world, and had no chart,
> Save one that faith deciphered in the skies:
> To trust the soul's invincible surmise
> Was all his science and his only art.

A builder—like a farmer or an enterpriser who takes risks with the pioneering kind of spirit that built America—certainly must practice faith and also patience. During World War I, we were faced with inflation. Each year for five years, although I raised my bids trying to anticipate the constantly increasing wages and prices of materials, I never quite caught up with the soaring costs. The result was that for five years I made no money; in fact, was broke. In making the comeback, I learned that it takes patience to maintain faith. There is no precise timetable for reaching faraway goals at the immediate moment you may want to, but patient believing will carry you past detours and delays, giving faith the time to work its miracles.

Once a Mississippi River flood swept away, overnight, a levee we had been building. I waded out afterward knee-deep into a sea of mud to find all our earth-moving equipment almost buried and our men looking as down-at-the-mouth as if the bottom of the world had fallen out. When they saw I wasn't disheartened, they asked what I could find cheerful about the disaster. I said, "I don't see any mud." They answered, "Just look—mud everywhere: we're buried in it!" I said, "The difference is this: you're looking down and can't see anything but mud. But I'm looking up, where I see nothing but sunshine and the clear blue sky." So, with the aid of the sun in drying out the mud and with courageous planning, faith restored, and the will to work—we dug ourselves out, and our problems were licked.

Later, when our young men built the great Bonneville Dam in the West, which had been declared "impossible," an official said, "The kids succeeded because they never had been licked." They had no fear of failure, which prevents accomplishment. Faith overcomes baseless fear and says you *can* do it. As the Apostle Paul wrote in his Epistle to the Romans (8:31): "If God be for us, who can be against us?"

Faith generates a wider and wider circle of faith. I remember in 1940 when Britain was pleading desperately for the building of ships for the war. The visiting English purchasing commissioners, who were negotiating with us to build thirty ships, asked me to show them our shipyards. I took them to a vast mud flat across the bay from San Francisco, and said, "There are our shipyards! It's true you see nothing but mud here. But it's space—space for thousands of workers to come together, build homes, park their cars and mass materials. Just envisage the shipyard that can be built in a matter of

months to pour out ships." The British accepted our faith; they
decided that what we promised, our boys *could* do and *would* do.
When faith and work demonstrated what could be done, the United
States gave us the opportunity to build not one, but seven shipyards; not just thirty ships but nearly fifteen hundred. The employment of 180,000 people in the shipyards developed a good understanding of the human needs waiting to be filled and the reason for
always having faith in the future.

In commerce and industry there are limitless possibilities of raising the standard of living constantly. Seeing the opportunities on
every hand to fill human needs give you a faith in the future and
also the will to work, for "faith without work is dead." Skeptics
said that a new cement plant could not be built and operated successfully in a certain area of California. Hardheaded men said the
Pacific Coast could not supply the raw materials and markets to
justify an integrated iron and steel industry. Disbelievers said aluminum would be running out of our ears after the last war and that a
new producer would be doomed to failure. All three of these industries became realities, and today are helping fill great needs. Yet,
the power of faith in our workaday lives goes much deeper than
merely being a way to accomplish our personal ends and ambitions.
For, as Matthew wrote: "What is a man profited, if he shall gain the
whole world, and lose his own soul?"

Each human being needs to give a chance not only to the divine
spark of spirit within himself, but to see it in others, for as John
Masefield penned:

> God dropped a spark down into everyone,
>   And if we find and fan it to a blaze
> It'll spring up and glow, like—like the sun,
>   And light the wandering out of stony ways.

The spark that God has dropped into everyone can light our way
to the fully satisfying life—the life of love, courage, confidence and
creative, adventurous spirit—the life of inner peace with God and
our fellow men.

Faith in God leads to the fullest life. We can find God wherever
we turn our sight and our insight. God speaks through "the flower
in the crannied wall"—through the beauty of a garden or a flaming

sunset—through every mystery of life—through the wonder of a child—through the spirits of fellow men created in His image. It takes strength of character to practice religion. Yet the more it is used, the more it keeps forever building greater strength of character. It gives beliefs you can hold fast to when everything else may be crumbling.

Tremendous faith is needed in the kind of world in which we are living, where civilization has invented the means of its own utter destruction. Totalitarian systems are trying to crush out belief in God and substitute the state and a dictator as master over all the thoughts, aspirations and lives of the people. The faiths that men and nations live by are at stake—faith in God and worship, faith in achieving lasting peace, faith in freedom and the sanctity of the individual. These are the priceless values of the human spirit that we struggle to keep alive today.

Can the faith of free peoples, the world around, grow strong enough to restore the hearts of millions of bewildered, despairing people who already have surrendered or are threatened with doom? It is my conviction that faith is stronger than disbelief, that faith can overcome fear and hopelessness, just as the history of mankind has been lighted up by the faiths that always have triumphed over the forces of darkness. George Washington prayed to God during bitter winters from 1775 to 1780 when his soldiers were cold, hungry, tattered and barefoot—their marches through the snow traced by blood from their bleeding feet. Yet faith carried Washington's ragged band of patriots to victory for American independence and those values of the spirit that enter into the pursuit of genuine happiness.

Again, today, young men and their loved ones are making sacrifices for their faith in freedom and for a world in which justice and peace shall prevail. Surely mankind needs a rebirth of faith during the present war for men's minds. As a people, we need a reawakening of faith; we look for leaders who inspire faith. Yet, for each individual, the paramount need is to develop within himself the rounded faith without which nothing *really* worthwhile is accomplished.

Your plan for work and happiness should be big, imaginative, and daring. Strike out boldly for the things you honestly want more than anything else in the world. Certainly your objective and well-thought-out plans will seem beyond your reach. But, as Robert Browning declared:

> Ah, but a man's reach should exceed his grasp,
> Or what's a heaven for?

The mistake is to put your sights too low, not to raise them too high. The definite, faraway goal will supercharge your whole body and spirit; it will awaken your mind and creative imagination, and put meaning into otherwise lowly, step-by-step tasks you must go through in order to attain the final success.

In the grand adventure of self-discovery and of formulating a plan for your future, count upon harnessing certain amazing spiritual powers that are yours for the using. Think of it—a power greater than any power on earth! As the psychologist William James said, "Men habitually use only a small part of the powers which they possess and which they might use under appropriate circumstances."

Only you can work out a code to live by and a faith that means you need never be defeated. See if you cannot find for yourself the faith that says, as does Philippians 4:13: "I can do all things through Christ which strengtheneth me." I have seen demonstrated, beyond possibility of doubt, the words of Jesus written in Mark 9:23: "If you canst believe, all things are possible to him that believeth." What a man can imagine or conceive in his mind, he can accomplish. Impossibles are only impossibles as thinking makes them so. Faith can unleash the power that enables you to accomplish whatever you really set out to do.

Faith, it is my conviction, is the key to unlocking limitless powers of the mind, the heart, the soul: faith in God, faith and belief that right triumphs over wrong, faith and belief that you can win out over disasters and setbacks, faith and belief that smash fear, faith and belief in the ultimate realization of your hopes that are right.

Faith tells us that America's greatest days lie ahead, and they do lie ahead. What faith can mean to your own future is summed up in a brief quotation from an author whose name I regret I do not know. He declared:

All things are possible to him who has faith.
Because faith sees and recognizes the power
That means accomplishment. Faith looks beyond
All boundaries. It transcends all limitations.
It penetrates all obstacles. And it sees the goal.
Faith never fails. It is a miracle worker.

I believe that with all my heart.

Brother Mandus

It begins to look like practical common sense that we identify ourselves and our personal and world creativeness with the Mind, Spirit, Christ, God through whose Being we all exist and through whom we have any capacity to think at all.

More than twenty years ago a young British businessman experienced a spiritual illumination which transformed his life and guided him to become an adventurer in faith. Now sixty years old and known throughout the world as Brother Mandus, he is one of England's most remarkable religious and ecumenical leaders. Prolific author and indefatigable lecturer, Brother Mandus inspires millions around the globe as a crusader for Christ and speaks as both workman and witness to the divine awakening which today stirs all humanity.

Brother Mandus, who now makes his headquarters in Blackpool, England, is founder and leader of the World Healing Crusade. He left school at age fourteen, worked as a clerk and became a chartered ship broker, and then served for five years with Grace Line and Pan American Grace Airways in South America. During World War II he served in the British Ministry of War Transport. With the war over and his own business under way, he experienced "a spiritual illumination which decreed following a way the Lord opened and a work essentially devoted to the Christ way of love, faith and prayer."

Brother Mandus believes with Dr. William Fletcher, former Archbishop of Canterbury, that "throughout the world and especially through the churches there are breaking forth new streams of living water and new outgrowings of Christ's risen life." This dedicated Christ servant not only strengthens that new life through his inspirational talks and travels but also publishes the magazines *Power Lines* and *The Crusader*, which go to his world-wide following. His ministry of prayer also is carried on tapes and records to individuals and groups in Africa, Asia, Australia, New Zealand, South America, Canada and the United States.

The Divine Awakening

The beautiful islands of Britain, spilling over with a population of over fifty-two million people, still stand as a citadel of freedom for the world. Every culture or civilization rises through the mistakes, successes and experiences of its people over long periods of time. And, whatever else, these island tribes have a history unique in world-wide adventures and organization on the one hand, and on the other of creative ingenuity in their hitherto seabound isolation.

Like individuals, nations too have their special personalities and gifts of creativeness. Even as men and women in a community share and express the national life, so does each country or continent form part of a perfect pattern ultimately to be woven into the fabric of the whole. Therefore, the wise man of this generation will always work to that end, eager to recognize the virtues and values inherent in the peoples of every land, equally ready to be compassionate, understanding and tolerant with their traditions, mistakes or weaknesses which do not square with his own outlook and experience.

The world traveler increasingly begins to comprehend the national characteristics and aspirations of both the advanced nations abroad, and those as yet backward in their evolution. There is an urgent yearning everywhere to find enduring solutions to intolerable world problems, as more and more nations struggle for freedom or prosperity, and often for domination over others.

In these battered islands of Britain during the last war, conservative Englishmen demonstrated, perhaps as never before in world history, how strong is the human spirit in determination and endurance when it believes in some great ideal. And, while everyone, everywhere, hates warfare and all that it means, countless men and women of ordinary family homes gave their all, including life, rather than submit to tyranny. The evolutionary awakening still moves inevitably toward predestined fulfillment. In spite of the gravity of world conflicts, crystallized clearly to our general view in the East-West Communism versus the rest, and the bloodletting wound in the side of all nations through massive armaments, thinkers everywhere are for the first time seriously awakening to the need for absolute peace based on equality, justice and mutual help.

How small, then, our world has become to the modern traveler. By jet plane, London to New York—six hours. New York to San Francisco—five hours. To the other side of the world, east or west, in another handful of hours. And soon, no doubt, we shall have rocket planes and spaceships. All this, and a million things more, constantly magnify our experience through the invisible power of human minds, intent on creating greater and ever-greater expression of man's infinite and invincible nature.

An important lesson can always be learned by anyone, no matter how evolved or humble the intellect, who cares (or dares) to pause long enough to consider the miracle of mind, its central significance in human achievement, and its inevitable relationship with the infinite Mind of God which makes every aspect of creation and the experience of man possible at all. The most urgent need of all people today is to turn their attention inward to seek a deeper understanding of this mental mystery, and its tremendous powers in the creativeness that is certainly man's heritage.

Hypnotized, as we are, by the outward flow of events and things we create, we tend to forget the mighty powers of love, imagination, will and intellect which are the motivating causes of every effect we have ever seen or experienced. Behind the Taj Mahal, the citadels of New York, St. Paul's Cathedral in London, the ships and planes, machines and every building, are the invisible minds which patterned them long before they could be expressed in material form.

The very chair upon which we sit, or the artist's picture we behold, could never exist apart from the thinker who first found the pattern in his mind. The thought, therefore, was the vital factor, and, inevitably, the product of chair or picture will always conform to and express the invisible motivating love, imagination and thought. It becomes increasingly clear that the supreme objective of man must be toward the highest development of his inward faculties, because his life achievements will be governed strictly by the potency

of his mind and the degree of his ability to react powerfully to the
environment and people through which his potential must unfold.

Man, the thinker, is awakening en masse now with a speed that
staggers the imagination, and often affrights us all. In the last hundred years he has advanced his intellectual capacities and correspond-
ing knowledge more than in all the preceding thousands of years
of his long climb from the cave to the modern city. Unfortunately,
so much of his mental development has been achieved without
regard to the basic spiritual principles and laws which inevitably
govern his entire existence. Just as the jet plane in the skies represents the jet-plane thinker, so is the thinker himself the outward
form of the Invisible Thinker of the entire universe. It begins to
look like practical common sense that we must identify ourselves,
and our personal and world creativeness, with the Mind, Spirit,
Christ, God, through whose Being we all exist and through whom
we have any capacity to think at all.

We live, however, in a very exciting and adventurous age. We
are actually beginning now the next phase of development. In the
very early periods of awakening our long-past forebears concentrated
mainly on survival. Slowly they evolved better ways of obtaining
food and shelter, and art began to appear. Isolated tribes found
greater power and protection by merging and communities began to
grow. The story of the birth of nations is an age-long history of
awakening man but, even today, we have not outgrown our animal
natures, still so dangerously reflected through our wars, armaments
and economic strife.

Always, in the midst of an ever-increasing sense of power and
material objectives, inspired leaders have provided their people with
the vision of spiritual truth and principle. All the great religions on
earth have stressed these basic factors in human nature. Then came
Jesus Christ with the highest, most profound and yet the simplest
spiritual revelation the world has ever known. Here, indeed, was the
revelation of love, faith, atonement, redemption and eternal life in
which is the salvation of man, and it reaches its highest expression
in the Cross of Christ as the way of life divinely ordained for man.

Today a new light is appearing on the horizon. All over the world
a spiritual awakening is taking place. A new army of disciples has
arisen, both within and outside the Christian church. They come

with new vision and report "signs and wonders" very similar to the
works of Christ and the early Church.

In this age of intellectual enlightenment, the approach of these
new disciples to the exploration of spiritual principles and prayer
has been highly scientific. They sought their knowledge in human
lives and observed the causes of so much tribulation, disaster and
disease. Beginning from the concept of communion with God, they
have analyzed and traced through countless experiments the fact
that an astonishing percentage of physical disease was caused by lack
of love, frustration, fear, worry, resentment, sin, and any kind of
negative attitude to people, environment or events; and that an
equally astonishing degree of healing took place when people were
helped to practice the presence of God in love, faith and prayer.

A library of books has been written proclaiming their findings in
this supremely important field of research. Thousands of case his-
tories witness to the truth of divine healing, and to the simple fact
that man cannot live satisfactorily by bread alone. He is a spiritual
being, living in a spiritual universe, dependent FIRST upon God for
everything. Our common discovery has been that love, in all its mani-
fold forms of expression, and a childlike faith in God, are the
absolute essentials of life itself.

With the advent of nuclear physics, the old belief in a materialistic
universe has been exploded forever. As the scientist, in every branch
of research, probes deeper into matter, he meets the invisible but
all-powerful laws which govern its appearance. He is committed,
however reluctantly, to an exploration in the realm of invisible
CAUSE, into the very Mind of God. And this, without question,
someday will lead him to conceive and believe that LOVE is the
central motivating power in all creation, and that communion with
Infinite Intelligence can only become known through the ever-
widening reach of personal love, faith and prayer. As Sir James
Jeans says: "The universe begins to look more like a great thought
than a great machine."

The economic system of our modern society will also come into
a new era of expansion and creativeness when divine laws are fully
understood. It has long been a fallacy that "big business" and
spiritual principles are in opposing camps. In our new understanding,
it becomes clear that any business can only be infinitely more
successful for everyone concerned when it is directed and expressed

through love, faith and prayer which release infinite GOOD into everything without exception.

We move into a new age of such heights of potential and understanding that the next great concentration of personal, national and international aspiration will be to develop as quickly as possible the scientific use of a spiritual principle in every aspect of education. We know already that the Christ-filled mind is infinitely more potent in its creative power than a mind, however highly developed intellectually, that is divorced from an awareness and expression of spiritual principles.

The essence of our modern discoveries is the intensely practical nature of all that Jesus Christ revealed. Here is the complete answer to poverty and disease, when we learn fully how to conform to the laws which govern a divine response to our needs. Here is the secret of inspiration, guidance and higher creativeness on every level. Here we have the true way to peace on earth, the feeding of the starving millions, the health and well-being of every soul on earth. As a demonstrated reality, as a potential awaiting our exploration and acceptance, is the abundant life which, after all, is what everyone is so feverishly seeking.

If communion with God is possible—and we categorically state that modern research in prayer has proved it to be so—then we must logically begin to consider what is the true pattern and high objective in our personal life, when thus open to all the love and infinite resources of God. If we follow the teaching of Jesus Christ, we are told that "all things are possible." From beginning to end of His Word we are taught that according to our faith and love the Father will bring infinite and perfect everything into our experience. We do not need to depart from one word of His life and Gospel to enter into the dynamic experience of God's power flooding our lives with good.

It would seem that our real need is to believe completely in what is taught, and to lift the vision of our faith to accept and expect "mighty works." As long as we continue to limit ourselves by the range of our personal power and vision, we can *only* experience life on that level. Jesus tells us that the Power great enough to mold universes and all life, is not only able, but willing, to come into the little human life and transform it through His strength. Indeed, expect a miracle!

When we seriously begin to "dream our dreams" with God, and link our imagination with His Almighty thinking, then we shall see the outward signs of His power working through us, just as presently we see the outward results of our own thinking. In the Father lies all the knowledge of all the laws of creation. There is only one Power, and His Spirit fills everything that ever was or will be, including you and me. With Jesus, we can truly believe "the kingdom of Heaven is within you" and "all that I have is thine."

"In Him we live, and move, and have our being." "Behold, I make all things new." "It is the Father who doeth the works."

Mohammed Reza Pahlevi

Besides saying my Moslem prayers five times daily, I sometimes call on God to help me. Without claiming any sort of telepathic communication with the Divine, I can simply say that these calls do not go unheeded.

His Imperial Majesty Mohammed Reza Pahlevi, for the past twenty-six years *Shahanshah* or king of kings to the Iranian people, rules as the undisputed leader of his ancient nation. Trim, tough and a graceful soldier-athlete at forty-eight, the Shah is respected as one of the most progressive rulers in the Middle East. Today his strong-willed "revolution from the top" surely, if painfully and slowly, transforms his sprawling, semiarid land into a modern state.

World War II was raging and his country occupied by Great Britain and Russia when young Mohammed Reza ascended Persia's Peacock Throne in 1941. Boldly assuming full direction of his country and twenty-three million subjects at war's end, the Swiss-educated, military-minded Shah set about freeing the people from three thousand years of fusty feudalism and putting their backward society on the high road into the twentieth century. He threw a Soviet puppet regime out of northern Iran, three times escaped assassination attempts by left-wing fanatics, soberly began to plan the successive crash programs which are modernizing a primitive economy.

By 1962 the "elected" as well as the hereditary monarch of Iran after the overthrow of Socialist Premier Mossadegh, the *Shahanshah* launched a revolutionary social program to promote the welfare of the people, including farmer-peasants, industrial workers, and the women of the country. The major points, adopted in a nationwide referendum on January 26, 1963, are: abolition of the feudal landlord-peasant system; ratification of the law nationalizing forests, thereby providing a valuable new source of national wealth; ratification of the law for the sale of government-owned factories to former landlords to underwrite the land reform program; ratification of the profit-sharing law, whereby workers will share in the profits of industrial and productive enterprises; amendment of the electoral law to eliminate deficiencies which in the past led to election malpractices; creation of a Literacy Corps to facilatate compulsory national education in a nationwide campaign against il-literacy. "The most important thing," the Shah says, "is that today in

Iran there is a new spirit of enthusiasm for improvement and for a better life."

In the summer of 1966, the Shah kindled world-wide admiration when he contributed his country's equivalent of one day's military budget, or $700,000, to the UNESCO campaign against illiteracy. The most far-traveled ruler in the history of a fabled land that gave the world Zoroaster, Cyrus the Great and Omar Khayyam, the Shah has visited Pakistan, India, Japan, the U.S. and all of the Middle East and western Europe to strengthen Iran's international position. In 1959, after two divorces, he married the daughter of an Iranian army officer who as Empress Farah Pahlavi now devotes herself to many of the country's new social reform activities. Devout Moslems who have made the hadj or pilgrimage to Mecca, their Imperial Majesties have three children—Crown Prince Reza, six, Princess Farahnaz, three, and an infant son, Prince Ali Riza—and they live in the Marble Palace in Teheran where the Shah recently crowned himself and his beauteous Empress.

The White Revolution

Since my early childhood in Teheran I have known that it was my destiny to become a king, and to preside over a land whose ancient and magnificent culture I venerate. From my first youthful days as crown prince in the late 1920s, I wanted to improve the lot of my people, especially the common folks, and today I feel that my Moslem faith supports me in this difficult task. Indeed, I should consider it self-centered and arrogant to believe that I could accomplish my lifework—my twenty-five-year-old white revolution to modernize a five-thousand-year-old country—without God's help and without daily reliance on the wisdom of our holy book, the Koran.

In September, 1931, as a boy of twelve, I was enrolled in the Le Rosay School in Roll, Switzerland, in line with my father Reza Shah's determination that I should have a western European education and thus be prepared to direct the upbuilding of Iran. During my first two years abroad, with so much to digest in my new environment, I did not think much about religion. But then, with more interest than ever, I returned to it. I started to recite the Moslem daily prayers, and during my last three years I said them with real fervor and conviction. I was determined that when later I came to the Persian Peacock Throne, my conduct would always be guided by a true religious sense.

Like devout Moslems from Spain to the Philippines, I believe in the creed of Islam: "There is no God but Allah and Mohammed is his messenger." I believe—and try earnestly to live by—the Five Pillars of Islam: belief in one God, prayer five times daily, regular almsgiving, frequent fasting including our great religious month of Ramadan, and the hadj or pilgrimage to Mecca. Indeed, much of the vision, fervor and perseverance of my "revolution from the top," with its abolition of the feudal landlord-peasant system, nationalization of the forests, reform of the electoral law to grant voting rights to women, ratification of profit-sharing laws whereby workers may share in the profits of industry, and distribution of thousands of acres of government lands to the poorest farmers, can be said to derive directly from my Moslem faith.

Thus, it is my religiously inspired plan to produce a new society. It is a program that will liberate the people from the chains of exploitation through land reform and mass education. We must accomplish many centuries of advance in twenty years at the most, in ten years if possible. Our aim is nothing less than a modern state with a standard of living comparable to Europe's and I have no doubt that with work and self-sacrifice we can achieve it.

I am convinced that I have been able to accomplish things which, unaided by some unseen Hand, I could never have done. I make no apologies for my religious faith. But that does not mean that I consider myself as an indispensable instrument of God or anything of that sort. I want to make it perfectly clear that I do not.

Until now I have never publicly revealed it, but it was during an acute childhood illness with typhoid fever that my religious life began. I then had a dream about Ali, who in our faith was the chief lieutenant of Mohammed (much as, according to Christian doctrine, St. Paul was a leading disciple of Jesus Christ). Ali was the husband of Mohammed's daughter and one of his bravest followers.

In my dream, Ali had with him his famous two-pronged sword, which is often seen in paintings of him. He was sitting on his heels on the floor, and in his hands he held a bowl containing a liquid. He told me to drink, which I did. The next day, the crisis of my fever was over, and I was on the road to rapid recovery. Although I was only seven at the time, in my childish way I recognized that the dream and my recovery were not necessarily connected. But this experience was within the same year followed by two other events which were also significantly to influence my life.

Almost every summer my family and I made an excursion to Emamzadeh-Dawood, a lovely spot in the mountains above Teheran. To reach it one had to follow a steep trail on foot or on horseback; and since I was so young, a relative who was an army officer placed me in front of him on the saddle of his horse. Some way up the trail, the horse slipped, and I was plunged head first on to a jagged rock. I fainted. When I regained consciousness, the members of the party were expressing astonishment that I had not even a scratch. I told them that as I fell, I had clearly seen one of our saints named Abbas, and that I had felt him holding me and preventing me from crashing my head against the rock.

My father was not present, but when he later heard the tale of this vision, he scoffed at my story. Knowing my father to be a very strong-willed man, I did not argue with him but I never doubted that I had seen St. Abbas.

The third event occurred while I was walking with my guardian near the royal palace in Shimran. Our path lay along a picturesque cobbled street. Suddenly I clearly saw before me a man with a halo around his head—much as in some of the great paintings of Jesus by Western masters. As we passed one another, I knew him at once. He was the Imam or descendant of Mohammed who, according to our faith, disappeared but is expected to come again to save the world.

I asked my guardian, "Did you see him?"

"But whom?" he inquired. "No one was here. How could I see someone who was not here?" I felt so certain of what I had seen that his reply did not bother me in the least. I was self-confident enough not to be bothered by what my guardian, older and wiser though he was, might think.

Long after I had emerged from childhood fantasies (if any among my readers feel more comfortable to call them that), there occurred four other incidents which may help explain why my childhood faith has continued strong within me. The first was in 1948 when

I went to visit a place called Kuhrang, near Isfahan, to inspect the site for an irrigation dam. When I was ready to return, I climbed into my plane at the small airstrip; with me was the general in command of the area. I was at the controls, for I am a licensed pilot and enjoy flying my own planes or indeed any plane. Because the airstrip was so small, we were using a light single-engined plane, and some ten minutes after we took off the engine went dead. We had to make a forced landing in a mountainous region in a ravine full of rocks and boulders.

As every pilot knows, a plane has a stalling speed below which it will go into a spin. With the engine gone I had no throttle, nor could I maneuver within the narrow confines of the ravine; the only thing was to maintain my speed by going down then and there. Just before we struck, I pulled on the stick to raise the plane's nose and avert a head-on collision with a barrier of rock lying directly in front of us. The plane had barely enough speed left to clear the barrier, and could not surmount a big stone lying just beyond. When we collided with it the undercarriage was completely torn off, but at least that helped to reduce our speed. The plane started to slide on its belly over the rock-strewn ground. A moment later the propeller hit a large boulder, and the plane turned a slow and deliberate somersault, coming to a halt with the fuselage upside down. There we were, hanging by our seat belts in the open cockpit. Neither of us had suffered so much as a scratch. I remember that the scene amused me so much that I burst out laughing, but my upside-down companion didn't think it was funny.

Was that narrow escape good luck, or was it good luck bolstered by something else . . . ?

The second incident was the wresting of our rich Azerbaijan Province from alien control. This is a wonderful story of Persian nationalism, reinforced, as I maintain, by divine guidance. In the final resolution of the problem, I ordered the Iranian Army into action, personally supervised the military operations and destroyed the Azerbaijan "Democratic" party which had been manipulated by the Communists.

The third incident was when, in February of 1949, I was attending the annual commemoration of the founding of the University of Teheran. In military uniform, I was just about to enter the Faculty of Law Building, where the ceremony was to be held, when suddenly shots rang out and bullets came in my direction. Fantastic though it may seem, three of them passed through my military cap without touching my head. But the gunman's fourth shot penetrated my right cheekbone and came out under my nose.

My would-be assasin, who had been posing as a photographer, was within six feet of me. He was now aiming his revolver at my heart. Both he and I were sufficiently apart from the crowd for me to know he had a good clear field of fire. At such point-blank range, how could he miss? I suddenly started shadow-dancing or feinting. He fired again, wounding me in the shoulder. His last shot stuck in the gun. I had the queer and not unpleasant sensation of knowing that I was still alive. . . . Perhaps I may be forgiven for thinking that this incident seemed to fit into the pattern, which had so early taken shape in my mind, of God's support. I know that many will deny that God supports anything or anybody. But now, as in my childhood days, my reliance on God affords me a firm foundation for thought and for action.

The fourth incident was the miracle, as today it still seems to me, of how we in Persia recovered from former Prime Minister Mossadegh. I defy anybody to prove that the overturn of Mossadegh was not basically the work of the common people of my country—people whose hearts held a spark of the divine.

When I travel abroad, people often ask me if a king's life is not a lonely life. I think not. My affection for my wife and children, for my people as a whole, and for nature helps prevent that. Furthermore, I really love my work, the challenge it offers, and the satisfactions it brings.

But there is still another reason why my role as king does not leave me lonely. I spoke earlier of my conviction that God is guiding me and that I can rely upon God's support. I think my assurance of His direction in no way makes me arrogant or fanatical; instead it gives me the quiet confidence of somehow being in tune with the universe. Besides saying my daily prayers, I sometimes call on God to help me. Without claiming any sort of telepathic communication with the divine, I can simply say that these calls do not go unheeded.

Pearl S. Buck

To know the Law and to use it for one's own fullest development—that is the wisdom which alone brings the contentment we call happiness.

Miss Pearl S. Buck, America's most renowned and prolific woman novelist, has won both the Nobel and Pulitzer Prizes for Literature. The Pulitzer Prize was given to her in 1932 for her famous novel *The Good Earth*, while the Nobel award was made in 1938 not for one book but for the body of her work. In citing Miss Buck as the first American woman to be so honored, the Nobel Committee praised her "rich and genuine epic portrayals of Chinese peasants' life and her masterpieces of biography."

The daughter of Presbyterian missionaries stationed in China, Pearl Buck was the only one of their seven children to be born in the old family mansion in Hillsboro, West Virginia. Her childhood was spent in the historic city of Chinkiang where she learned to speak Chinese before English. She attended boarding school in Shanghai, remembers vividly the Boxer Rebellion in 1901, and at age seventeen returned to America to attend Randolph-Macon College. In 1915 she rejoined her family, taught English literature in Chinese schools and began planning and writing the sixty-odd books that were to come from her pen.

East Wind, West Wind, her first novel, was published in 1930. Other best-selling Buck books on Chinese life include *The Good Earth, Dragon Seed, God's Men, Letter from Peking, The Promise, Sons, The Mother* and *Imperial Woman*. Her two biographies, *The Exile* and *Fighting Angel*, are the life stories of her own parents. *This Proud Heart*, published in 1937, was her first novel dealing wholly with American characters and the American scene. A series of short stories and novels about Americans followed, the most famous of which is *The Townsman*. In 1954 she published her internationally acclaimed autobiography, *My Several Worlds*.

Today, in addition to her writing, the activities of seventy-five-year-old Pearl Buck are youthfully varied. She is founder and chairman of the board of Welcome House, an adoption agency which finds homes and parents for children of mixed Asian-American blood. She is chairman of the board of the Pearl S. Buck Foundation which she founded in 1964 to succor homeless children born of Asian mothers and G.I. fathers. In collaboration with producer Ted Danielewski, she recently completed her second motion picture, *The Guide,* a drama of modern India for which she wrote the script. As Mrs. Richard Walsh in private life, white-haired, handsome Pearl Buck now lives in Dublin, Pennsylvania, with nine adopted children.

A Bridge for Passing

It was a visit I shall never forget, the inspiring hour in my life when I was about to meet the Dalai Lama, the young god-king of Tibet, in New Delhi, India. He was a Buddhist and I had followed his life story with intense interest ever since at age two he had been chosen as the reincarnation of Tibet's thirteenth Dalai Lama.

Whether or not I believed in the subtly-just doctrine of reincarnation, I had long kept in touch with the actions and omens of his ten-year reign as the combined head of a nation and a national religion; now that he and his people had been driven into cruel exile by the Communist Chinese, I wanted to hear directly the story of his perilous escape from Lhasa as well as his own interpretation of Buddha's message of peace and nonviolence.

So it was two years ago that I had come to the high mountain town of Darjeeling, not only to see the Dalai Lama's people there but also the mountains over which they had come into India. Therefore I got up early one morning in the darkness before dawn and went by Jeep to Tiger Hill. We took shelter in a small building and waited for the sunrise. When the sun came blazing out of the east, we gazed westward. Out of the darkness we saw the snowy Himalayas appear in the sky, rose-tinted in the sunlight. I count this among the rarest sights of my life. We were awed and silent before such beauty, such majesty, such terror.

It was across those vast ranges that the Tibetans came, most of them on foot, many of them carrying children and helping the old as they followed their young leader and god-king, the Dalai Lama. Standing there in the chill dawn, I marveled at their heroism and their endurance. How had it happened that they were driven out of their homes and out of their country? It is an old story begun long ago and not yet ended. The strife between Tibet and China is not a new one. Chinese and Tibetans are very different. Even their languages are different. Tibetans have an alphabet; they have never used the characters or ideograms of the Chinese. Their food, their clothing, their ways of living, their government all are different from those of the Chinese. Certainly the landscape of Tibet is different from that of China, bordered on the south as it is by the Himalayas.

I was remembering those mountains, soaring white against the sky, their snows eternal, when suddenly at the far end of the room where I sat, a dark-blue curtain was put aside, and I saw the Dalai Lama. He had the look of a king and something more. I have seen kings in my life, and while they each have majesty, this king had also a god-look about him. He was king and high priest.

I rose to my feet, seeing with my woman's eyes that he was young and tall and strong and very handsome, his skin a clear tan, his eyes black and sparkling, his cheeks red. Suddenly he smiled, and walked toward me so swiftly that his dark yellow robe rippled about him. I bowed; he put out his hand and took mine in both of his. It was an unusual gesture—Asians do not touch hands—but he was Western enough to use the gesture to which he thought me accustomed.

For the next several hours, we talked long and earnestly, I listening and learning, and all the while I knew I was in the presence of a superb human being. The twenty-six-year-old Dalai Lama has that indefinable quality which I can only call presence or star quality. It is born in a human being and cannot be acquired. The possessor is himself, seeming simple yet comprehending all, natural and yet dignified. We talked of his deeply grounded faith in God and a moral universe, and in his illuminated presence I felt my own spiritual sensibilities grow.

The day ended, as all days must, and I could not forbear a final question.

"Do you see the end of your exile?" I asked.

"Who can see the end?" he replied. "One thing I know. When we return to our country, we cannot separate ourselves again from the rest of the world. We must join the human family."

"Then you have faith that you will return?" I persisted.

He looked down from his height. "One thing I know," he told

me. "I know that evil will be vanquished and that good will prevail. Do not ask me when. So long as we believe, we can wait."

The world is an old, old place. Each generation is as young as springtime, and yet spring itself follows the laws of birth and growth and death. To know the Law and to use it for one's own fullest development—that is the wisdom which alone brings the contentment we call happiness.

When my first husband, John L. Buck, an agricultural teacher in China, died in 1929, a chapter in my life ended. Together we had lived in various parts of China for fifteen years. After that time, except for brief visits to the Orient, I was to make my home in America. At that time, my mind, unable as yet to face the profound change in my own life, explored the meaning of eternity, time without beginning and without end. Einstein had just proved to us that mass is interchangeable with energy. This sentence resulted in the awakening of my own mind to the new age. It was more than an awakening of the mind. It was the conversion of my soul, the clarification of my spirit, the unification of my whole being.

Gradually I had a new conception of death, a new approach to life. Like Saul of Tarsus, I was proceeding on my way when a light broke upon me, a burning illumination that changed my course. This equation, which Einstein crystallized into a few brief symbols, is the key to our universe and doubtless to many more beyond. What was once mass can become energy, is potential energy even while it is mass. Is this the scientific proof of what we call soul?

If I am right (and there is a hereafter), my first words to him as I step over will be spoken in love and triumph.

"Here I am. Now we know."

Until then I continue as we were before, he doubting, I believing. Yes, I think I still believe, although I have not yet discovered how to know. Faith, the saints have told us through the ages; possibility, the scientists are saying today, because so much we once thought impossible is now possible. Saints and scientists . . .

Someday we shall know. What day? That day, perhaps, when saints and scientists unite to make a total search for truth. It is the saints, the believers, who should have the courage to urge the scientists to help them discover whether the spirit continues its life of energy when the mass we call body ceases to be the container. Faith supplies the hypothesis, but only science can provide the computer for verification. The unbeliever will never pursue the search. He is already static, a pillar of salt, forever looking backward. ⌈There are no miracles, of that I am sure. If one walks on water and heals the sick and raises the dead to life again, it is not a matter of magic but a matter of knowing how to do it. There is no supernatural; there is only the supremely natural, the purely scientific. Science and religion, religion and science, put it as I may, they are two sides of the same glass, through which we see darkly until these two, focusing together, reveal the truth. ⌉

Martin Luther King, Jr.

❖

*Whatever the name, some extrahuman Force labors to
create a harmony out of the discords of the universe. There
is a creative power that works to pull down mountains
of evil and level hilltops of injustice. God still works
through history His wonders to perform.*

Dr. Martin Luther King, Jr., of Atlanta, Georgia, the Negro Baptist
minister and apostle of nonviolence who had something of the Old
Testament prophet in him, led the civil rights movement in America
until his tragic death by an assassin's bullet in Memphis, Tennessee,
in April, 1968. His ironically violent death not only set off recurring
demonstrations of burning, looting and civil disorders across the land,
but also removed from the national scene the one black American with
the character and charisma to mediate between Negroes and whites.
As a Gandhian evangel of love, hope and brotherhood, Dr. King
lived and died in the service of God and man and in the advancement
of mankind's immemorial vision, "Let freedom ring."

In 1964 this widely admired, wildly assailed Christian leader won
the Nobel Peace Prize. The Reverend Dr. King, at age thirty-five,
the third Negro and the youngest person ever to receive the award,
was nominated by the Swedish Parliament "because he had succeeded
in keeping his followers to the principles of nonviolence." For nearly
fourteen years, as president and founder of the Southern Christian Leadership Conference. Dr. King pressed his nonviolent protest against racial
discrimination from backwater Southern towns to Northern city slums
to the halls of the U. S. Congress.

An ordained Baptist minister since 1951 and an ardent advocate of
the moral doctrines of Jesus, Thoreau and Mahatma Gandhi, King first
put his Christian philosophy and operating technique to the test in
Montgomery, Alabama, in 1955 when frustrated Negroes won their
first significant struggle against bus segregation after a long, bitter battle.
Although his home was bombed and his life threatened, only King's
calm preaching of nonviolence and love prevented Montgomery from
becoming a civic blood bath. Armed with the miraculous thrust of
ahimsa and adding such new nonviolent weapons as sit-ins and freedom
marches, the heavy-set, dark-suited minister successfully extended the

Negro revolution to Albany, to Birmingham, to Jackson, Mississippi, to Washington, D.C.—until by 1963 he had become world-famous and the symbol of that revolution to millions, black and white, around the earth.

By preachment, precept and mass protest, the King-keyed crusade to "redeem the soul of America and secure the right of individuals to govern themselves" continues unabated in the North as in the South. In 1964 *Time* magazine named Dr. King "Man of the Year," and a recent Gallup poll revealed him as one of the world's most admired religious leaders. In impassioned pursuit of his dream of a just society for all men, the recipient of twenty honorary degrees, Dr. King traveled extensively in Europe, Asia and Africa, and won the reverent respect of both the great and humble everywhere. Among his best-selling books are *Stride toward Freedom, Strength to Love* and *Why We Can't Wait*. Dr. King's great work, as well as the activities of the Southern Christian Leadership Conference, are perpetuated today by his widow and by his friend and successor, the Reverend Dr. Ralph Abernathy.

The Religion of Nonviolence

Worship at its best is a social experience with people of all levels of life coming together to realize their oneness and unity under God. Whenever the church, consciously or unconsciously, caters to one class it loses the spiritual force of the "whosoever will, let him come" doctrine, and is in danger of becoming little more than a social club with a thin veneer of religiosity.

Certainly, otherworldly concerns have a deep and significant place in all religions worthy of the name. Any religion that is completely earthbound sells its birthright for a mess of naturalistic pottage. Religion, at its best, deals not only with man's preliminary concerns but with his inescapable ultimate concern. When religion overlooks this basic fact it is reduced to a mere ethical system in which eternity is absorbed into time and God is relegated to a sort of meaningless figment of the human imagination.

But a religion true to its nature must also be concerned about man's special conditions. Religion deals with both earth and heaven, both time and eternity. Religion operates not only on the vertical plane but also on the horizontal. It seeks not only to integrate men with God but to integrate men with men and each man with himself. This means, at bottom, that the Christian gospel is a two-way road. On the one hand, it seeks to change the souls of men, and thereby unite them with God; on the other hand, it seeks to change the environmental conditions of men so that the soul will have a chance after it is changed. Any religion that professes to be concerned with the souls of men and is not concerned with the slums that damn them, the economic conditions that strangle them, and the social conditions that cripple them is a dry-as-dust religion. Such a religion is the kind the Marxists call "the opiate of the people."

A Christian text for the current crisis in civilization might be taken from the Gospel of St. Luke. The familiar parable reads as follows:

> And he said to them, "Which of you who has a friend will go to him at midnight and say to him. 'Friend, lend me three loaves; for a friend of mine has arrived on a journey, and I have nothing to set before him'; and he will answer from within, 'Do not bother me; the door is now shut, and my children are with me in bed; I cannot get up and give you anything'? I tell you, though he will not get up and give him anything because he is his friend, yet because of his importunity he will rise and give him whatever he needs."

Although this parable is concerned with the power of persistent prayer, it may also serve as a basis for our thought concerning many contemporary problems and the role of the church in grappling with them. The first thing we notice is that it is midnight in the parable; it is also midnight in our world today and we are experiencing darkness so deep we can hardly see which way to turn.

It is midnight within the social order. As we look out on the international horizon we see the nations are engaged in a colossal and bitter contest for supremacy. Within a generation we have fought two world wars and the threat of another hangs ominously low. Atomic warfare has just begun and bacteriological warfare remains yet unused. That is the danger: that all these things will yet conspire to bring an untimely death to the human family on this globe. It is midnight.

The midnight in the social order is nowhere expressed more than in the racial crisis confronting our nation. We must face the melancholy fact that one hundred years after the Emancipation Proclamation the Negro is still dominated politically, exploited economically, humiliated socially. Negroes, north and south, still live in segregation —housed in unendurable slums; eat in segregation, pray in segregation, and die in segregation.

What is more indicative of the midnight in our social order than the recent riots that have engulfed New York City, San Francisco, Chicago, Cleveland, and Jersey City, New Jersey? Certainly we must condemn lawlessness and violence wherever they occur. It is my firm conviction that the use of violence in the struggle for freedom is both impractical and immoral; it ends up creating many more social problems than it solves. But after condemning the violence, we must affirm that the important question facing the nation as a whole is not merely that there be shallow rhetoric condemning lawlessness, but that there be an honest soul-searching analysis and evaluation of the environmental causes which have spawned the riots. Nonviolence does not exist in a vacuum. If law and order are to be maintained in New York City, or Mississippi, it can only be done where there is an ever-increasing attempt, an ever-increasing measure of justice and dignity accorded all persons. As long as a Negro finds himself on a lonely island of poverty, in the midst of a vast ocean of prosperity, as long as millions of Negroes feel that they are exiles in their own land, to see their plight as a long and desolate corridor with no exit sign, as long as millions of Negroes are forced to accept educational situations that are grossly inadequate, as long as millions of Negroes see life as an endless flight with powerful head winds of tokenism—token handouts her and there—there will be the ever-present threat of violence and riots.

And so all men of good will must see the necessity of working passionately and unrelentingly to get rid of the conditions that bring about the frustration and despair and cause individuals to respond to such impractical and immoral approaches. It is one of the ironies of history that in a nation founded on the principle that all men are created equal, men are still arguing about whether the color of a man's skin determines the content of his character. And so our nation faces a dreary and frightening midnight in the social order.

But it is not only midnight in man's external collective life, it also is midnight in his internal individual life. It is midnight in the psychological order. Everywhere paralyzing fears harrow people by day and haunt them by night. Deep clouds of anxiety and depression are suspended in our mental skies. People are more emotionally disturbed today than ever before. The psychopathic wards of our hospitals are full and the most popular psychologists today are the psychoanalysts. Best sellers in psychology are books such as *Man Against Himself, Modern Man in Search of a Soul,* and *The Neurotic Personality of Our Times.* Best sellers in religion are such books as *Peace of Mind* and *Peace of Soul.* Often the most popular preachers are those who can preach soothing sermons on "How to Be Happy" and "How to Relax." Some have been tempted to revise Jesus' command to read, "Go ye into all the world, keep your blood pressure down, and, lo, I will make you a well-adjusted personality." All of this is indicative of the fact that it is midnight within the inner lives of men and women.

Not only that, it is also midnight within the moral order. Midnight is a time when all colors lose their distinctiveness and become merely a sullen shade of gray. Certainly in the modern world in so many instances moral principles have lost their distinctiveness. Right and wrong in so many quarters are merely relative to our likes and our dislikes and our appetites and to the particular community in which we live, and so we have reduced morality to group consensus. We have come to believe that you discover what is right by taking a sort of Gallup poll of the majority opinion. Everybody is doing it so it must be all right. This is the philosophy that pervades so many of our communities. Midnight is a time when men are concerned mainly about getting by, and so at midnight the only thing important is to keep from getting caught. In so many instances today nobody is concerned too much at obeying the Ten Commandments. They are not important. Everyone is busy trying to obey the eleventh commandment: "Thou shalt not get caught." It is all right to lie, according to this ethic, but lie with a bit of finesse. It is all right to exploit but be a dignified exploiter. It is all right even to hate, but dress your hate in the garments of love, and make it appear that you are loving when you are actually hating. Just get by. In our day and in our age we have developed a sort of philosophy of the survival of the slickest. This has left us in a tragic midnight in the moral order. This is the problem modern man confronts, a threefold midnight: midnight in the social order, midnight in the psychological order, midnight in the moral order.

As in the parable so in our world today the deep darkness of the midnight is interrupted by the sound of a knock. On the door of the church millions of people knock. In this country the roll of church members is longer than ever before. More than 125,000,000 people are at least paper members of some church or synagogue. This represents an increase of more than 100 per cent since 1930, although the population has increased by only 31 per cent in that time.

The traveler asks for three loaves of bread. In the parable the traveler was asking for three loaves of physical bread. In the world today the weary traveler is in quest of three loaves of spiritual bread. He wants the bread of faith. In a generation of so many colossal disappointments, men have lost faith in God, faith in man, and faith in the future. In the midst of staggering disillusionment many cry out for the bread of faith.

Then there are those who are seeking the bread of hope. Certainly we all need this bread. Many people have concluded that life has no meaning. Many people find themselves crying out with the philosopher Schopenhauer that life is an endless pain with a painful end. But others cry out with Shakespeare's Macbeth that

> Life . . . is a tale
> Told by an idiot, full of sound and fury,
> Signifying nothing.

Still others cry out with Paul Laurence Dunbar:

> A crust of bread and a corner to sleep in;
> A minute to smile and an hour to weep in;
> But never a laugh but the moans come double.
> And that is life.

In the midst of this hopelessness, men cry out. For even in the moments when all seems hopeless, men know that without hope, they cannot really live, and in agonizing desperation they cry for the bread of hope.

And there is a deep longing for the bread of love. Everybody wants this bread. Everybody wishes to love and to be loved. He who feels that he is not loved feels that he does not count. Living in a world which has become oppressively impersonal, many of us have come to feel that we are little more than numbers. As we look out in life we see so many things to remind us of this. The mother who gives birth to a child is often maternity case No. 8434 and her child after being fingerprinted and footprinted becomes case No. 8225. The child grows up and gets a job. He becomes No. 5260 in some industrial plant. If he happens to go in the army he becomes No. 8576 in regiment 975. And finally when death comes, a funeral in a large city is an event in Parlor B with Class B flowers and at which Preacher No. 14 officiates and Musician No. 84 sings Selection No. 174. Bewildered by this tendency to reduce man to a card in a vast index, man desperately searches for the bread of love. In the darkness of midnight thousands and millions of people find themselves in quest for the bread of faith, the bread of hope and the bread of love.

Now let us notice another thing in this parable. When the man in the parable knocked on his friend's door and asked for the three loaves of bread, he received the impatient retort, "Do not bother me; the door is now shut, and my children are with me in bed; I cannot get up and give you anything." So at the most difficult period of his life this man was left disappointed. How often have men experienced a similar disappointment when at midnight they knock on the door of the church. Millions of Africans, patiently knocking on the door of the Christian church where they seek the bread of social justice, have either been altogether ignored or told to wait until later, which almost always means never. Millions of American Negroes, and other minority groups, starving for the want of the bread of freedom, have knocked again and again on the door of so-called white churches, but they have usually been greeted by a cold indifference or a blatant hypocrisy. We must face the shameful fact that at eleven o'clock on Sunday morning when we stand all over this vast country singing "In Christ there is no East or West," we stand in the most segregated hour in America. The most segregated school of the week is the Sunday school. This reveals that too many Christians have had a high blood pressure of creeds, and an anemia of deeds. This reveals that so many people have been left disappointed at the midnight hour. One of the most shameful tragedies of history is that the very institution which should remove man from the midnight of racial segregation participates in creating and perpetuating the midnight.

In the terrible midnight of war men have knocked on the door of the church to ask for the bread of peace, but the church has often disappointed them. What more pathetically reveals the irrelevancy of the church in present-day world affairs than its witness regarding war? In a world gone mad with arms build-ups, chauvinistic passions, and imperialist exploitations, the church has either endorsed these activities or remained appallingly silent. Oh, how tragic this is! It reveals that as people knock with determination, they are so often left disappointed. A weary world, pleading desperately for peace, has often found the church morally sanctioning war.

Those who have gone to the church to seek the bread of economic justice have been left in the frustrating midnight of economic deprivation. In many instances the church has so aligned itself with the privileged classes and so defended the *status quo* that it has been unwilling to answer the knock at midnight. We've seen this in other countries. The Greek Church in Russia allied itself with the *status quo* and became so inextricably bound to the despotic czarist regime that it became impossible to be rid of the corrupt political and social system without being rid of the church. Such is the fate of every ecclesiastical organization that allies itself with things-as-they-are.

There is another thing that I would like you to see in this parable. We notice that even after this man was disappointed, even after the man within left him standing outside, in agonizing disappointment he continued to knock. There is a big word used in that parable. It says "because of his importunity," which says in substance "because of his persistence," his determination, his stick-to-it-iveness, because he decided to keep on trying, he finally brought the man within to the point of providing bread. Now, we can use our imagination a great deal concerning why that man continued to knock, but I have a theory. That man continued to knock on that door because deep down within, he knew some bread was there. He wouldn't have knocked, he would have moved on if for one moment he had felt that the man within didn't have any bread, but deep down within he knew that even though he had been left disappointed, there was some bread in that house. Even though millions of people have been disappointed with the church, they continue to knock because they know somehow the bread of life is here. The great challenge of churches all over this nation is to keep the bread fresh. Many will continue to come in quest of answers to life's problems. Many young people who knock on the door and are perplexed by the uncertainties of life, are confused by daily disappointments, and disillusioned by the ambiguities of history. Some who come have been taken away from their schools and careers and cast in the role of soldiers. We must provide them with the fresh bread of hope and imbue them with the conviction that God has the power to bring good out of evil. Some who come are tortured by a nagging guilt resulting from their wandering in the midnight of ethical relativism and their surrender to the doctrine of self-expression. We must lead them to Christ who will offer them the fresh bread of forgiveness. Some who knock are tormented by the fear of death as they move toward the evening of life. Somehow we must provide them with the bread of faith in immortality, letting them know that death is not a period which ends this great sentence of life, but a comma which punctuates it with more lofty significance. Death is not a blind alley which leads the human race into a state of nothingness, but an open door that leads men into life eternal. This earthly life is merely an embryonic prelude to a new awakening.

Midnight is a confusing hour when it is difficult to be faithful. The most inspiring word that the church may speak is that no midnight long remains. The weary traveler by midnight who asks for bread is really seeking the dawn. Every word that we must have for men and for the world is that morning will come. This is the need. During the dark days of slavery, our slave foreparents saw the midnight of life. They had nothing to look forward to morning after morning but the sizzling heat, the rawhide whip of the overseer, and long rows of cotton. Somehow they saw something beyond that. When they would think of midnight, they would sing: "Oh, nobody knows de trouble I've seen; . . . nobody knows but Jesus." Then they thought of the fact that midnight would not remain forever. They thought of the fact that morning would come and so they could sing on the other hand; "I'm so glad trouble doesn't last always."

This is our word and this is our faith. I've seen this so often in our struggle for justice and human dignity all over the South and over the nation. We have developed a little theme song for our movement, and it grows out of this deep belief that midnight cannot last forever:

> We shall overcome, we shall overcome,
> Deep in my heart I do believe
> We shall overcome.

So often we've joined hands to sing it. Behind the bars of crowded jail cells—often made for twelve people, and thirty or thirty-five packed in there—in the midst of these packed conditions we could so often lift our voices and sing, "We shall overcome." So often we have had to face the jostling winds of adversity; so often we've had to face violent and vicious dogs and yet we could still sing it. I never will forget three years ago we were in the midst of a struggle in Alabama, and I remember one Saturday night that I had returned to Atlanta, Georgia, to preach in my church, and late that night I had a call from Birmingham from my brother, who pastors a church there, and he was telling me that his home had just been bombed, and as he was talking with me, I heard sounds, I heard a little noise. I said, "What is that?" And he said, "Listen just a moment." As he turned the phone in that direction, I could hear voices singing, "We shall overcome. We are not afraid. The Lord will see us through." So often we have been able to stand amid the smoldering ruins of our churches and our homes, and sing, "We shall overcome." Just last year I was journeying through the state of Mississippi, and I never will forget day after day I met people in tragic oppression; I met Negro families literally earning less than six hundred dollars a year, never having the opportunity of voting in their lives—they could still in their meetings sing, "We shall overcome." Strange, isn't it? Deep down within they could sing that because they knew that midnight was only a temporary phenomenon in the universe. For some reason there is something in the universe that makes it possible for morning to come. The arc of the moral universe may be long but it bends toward justice. Thus I can say to you there is something in this universe which justifies Thomas Carlyle in saying, "No lie can live forever." There is something in this universe which justifies William Cullen Bryant in saying, "Truth, crushed to earth, shall rise again." There is something in this universe which justifies James Russell Lowell in saying,

Truth forever on the scaffold,
    Wrong forever on the throne,
Yet that scaffold sways the future,
    and, behind the dim unknown,
Standeth God within the shadow,
    keeping watch above his own.

This is our faith. The psalmist is right. Midnight may come, "weeping may tarry for a night, but joy cometh in the morning." With this faith we will be able to move out of the dark and desolate midnight, and to a beautiful daybreak. With this faith we will be able to adjourn the councils of despair and bring new light into the dark chambers of pessimism. With this faith we will be able to transform the jangling discords of our nation into a beautiful symphony of brotherhood. With this faith we will be able to transform dark yesterdays into bright tomorrows and speed up that day when "every valley shall be exalted, and every mountain and hill shall be made low; and the crooked shall be made straight, and the rough places plain: and the glory of the Lord shall be revealed, and all flesh shall see it together." And when this happens, morning stars will sing together, and the sons of God will shout for joy.

Sarvepalli Radhakrishnan

Properly understood, religion is a summons to spiritual adventure, to individual regeneration, to a change of consciousness from the ordinary ignorant state when we are cut off from our true self.

In tall, scholarly S. Radhakrishnan, recently retired president of the Republic of India, the dream of the Greek genius Plato has been fulfilled—the philosopher as head of the state. For, before being elected the second president of free India in 1962, Dr. Radhakrishnan had taught in universities from Madras to Oxford, served as president of UNESCO and written a score of widely acclaimed books on Hindu religion and philosophy. Today, at age eighty, he is regarded as one of the foremost thinkers of the world and one of the ablest exponents of the Far East's philosophical tradition.

Although admired the world over for learning and statecraft, Dr. Radhakrishnan was born in the tiny town of Tirutani in southern India. As a young student at Madras Christian College, philosophy was his major subject and he wrote his master's thesis on "The Ethics of the Vedanta." During the next thirty years he taught successively at Mysore, Calcutta and Oxford universities and lectured and received honorary degrees at such American universities as Columbia, Pennsylvania, New York and Chicago. The far-traveled Indian sage was elected to the Indian Constitutional Assembly in the late 1940s, served three years as ambassador to Russia and in 1952 was named vice president of India.

Beyond his momentous role as the leader of democratic India, Dr. Radhakrishnan becomes more and more the great subcontinent's cultural ambassador and the eloquent advocate of a spiritual meeting of East and West. ("I think today," the philospher-statesman says, "Indian wisdom is not only essential for the revival of the Indian nation but also for the re-education of the human race.") Among his best-known books are *Indian Philosophy, Religion and Society, The Hindu View of Life, East and West in Religion,* and *Eastern Religions and Western Thought.* As an educator, he has served as president of the All-Asia Education Conference.

"Never in the history of philosophy," states Professor George P. Conger, "has there been such a world figure as Dr. Radhakrishnan.

With his unique dual appointment at Benares and Oxford, like a weaver's shuttle he has gone to and fro between East and West, carrying a thread of understanding, weaving it into the fabric of civilization. Except for an occasional Marcus Aurelius, philosophers never will be king but sometimes a philosopher wields among his contemporaries an influence which any king might envy."

The Religion of Righteousness in Action

Religion for the Indian mind is life in God, love of man and charity for all. If modern religion becomes unique and universal, as I believe it must—a flame which cleanses mankind and so cleanses the world—then will the cry of St. Joan in Bernard Shaw's play be fulfilled: "O God, that madest this beautiful earth, when will it be ready to receive thy saints?" Then will come a time when the world will be inhabited by a race of men with no flaw of flesh, no error of mind, freed from the yoke not only of disease and privation, but of lying words and of love turned into hate.

From the beginning of her history India has looked upon religion not so much as a revelation to be attained by faith, but as an effort to unveil the deepest layers of our being and get into enduring contact with them. Religion is spiritual life, which is different from a vague religiosity or conventional piety. Religion is not a solemn routine or a superstitious faith. It is not submission to authority or subscription to a formula. Properly understood, religion is a summons to spiritual adventure, to individual regeneration, to a change of consciousness, from the ordinary ignorant state when we are cut off from our true self, to a greater consciousness in which we find our true being. To uncover the inner springs of regeneration we must turn inward, deepen our awareness, grow into completeness, develop a more meaningful attitude toward life, an attitude which will free us from bondage to the external forms and hardening of the spirit.

Religion, if authentic, means an illumined mind, a changed heart and a transformed will.

Such an intensification of religious consciousness will naturally be accompanied by an intensification of social consciousness. The great Indian thinker Shankara tells us that one has first a consciousness of the Divine in oneself and next the consciousness of the Divine in all. We must first grasp the kingdom that is within us all, and then it becomes manifest in our relations with the world. "When we realize the one Lord in whom we all dwell, how can there be any talk of friend and foe?" Oneness with our fellows becomes then the leading principle of our life, not merely a policy for economic cooperation and political unification. It becomes a principle of deeper brotherhood, an inner realization that only in the life of our fellow men is our own life complete. Such a feeling, which is not only an idea but the truth of our being, is the only secure base for human unity.

It is a truism to say that mankind is today in the midst of one of the greatest crises in history. Our predicament is due to the lack of adjustment of the human spirit to the startling developments in science and technology. In spite of the fact that the great scientific inventions have liberated us from servitude to nature, we seem to suffer from a type of neurosis, from cultural disintegration. Science has relieved us of grinding poverty, mitigated the tortures of physical pain. Yet we suffer from an inward loneliness. All growth is marked by pain. All transition belongs to the realm of tragedy. The transition that we have to effect today, if we are to survive, is a moral and spiritual revolution which should embrace the whole world.

We have had other revolutions in human history, when we discovered how to make a fire, when we invented the wheel, when we applied steam, when we discovered electricity. These are reduced to insignificant proportions compared with the present revolution brought about by the development of nuclear energy. The discovery of nuclear energy presents not only great possibilities of human progress but also the risk of immediate and utter destruction. It can move mountains, dig tunnels, build harbors, increase food production, bridge the gap between the well-fed and hungry peoples of the world and remove some of the major causes which hitherto led to wars; or it can bring death and destruction to the peoples of the world. Modern science enlarges the power of man to do evil as well as to resist evil. We can meet the challenge and build an international order which allows freedom of development to all the constituent states under a rule of law which is enforceable by a world authority, or the great power which we wield may destroy us in the duel between the two armed groups led by two great powers.

The root cause of the cold war is fear and hatred of each other and not greed for possessions. So long as it continues, a war may result through a navigational error, a wrong image on a radar screen, a tired pilot, a sick officer or any other accident. There is conflict today between the goal of humanity as a family of nations, cooperating with each other in peace and freedom, and the present system, which gave us global wars, universal advance into the machine society and militant materialism. The future requires a radical change in our attitude to international relations.

While we recognize the need for giving up the military approach to the settlement of international disputes, for subordinating our national loyalties to the good of humanity, our political leaders are continuing the old intrigues and threats, bargaining and maneuvers as if the old weapons of bows and arrows, guns and grenades would prevail. Power politics, which has been the guiding principle of the traditional system of intergovernmental relations, still survives though disguised in different ways. The logical outcome of power politics in the nuclear age will be not world supremacy but universal genocide. An all-out nuclear war would mean victory not for any nation or group of nations but for death and darkness. Even if there is no war, the tests themselves are disastrous to human welfare. In a recent issue of a British magazine, we read of the agony of future generations of little children who struggle in vain to live. Our misdeeds will blast their whole future. We must recognize that we have reached the end of the military road. When Calvin burned Servetus, Costello observed: "Burning a man is not defense of Faith, but the murder of a man." To burn men, women and children by atom bombs is not the defense of a nation but murder of men, women and children. We are devising weapons for our defense against the enemies around us, but the enemy is within us.

The aim of human endeavor is the development of the whole man. An ancient Upanishad tells us that he is a whole man who has a balanced development of the different sides of his nature. He should have the play of life, the satisfaction of mind and tranquillity of spirit; humanity, fullness of being, completeness of development was the ideal. The Greeks had a similar conception. Pliny said to a friend setting out for Greece, "You are going to visit men who are supremely men." Pythagoras, for example, was an artist, mathematician and mystic. The Greeks exalted sages more than saints.

Those who are lacking in wholeness suffer from neurosis, unease, disease, despair. In *Faust,* Goethe gives us a representative figure of modern life, a divided man. Faust is the ambitious spirit who aspired after all knowledge and all power:

> From heaven he demands the brightest stars,
> And from earth its every strongest joy.

When we first meet him he is a master of every field of knowledge but has not had an insight into the meaning of it all. His knowledge is vast but diffused and directionless and he is distraught in mind. He knows his limitations and is lost in profound despair. He even contemplates suicide. But at the moment of surrender he is held back by a sudden recollection of childhood memories of Easter bells which give him the determination to live.

Modern man is restless with all his knowledge and power. His unrest is traceable to the increased tempo of scientific discovery. Our age differs from others in the unprecedented betterment of the human condition, in the scale and impetus of social progress. Science has relieved us of grinding poverty, mitigated the tortures of physical pain. Again, we have today a large-scale intercourse among the peoples of the world owing to intellectual awakening and mechanical invention. What happens anywhere in the world affects the fortunes of people everywhere, however remote. Whether we realize it or not, we are "members one of another." Unfortunately, there are certain historical attitudes to which we are wedded which prevent the consolidation of the human race, such as faith in military methods and sovereign nation-states. The past half-century has witnessed a regression of humanity, an increased insensibility, a frightening decrease in civility, decency and justice. The suffering and degradation which human beings are capable of inflicting on one another often lead one to despair of the future of humanity.

A scientific study of the cosmic process reveals to us a mystery at the heart of the universe. The men associated with the Royal Society in its early days believed that "the Heavens declare the glory of God." John Beale wrote of "the lawful and religious delight which should result from beholding the curious and wonderful frame of this our visible world." For Isaac Newton space was the *sensorium Dei.*

"The wonderful contrivances" of the great Creator held Hermann Oldenberg in awe. The great naturalist John Ray gave his book the title *The Wisdom of God Manifested in the Works of the Creation.*

Faith must be related to reason. There can be no conflict between reason and religion. Faith in contrast to superstition cannot be irrational. Nor is reason wholly devoid of faith. Science, philosophy and religion all attempt to reveal the truth which is ultimately one and all-inclusive. We cannot have different truths covering the same ground. Religion is the name for man's total conscious attitude toward life as it is found and enlightened by rational awareness and knowledge. The data of faith must have affinity with the natural knowledge which man has of himself and the world. The religious view requires to be harmonized with the picture of the world and of man which modern science gives us today. "I am the mover of the tree," the Upanishad says, *aham vrksasya reriva.*

All great scientific achievements are the work of the living spirit in man. The cosmic mystery is also the inmost being of man. The free human individual has a social side to him but so long as he remains a human being, there is a certain innocence at the heart of his being which defies all analysis. It is the subject in us which makes us capable of individual freedom and responsibility. We must reassert our ultimate power to redeem ourselves. We are not completely the victims of necessity. Kant's doctrine of transcendental freedom affirms a wholly free, noumenal self, located in a realm transcending the causally connected phenomena projected by the knowing mind. If we realize that we are not simply objects but subjects also, every day gives us a new chance, heralds a new life, even a new order of society.

God is not only transcendent to the world but is immanent in it. One of Kabir's songs represents God as saying:

> O servant, where dost thou seek me?
> I am beside thee.
> I am neither in temple nor in mosque.
> I am neither in rites and ceremonies.
> If thou art a true seeker,
> Thou shalt at once see me.

Kabir also says: "God is the breath of all breath."

We must use our reason to fight the superstitious beliefs and practices which have crept into religion. We can believe only in a just God, who is impartial to the saint and the sinner even as the sun shines on those who shiver in cold or sweat in heat. God is not angered by neglect or placated by prayers. The wheels of His chariot turn unimpeded by pity or anger. God is not mocked. He is *karmadhyaksa*, the lord or supervisor of karma. If we repent of our sins and change our behavior, God takes note of it, and assists us in our endeavor to improve.

Heaven and hell are not physical areas. A soul tormented with remorse for its deeds is in hell, a soul with the satisfaction of a life well lived is in heaven. The reward for virtuous living is the good life itself. Virtue, it is said, is its own reward.

Paul G. Hoffman

*If we agree in brotherly love, there is no disagreement
that can do us any injury; but, if we do not, no other
agreement can do us any good.*

Paul G. Hoffman, administrator of the United Nations Development
Program, has fashioned two distinguished careers in his professional
lifetime—one in American industry, the other in international affairs.
He has headed the U. N. Special Fund, the largest of all its agencies
rendering international technical assistance, since its inception in 1959.
Before his public service career, he served as president of the Studebaker
Corporation.

Mr. Hoffman's involvement in international development began with
his appointment by President Truman in 1948 as the first administrator
of the Marshall Plan (ECA). Resigning from this position in 1950, he
served for two years as president of the Ford Foundation. In 1956 he
was a member of the U.S. delegation to the U. N. General Assembly,
concentrating his activity in the work of the Economic and Social
Committee. He served three terms as president of the Society of International Development, a leading professional organization in the
field. From 1942 to 1948 he was chairman of the board of trustees of
the Committee for Economic Development. He also played a leading
role in organizing the Automotive Safety Foundation, and served as
its chairman from 1936 to 1948.

Mr. Hoffman, who studied at the University of Chicago, holds a
number of honorary degrees. He is the author of *Seven Roads to
Safety* (1939), *Peace Can Be Won* (1951), *One Hundred Countries
—One and a Quarter Billion People* (1960), and *World Without
Want* (1962). The recipient of numerous national awards, including
that of Freedom House in 1951, he has been decorated by several
foreign governments. Mr. and Mrs. Hoffman (the former Anna M.
Rosenberg) live in New York City.

The World on Your Shoulders

I am not a member of the Unitarian Universalist Church, but I share with its members a deep positive faith in the goodness of man and our destiny here on earth. I subscribe also to the aims and objectives of the new Unitarian Universalist Association as they were set forth at the time the two denominations were united.

(1) To strengthen one another in a free and disciplined search for truth as the foundation of our religious fellowship;

(2) To cherish and spread the universal truths taught by the great prophets and teachers of humanity in every age and tradition, immemorially summarized in the Judeo-Christian heritage as love to God and love to man;

(3) To affirm, defend and promote the supreme worth of every human personality, the dignity of man, and the use of the democratic method in human relationships;

(4) To implement our vision of one world by striving for a world community founded on ideals of brotherhood, justice and peace;

(5) To serve the needs of member churches and fellowships, to organize new churches and fellowships, and to extend and strengthen liberal religion;

(6) To encourage cooperation with men of good will in every land.

How can one put these tenets into action? We can do so and at the same time be true to our great American and world heritage, only by accepting a responsibility more urgent, more demanding and potentially far more rewarding than any previous generation has had thrust upon it. We must perceive the supersonic speed with which technology is sweeping us along, and we must face up to what it means. Unless we do, all the triumphs of technology will turn into a tragedy for humanity. For in breaking the sound barrier, we have broken age-old barriers of isolation between peoples so that hundreds of millions of strangers are being turned into neighbors whether they will or no. In this, there is as much peril as promise.

Even the first essential step—grasping the fact that we have three billion neighbors—calls for a most difficult feat of imagination. What has helped me to accomplish it is to scale things down to more manageable proportions—to think of the world as though it were a small country with only three *million* inhabitants each of whom stands for a thousand people of similar economic or social status. One-third of this nation lives quite well, some even luxuriously, with health, education, economic welfare, and almost seventy years of life expectancy in which to enjoy these blessings.

It is encouraging to note that 90 per cent of all the research scientists who ever lived are alive and working today, and that the sum total of all human knowledge now doubles every four years. But, perhaps an even more hopeful sign is the attempt, now being made for the first time in history, to use some fraction of this incredible intellectual reservoir on a planned, programmed, internationally cooperative basis for the tasks of development so urgent and so vital to the maintenance of peace.

Thirteen years ago, I asked the late Dr. Carl Compton, then president of M.I.T., whether it wouldn't be possible to divert just a small segment of our scientific brainpower from making bigger bombs to the task of making a better life for the people of this earth. He wanted to know what I had specifically in mind. I told him that, among other things, I was thinking of the need to find economically feasible ways to desalinate water. Without hesitation, he replied that if only 10 per cent of the effort, ingenuity and financing poured into development of the atomic bomb were devoted to this enormously pressing problem, fresh water could readily be extracted from the sea at commercially practical costs.

Similarly, Americans especially must make fuller use of their actual and potential capacities in releasing the intellectual, scientific and material abundance which the underdeveloped countries so desperately need. Actually my own attitude can be summed up in one biblical phrase: "To whom much is given, from him is much required."

First of all, we are required to learn, and to learn, and to go on learning. For the first time in history a whole people has been freed from devoting all its time to making a living. In fact, there are a thousand pressures on us to make being comfortable our principal business. There is nothing wrong with comfort, and *discomfort* for its own sake is pure foolishness. But, equally, we must understand our own need to use leisure not simply for recreation but for "re-creation"; for the continuous growth that alone can prevent us from shrinking. And growth means learning—the acquisition of intellectual, spiritual and emotional wisdom that must be ours if we are to live a fully human life.

Second, we must "trust in work." For each of us must shoulder the burden of making something of himself, before he can contribute something worth while to remaking the world. I realize that nowadays men are supposed to be the plaything of internal pressures and external forces about which they can do nothing. This is simply not true. Each of us is absolved or condemned by our own continuous creation; we make ourselves every day of our lives; we are responsible for what we do or fail to do; and what happens to us, what we become, is the result of our regular and inescapable acts of everyday choice.

Third, you are urgently required to "love thy neighbor as thyself." You cannot, of course, even begin to love three billion neighbors in any personal sense. But you can, indeed you must, love the fact of our common humanity enough to commit yourself fully to the struggle for its preservation. I have to confess that I find it difficult to understand why some people look upon the idea of "one world" as vaguely subversive, unpatriotic, un-American. Not only does this show a narrowness of spirit that truly violates the American tradition; it completely disregards the plain facts of the twentieth century which no one can ignore, and of which we have time and again received the most painful kind of proof. Since even if we wished, we can neither pack up and move out of our world neighborhood, nor remain untouched by trouble in any part of it, we must, in this sense, love our neighbors.

Our fourth requirement is to be brave. Our national anthem says that America is "the land of the free and the home of the brave." This is more than a lyric. It states a vital relationship that America will be the land of the free only so long as it is the home of the brave. Being brave doesn't mean being without fear. If you don't get plain scared at times, there is something wrong with you. It does mean pushing ahead, doing what you should do, even if you are afraid. That is real bravery.

But neither learning, nor work, nor love, nor bravery, nor all these together will serve and save you unless you meet the fifth require-ment—to participate in making the world a better one. For we are facing a real danger. Indeed it is my own conviction that, in helping others to acquire the privileges and the opportunities we now enjoy, we will be serving our own best self-interest. I am also convinced that if we stand aside from the struggle, we will cheat ourselves of an enormous personal satisfaction. Worse, we will run the gravest risk of squandering a future we have no right to throw away—since, after all, we are only minority shareholders in the human company. To me, the idea of being committed to a cause and working for it is not only a religious imperative but also a practical insurance against the threatening tide of tyranny. Today, we might say of the rest of the world as Hosea Ballou, great nineteenth-century Universalist thinker and leader, wrote: "If we agree in brotherly love, there is no disagreement that can do us any injury, but if we do not, no other agreement can do us any good."

Gordon S. Seagrave

The Christian determination to make available to the people of Burma the things—religion, education, medicine and democracy—which Americans hold precious persists in our family to this day.

Dr. Gordon S. Seagrave, the famed Burma surgeon who became an immortal of medicine in his own lifetime, was saluted by President John F. Kennedy in 1961 as "a symbol to the entire world of the American tradition of humanitarian service abroad." Ambassador Chester Bowles called him "the best of America overseas." When he died in 1965, he was treating twenty thousand patients a year who trudged to the hilltop Namkham Hospital he founded forty-three years before near the Burma-China border. Overworked and understaffed since he set up the Baptist mission hospital in 1922, he had become a legendary one-man "Peace Corps" who served patients of every race, creed and color—and who often received his pay in gifts of fruit, chicken and hard-boiled eggs!

The Seagrave tradition in Burma goes back 130 years. Beginning with his maternal great-grandfather who arrived in 1834, the family has furnished twenty-eight Christian missionaries to the Southeast Asia country. Born in Rangoon and educated at Johns Hopkins University, Dr. Seagrave was the last of his family to have lived and worked continuously in Burma. Of all the Americans who have labored in foreign places to free men from disease and ignorance, none have worked longer or more selflessly than this Yankee son of four generations of missionary preachers.

Today, following the nationalization of his hospital in Burma, Dr. Seagrave's name, fame and good works are enshrined in the Gordon Seagrave Memorial Hospital and School of Nursing in Kaejong, South Korea. Headed by a distinguished Korean physician, Dr. Young Choon Lee, and supported by funds from the American-Korean Foundation, the new surgical and postoperative hospital perpetuates the sacrificial Seagrave tradition in a poor rural province where the people's medical needs are immense. Dr. Lee, sixty-five, whose career closely parallels the Burma surgeon's and who hopes to add U.S. doctors and nurses to his staff as soon as monies are available, says of his expanding medical institute: "All this is like a dream come true. I had read the books of Gordon Seagrave and found in Burma an American who was a brother."

The Ideal of
Humanitarian Service

The year was 1902. The scene was Rangoon, Burma. I was about five years old. A great hulking Irishman stamped up the veranda steps of the house my great-grandfather had built out there after the British took over all of Lower Burma. The Irishman sat me on his lap and told me stories of wild jungles and great deeds: about service in the Royal Irish Constabulary as a young man; about his later adventures in Canada in the Royal Northwest Mounted Police; about stray rifle bullets that whizzed past him as he sat in his bungalow in the Shan States and that bored through the side of his bookcase. Then he grasped the top of a heavy dining-room chair in his teeth and swung it up over his head. I was fascinated! I tried it out on my tiny nursery chair, but it didn't work; my teeth couldn't have been much better then than they are now. Then he asked me for a glass of water to quench his thirst, and drank it down—standing on his head. I was completely overwhelmed!

After he had gone I asked my mother who the big chap was.

"He is Doctor Robert Harper, a medical missionary at Namkham on the border between the Northern Shan States and China."

That made it still more romantic.

"When I grow up I'm going to be a medical missionary in the Shan States," I declared.

Mother didn't say anything. The vaporizings of a five-year-old didn't worry her. After a few years her only son would undoubtedly become an evangelistic missionary to the Karens of Lower Burma like his father, grandfather and great-grandfather, and a smattering of uncles and aunts, great-aunts, and what not had been before him. Blood would tell . . . and it did with the exception that twenty years later I became a medical missionary to the *northern* Burma states!

The desire to serve Burma runs in my blood. I am the last of twenty-eight of my family who have spent their lives for Burma. When I called upon my sister Grace to come and join my work at Namkham, it was simply adding another link to a long chain reaching back into the past.

Our forebears—two lines of them, the Vintons and the Haswells—came to Burma 130 years ago to teach the Christian faith. And in all that span of time, there have always been Vintons and Haswells—and later, Seagraves—carrying on their work among the people. The children of this family, for four generations, had been born in Burma; then, following the family pattern, were sent to the United States to be educated; and when education was completed, or before if need arose, returned to Burma to take over the work from their elders. The Christian determination to make available to the people of Burma the things—religion, education, medicine and democracy—which Americans enjoy and hold precious, persists in our family to this day.

Throughout my life, nurtured by this calling and strengthened by this Baptist missionary background, I have felt an inner something that compelled me to teach people how to do things, no matter how eccentric or unorthodox—a sense of some great event ahead that would need every talent I could develop in all who came under my influence. Here at the Namkham Hospital in a far northeastern corner of Burma, that strange urge is still behind our every policy decision in our medical work, in our training of one hundred student nurses annually, in our treatment of twenty thousand patients every year for diseases ranging from malaria to amoebic dysentery. In my forty-three years as a Burma surgeon, I have performed more than thirty-five thousand operations on patients of every color and creed—Hindu, Buddhist, Moslem, Taoist, Protestant and Catholic.

My Burma hospital is now forty-three years old, and I am approaching sixty-eight. It is exactly twenty years since the Japanese army was driven out of Namkham and, after tramping out of the country with General Joe Stilwell, we were permitted to return to find all of our buildings bombed out by the U. S. Air Force. In 1946, during a lecture tour in the United States, I amiably dissolved my connection with the American Baptist Mission Society and with the help of such friends as General Frank D. Merrill, General "Wild Bill" Donovan and Dr. I. S. Ravdin of the University of Pennsylvania we organized the nonsectarian American Medical Center for Burma. Our new hospital complex, rebuilt through the generosity of the American people and their great drug companies, now has three hundred beds. The poor people again flock to us by the thousands—some walking on foot for fifteen days to get here—particularly following the planting and harvesting seasons when their rice crop is gathered in.

So, far from home, a stubborn, strangely inspired old fool carries on his work. Sometimes at night I lie awake for hours remembering my old dreams. I remember my dream of rebuilding the war-ravaged Namkham center so that my successor would start his work with a beautiful, modern hospital and not with a mass of rubble. And perhaps something still more wonderful might prove possible—a hospital of a thousand beds instead of three hundred; a hospital where young medical students could come for internship and surgical training, where the men of Burma would catch the spirit that seemed so beautiful to me in the girls of our unit; not a Baptist hospital alone but a Christian hospital; a hospital that would appeal to Americans whether church members or not; a hospital above denomination where Buddhists and Hindus and animals could come and receive loving care when sick and learn that peace comes only to men of good will.

It is a beautiful dream—and outside the stars are shining.

But today, with Communist China one air-mile away across the valley, with groups of bandits who call themselves insurgents trying to undermine the government and even attacking and robbing nurses on their way back from vacation, with a budget for a three-hundred-bed hospital about sufficient for one with a hundred beds, with a huge new Russian-built hospital in Taunggyi being run by my wartime protégé Dr. San Yee, with a personal salary of ninety dollars a month—with all these there is no security for an American doctor with a hospital at Namkham. But there is adventure. There is a real happiness to be obtained in loving the people of Burma and in curing them of their ills even without sufficient funds to do anything in the way we would like to do it.

The possibility of our soon adding more American doctors to the staff, if sufficient funds can be provided for them, is of immense encouragement to us all. And, even if none of my three sons ever studies medicine and returns to Namkham as the fifth generation of our family to serve Burma, I still shall be able to say with complete sincerity, "Lord, now lettest thou thy servant depart in peace."

Joseph R. Sizoo

When man separates himself from his fellow man, he cannot survive. When man separates himself from God, he cannot live.

The Reverend Dr. Joseph R. Sizoo, named by *Life* magazine as one of America's twelve great American preachers, filled the chair of Milbank Professor of Religion at George Washington University until his recent death at the age of eighty-one. For more than half a century, he had been a clergyman of the Dutch Reformed Church in America and the eloquent pastor-preacher of two of the country's greatest churches—the Collegiate Church of St. Nicholas in New York City and the New York Avenue Presbyterian Church in Washington, D.C. (often called "the church of the Presidents"). As a Holland-born American citizen and scholarly admirer of Abraham Lincoln, Dr. Sizoo later gained the unique distinction of being the minister who wrote a book on Lincoln, who buried Lincoln's son and who became pastor of the church Lincoln attended.

Long an ecumenical champion and advocate of interfaith harmony, Dr. Sizoo preached a universal doctrine which transcends the boundary of any one church. A world traveler and friend to Jewish, Catholic and Protestant communities in many lands, he spoke regularly to congregations of the Lutheran, Baptist, Episcopal, Methodist, Congregational, Presbyterian, Quaker, Moravian and Greek Orthodox denominations. During his early ministry he worked as a missionary in India, served as a chaplain with the U. S. Second Division in World War I, visited South Africa at the invitation of the State Department to make an analysis of apartheid.

Dr. Sizoo is the author of a dozen books including *The Way of Faith, The Kingdom Cometh, Not Alone, Preaching Unashamed, Make Life Worth Living, I Believe in the Bible,* and *Still We Can Hope.* A graduate of Hope College and New Brunswick Theological Seminary, he has received honorary degrees from Rutgers University, Lafayette College, Columbia University, Lake Forest College, Lincoln Memorial University and George Washington University where he also served as director of University Chapel. Other honors include the Religious Heritage of America's Clergyman of the Year 1958 Award; Freedom

Foundation's George Washington Honor Medal, 1956, 1957, 1958, 1959; and the Huguenot Cross (1954). In 1963 he received the award for the Best Public Address of 1963.

The Old Road to a New World

The confidence in the self-sufficiency of human knowledge is one of the frightening phenomena of our time. Modern man has made such fantastic progress that he has come to believe he can do anything; he needs nobody beyond himself to see him through. He has made himself believe that facts are more important than values, that science is the ultimate source of truth, that life is great in proportion as the sense of mystery vanishes, and that the absence of faith is a sign of intellectual acumen. On that basis, religion is a fifth wheel, a kind of nostalgic hangover of childhood.

All this has not turned out very well. The roots of life are nourished in the soil of a living faith. Civilization can no more survive without religion than a watch can run with a broken mainspring. Life without religion is like Jacob without a ladder. It is motion but not direction. It is rather tragic to know everything about a subject except what it means. In the past, the emphasis has been too much on how to make a good living, rather than how to live the good life.

Knowledge may broaden the base of culture, but only religion can deepen it. Education may rationalize life, government may nationalize life, business may mechanize life, but only religion can spiritualize life. Education divorced from religion is doomed to spiritual sterility, and religion divorced from educaton is doomed to superstition and bigotry. Good character is no substitute for wise learning, and wise learning is no substitute for good character. But when you have both good character and wise learning, the nation is secure and human life is at its best. Wherever education aspires to more abundant life, struggles for a social pattern which transcends mediocrity and conformity, religion calls out, "This is the way, walk ye in it."

Sometime ago a disturbed and confused university student asked me in great sincerity, "What is the good of your religion? What can it do which no other agency of society can possibly hope to accomplish? In some down-to-earth fashion tell me what the Christian faith can contribute to this kind of a world." In one way or another that question is often asked today, on and off the campus. People have a right to ask that question. We live in a world in which the race is to the swift, and the battle to the strong. We have no time for excess baggage. If the Christian faith has no answer, then we may well brush it aside. After all, Peter's last admonition was, "Always be able to give to everyone that asketh a reason of the hope that is in you." I want to address myself then to this question.

No one with intelligence enough to know, or heart enough to care, or courage enough to face the facts, can possibly doubt that we belong to a generation which has suddenly been hurled, willy-nilly, into a whole new setting. For good or ill we are living in the atomic age. New energies, hitherto undreamed of, have been released. New patterns of life, never before known to exist, have been placed in our hand. New skills, until now beyond the reach of any man, are available to all men. New fires are burning in the heart of the earth, and civilization is becoming molten again. New waters are rushing out of hidden springs in the hills destined to make their way to new and undiscovered seas.

What all this will do to us; what changes it will force upon our patterns and habits of living; whether all this will enrich life or impoverish it, who knows. We have no experience to fall back upon, and no precedent to guide us. That is our world, and it is the only world we will ever know. Whether that fills you with adventure or makes you cringe with fear; whether that makes your blood curdle or your nerves tingle, depends entirely upon the stuff of which you are made. We made this world and we will have to do something about it.

Whatever may be hidden from us, two simple facts are beginning to emerge in this atomic age indicating the shape of things to come. These two facts raise two grave problems with which the Christian religion must come to grip, and for which it must have an answer.

I. *When man separates himself from his fellow man he cannot survive.*

In the past the frontiers of nations have been geographical. The boundaries which separated nations were a broad river, a wide sea, a stretch of swampland, or a range of hills. So long as these stood nations thought themselves secure; nobody from within could go out, and nobody from without could come in.

The atomic age has made all these frontiers meaningless. We can fly a plane over any hump, span a bridge over any river, sail any sea with a ship, and tunnel any mountain. As of today there are no two places in all the world farther than thirty-eight to forty-two flying hours apart. How much that time quotient will be diminished in the foreseeable future, I can only leave to your imagination.

Boundaries are meaningless. Iron curtains and bamboo screens are figments of the imagination. The frontiers are down. No nation can climb into its ivory tower, look upon the heartache of the world and say, "What a mess," and draw the curtains upon it. It is idle for people to isolate themselves from all contact. What affects one affects all. A small psychopathic group in a Munich beer hall brought nine million graves and affected the life of many generations to come. Man cannot isolate himself from the cruelty of racism, the cry of the disinherited, and the suffering of the poor. The veil of the temple of humanity has been torn to shreds. People face one another though they come from the ends of the earth. The frontiers are down.

In the attempt to protect themselves, nations therefore are building new and dangerous frontiers. These new frontiers sink so deep before you become conscious of their existence. They are not in the area of geography, but in the realm of the mind. For the new frontiers of nations are fear, suspicion, hate, and misunderstanding. So long as these frontiers stand, we shall never have peace on earth. We may build a different world, but it will not be a better world. It may bring change, but it will not bring improvement. The first problem, therefore, of the atomic age is how can we remove these frontiers. Is it possible for people to live together in understanding? Can man restrain his passion and release his good will? That is the unanswered problem of the atomic age.

Do you ask now, "What can the Christian religion do for such an age?" The Christian faith rests upon the fundamental affirmation that God is no respecter of persons. He has made of one blood all nations. He does not separate peoples by the barbed-wire entanglements of political, social, economic, racial, or religious frontiers. We are all God's children and were meant to live with understanding toward one another. The atomic age has made the world a neighborhood, but the Christian faith can make it a brotherhood.

We may believe what Paul wrote to the Ephesians: Christ is the goal of history; He is the hope of the ages; in Him all created things subsist. Christ is our peace and "the head of all things"; in Him the whole structure is fitly framed together. At His birth men came from the East; at His death men came from the West; and East and West meet in Him who said, "And I when I be lifted up from the earth will draw all men to me." In Christ there is neither Jew nor Gentile, bond nor free. He is a Jew in Jerusalem, a Greek in Antioch, a Latin in Rome, a Slav in Moscow, and an Anglo-Saxon in London and in Washington. Kipling maintains, "Oh, East is East, and West is West, and never the twain shall meet." But the Christian faith shouts across the centuries:

> In Christ there is no East or West,
> In Him no South or North;
> But one great fellowship of love
> Throughout the whole wide earth.

Facing an age bewildered and frustrated by its own fears and dilemmas stands Christ saying, "I am the way, the truth, and the life." When man separates himself from his fellow man he cannot survive. In the search for unity the Christian faith has the answer.

> Only through me the clear high call comes pealing
> Across the thunder of the battle plains;
> Only through me shall life's red wounds find healing,
> Only through me shall earth have peace again.

> Only through me can come the great awakening,
> Wrong cannot right the wrong that wrong hath done,
> Only through me, all other gods forsaking,
> Can ye attain the heights that must be won.

II. *The atomic age is making us aware of another fact: when man separates himself from God he cannot live.*

One of the amazing facts of this unpredictable age is its fantastic progress. Modern man has gained unbelievable mastery over natural resources, whether the atom or stellar spaces. Words like satellites, energy, spaceships, electric charges, fission, are breathing down our necks. Indeed, we have become hypnotized by our skill and genius. We have made ourselves believe that so long as enough accomplishment tumbled out of the cornucopia of human genius we would be marching to the land of promise. We have almost concluded that chromium-plated doorknobs, cloverleaf superhighways, cantilever bridges, and air-conditioned cars would bring us peace on earth, good will to men. We believed ourselves self-sufficient, capable of doing everything, and needing nobody beyond ourselves to see us through. We began to look with fishy eyes toward poetry, philosophy, and religion.

All this has created a sort of dichotomy, maintaining that man can live in one of two worlds: the sacred or the secular; the material or the spiritual; the world of reason or the world of faith; the world of science or the world of religion. These worlds are mutually exclusive. A great gulf separates them and never the twain shall meet. I do not mean to suggest that the atomic age by some sinister design has plotted the outlaw of religion, but rather that by the sheer weight of accomplishments man gradually shifted the emphasis until he completely engulfed this illusive thing called religion.

All this has not turned out very well. What Max Müller said of his election to membership in the French Academy of Science is true of modern man: "The dream of reality was greater than the reality of the dream." It has bred faster horses, lengthened the span of human life, and increased the fertility of the soil; it has brought revolutions, wars, concentration camps, and ghettoes; it has also brought emotional instability, moral insensitiveness, and spiritual decay. Science without religion is motion without direction or Jacob without a ladder.

One of the most hopeful signs of this atomic age is that man is beginning to develop an uneasy conscience and an uncomfortable feeling about progress that has no point of reference outside itself. After all, what is the use of knowing everything if you do not know why. What is the good of a civilization whose art ends in comic strips; whose literature ends in red-backed magazine stories of smutted lives and soiled tempers coated over with psychoanalysis; whose music ends in rock and roll; whose science ends in man's capacity for self-destruction.

It is true the atomic age has unlocked many doors and made available to man unbelievable power. Science has conquered many enemies of man, and won for man many battles. But it has lost the greatest battle of all, the battle for serenity, peace, and faith. God and time are catching up with us. Man in the atomic age is seeking something he knows not what, but without which he will never know joy, peace, or strength. The moment a civilization cuts itself off from God, life becomes so complex and complicated that man does not know what to make of it or how to handle it.

The second problem of the atomic age is, therefore: How can man bridge the chasm between the secular and the sacred? Is it possible to remove this veil which separates man from God? In the language of the theologian the problem of man is, "What must I do to be saved?"

To such an age, wistful and bewildered, the Christian faith offers the good news, "God sent not His son into the world to condemn the world, but that the world through Him might be saved." In His infinite goodness and out of the inexhaustible resources of His power, God has made available and put within the reach of man forces for his recovery. When Matthew recorded the story of the Crucifixion, he wrote, "The curtain of the temple was torn in two, from top to bottom." Once and forever Christ removed the barrier which separated man from God. The veil in the temple which hung between the place where man worshiped and where God abode was completely torn, never again to close. Man is reconciled to God. The world in which we live has its setting and framework in the spiritual and timeless. Life is more than meat . . . man cannot live by bread alone . . . seek ye first the kingdom of God. Education may rationalize life, industry may mechanize life, social-ism may regularize life, politics may nationalize life, but only religion can spiritualize life.

We are often told that man has five senses. In reality he has six,

and the sixth is the most important of all. However wonderful may
be the gift of these senses which forever open new doors to the
world of color and beauty and design, none of these senses—touching, tasting, hearing, seeing, smelling—can possibly bring to life the
wonder and glory which floods it when the awareness of the love of
God enters into them. The simple conviction that life has its setting
in the framework of the eternal baptizes it with a sense of significance, emancipates it from fear, provides it with inner resources of
power, and makes living a glad adventure. John Barrymore paid his
brother a great compliment when he said, "What I envy about
Lionel is not his mind, but his ability to believe. If he never found
love, he would still go on believing there was such a thing." When
the things of time are placed in the framework of the timeless, you
will have something which no experience can impeach and no
temptation can imperil. John Masefield wrote it this way:

Only the road and the dawn, the sun, the wind and the rain;
And the watchfires under the stars; and sleep, and the road again;
Friends and loved ones we have none, nor wealth, nor blest abode,
But the hope of the city of God, at the other end of the road.

Science is not an end, but a means to the end. Its function is not
to usurp God, but to manifest God. The chief end of man is still
"to glorify God and enjoy Him forever." When science, therefore, is
true to its mission, and becomes the handmaiden of religion, opening
doors through which the splendor and grace of God may come to
man, unbelievable and undreamed-of glories may yet flood the world
of tomorrow. As the atomic age takes seriously its divine function
and becomes an instrument which God can use to fulfill His eternal
purpose, there may yet come to pass: "Eye has not seen, ear has not
heard, neither has it entered into the heart of man the things which
God has prepared for them that love Him." This is the promise of
the Apocalypse. When the atomic age, with all its potentialities and
possibilities, places itself in the will of God, we may indeed
realize "a new heaven and a new earth."

So it all comes back to this: are there enough of us left who
believe it? Are there enough of us left who won't walk out on it;
are there enough of us left who will stay with it to the end of the
end, until the inheritance is won, and Jesus Christ shall see the
travail of His soul and shall be satisfied?

Amiya Chakravarty

While we are engaged in the wonderful pursuits of our own religious commitment, let us from time to time look beyond our monastery walls, out of the windows of our homes, and beyond our prayer halls and fields of work, and see the great horizon of human fellowship.

Long revered as one of modern India's foremost philosophers, scholars and political scientists, Dr. Amiya Chakravarty today towers over East and West as an ambassador of the universal human spirit. Poet and peacemaker, friend and intimate of such twentieth-century giants as Gandhi, Schweitzer, Nehru and Einstein, he has taught at many of the world's great universities from Madras to Oxford to Melbourne to Yale. He began his illustrious career as literary secretary to Rabindranath Tagore, India's mystic poet of mankind, and studied and traveled with him in Asia, the Middle East, Europe and the United States until the seer's death in 1941.

Today Dr. Chakravarty, who is professor emeritus at Boston University and a one-time advisor to the Indian delegation to the United Nations, heads the Department of Eastern Philosophy and Literature at New York State University College. An author and specialist in the field of comparative religions, he has attended UNESCO conferences on religion and philosophy in Paris and San Francisco, lectured widely across Asia, Europe and the Americas, authored books that have won him Indian, British, Jewish and UNESCO literary awards. In the United States he was awarded a Rockefeller Foundation grant in 1950.

As a crusading associate of Mahatma Gandhi, Chakravarty joined him in his many "peace marches" through Indian villages during the national struggle for independence in 1945–1948. Similarly, he made periodic visits to Dr. Albert Schweitzer in Lambaréné, Africa, Boris Pasternak in Russia and S. Radhakrishnan in India in order to know better both the person and philosophy of these modern creative heroes. He also has traveled extensively in Africa, the Caribbean and the South Pacific to survey their multi-cultural and religious problems. Among his numerous literary and academic honors, Dr. Chakravarty has received the UNESCO Award for his Bengali prose volume *Chalo Jai*, the Indian National Award for his book of poems *Ghare Ferar Din* and the Doctor of Literature degree from the University of Tagore.

A Pilgrim's Faith

"I believe," my Hindu poet friend and mentor Rabindranath Tagore used to say, "that there is an ideal hovering over and permeating the earth—an ideal of that Paradise which is not the mere outcome of fancy, but the ultimate reality in which all things are and toward which all things are moving. I believe that this vision of Paradise is to be seen in the sunlight and the green of the earth, in the flowing streams, in the beauty of a human face and the wealth of human love. Everywhere in this earth the spirit of Paradise is awake and sending forth its voice. It reaches our inner ears without our knowing it. It tunes our harp of life, urging us to send our aspirations beyond the finite as flowers send their perfume into the air and birds their songs.

"Someday," Tagore continued, "I shall sing to thee in the sunrise of some other world. I have seen thee before in the light of the earth and in the love of man." So he does and so must we all. So today, in considering a proper relationship between personal religion and a world community, all of us must heed the example of such spiritual personalities as Tagore who combined the qualities of a prayerful life with the responsible fulfillment of citizenship in a transnational society and who over and over again emphasized his belief in a "spiritual world—not as anything separate from this world —but as its innermost truth."

A few years ago in Japan, for example, I had an interview with Dr. Suzuki, the saintly chief exponent of Zen, who died recently at the age of ninety-five. Dr. Suzuki compared death to the absence of a person who goes into the next room. He is unseen and unheard, yet he has not ceased to exist. Likewise when you and I die we do not just disappear. The personality, especially the enlightened personality, is central to Zen. One should try to make his life a bright mirror that reflects this higher light. Dr. Suzuki spoke of satori, the illumination experience, which comes not necessarily from long study of scrolls or years of meditation, but from an instantaneous recognition of the inward meaningfulness of reality in a small part of nature, representative of the whole universe. Sometimes even a blade of grass can be a symbol of life. A man who has arrived at this state of illumination reflects deep inward truth and is recognizable. Though not the product of intellectual labor, illumination cannot happen by accident or any short cut but only after careful preparation in quiet discipline and intense meditation, *dhyana*, the original Sanskrit word for Zen.

In China, the excited serenity of Taoism, the Heavenly Way, teaches that life is a waiting for the arrival of something valuable—a preparation for filling up, as in the analogy of the empty cup. The changed person is the answer. One strives to beautify one's self in thoughts and actions and to show in one's influence purity, strength and character. Man cannot do without the example of others. Some approximation of divine reality is made meaningful to us through the personality. Apparent reality is a garment; that which wears the garment does not change. Thus, beyond the fact of death is the truth of imperishable personality.

Also in China, Confucianism stresses familial relationships, neighborliness, the golden rule and the family of man. The principle of Tien represents a celestial order, much like that of Plato. Li is comparable to Logos. Confucians believe in translation of the underlying laws of the universe into meaningful action that uplifts society. The real thing is not the call, nor even the commitment, but the holy obedience that makes you pursue and prepare yourself for the undertaking. Thus, the very concept of life carries with it a continuity of personal reality.

China too, and other Eastern countries, are indebted to India for the great and widespread religion of Buddhism. Buddha was a praying man. Whole villages of people, who came out to hear him and to see him pray, were themselves transformed. He revealed divine law in the ethical action and truth of his entire life; he preached the doctrine that we ourselves create most of our ills by our cravings, which can never be satisfied and so would better be eliminated. But the elimination of the lesser ego does not destroy the true self; the higher self is achieved through a continuous process of transcendence. Nirvana was, for Buddha, not extinction, but a creative path toward the ultimate realization.

Hinduism, India's ancient religion, has many of the same images as the Greeks ("Deeply hidden as in a cave"). Yoga is a method of uniting the two currents of the material and the spiritual laws which meet in human life. It is a yoking of the human personality to the Divine through a series of disciplines which regulate and strengthen the body, the mind, and the higher consciousness. A favorite image of Hinduism is that of the light and the lamp, which exist together in symbiotic relationship. One can smash the lamp, but that was not the light. So with the body and the soul. Destruction of the body in death fills us with sorrow, but even in our grief we recognize that the person who is dead is not wholly identifiable with physical reality.

Like all other great religions, Hinduism as witnessed in the life of Gandhi or Tagore in our own times, expresses an unshakable faith in the value of human personality. Man attains immortality not only through the good deeds he has done on earth, but also through the further journey into fulfillment of which his present life is a part. Science and religion today are confronting this witness of humanity in the West as well as in the East, and discussing anew the unbroken continuity of man's humanity in this world. A half-century ago Tagore could write: "The religion that only comes to us from external Scriptures never becomes our own; our only tie with it is that of habit. To gain religion within is man's great lifelong adventure . . . we must know that it is only the revelation of the Infinite in us, which unlocks the identity and power of our individual selves."

Often I have thought how we are surprised by an inspiration arising out of the incense; it might be the stained glass; it might be the incantation. There is the lighted book, the eager faces, the sky outside—all of these together or separately. The authentic religious experience could be the effect of the mass in Latin, the litanies heard, the Gregorian chants offered in a Bavarian church or in Notre Dame. It could arise in the setting of Vedic hymns, of the reading of the Gita in a temple on a hill, perhaps in the high Himalayas. In Mount Carmel the vision of humanity was revealed; in Haifa or Safed, in a Judaic mystical order today, we can be challenged by a new and yet ancient vision of man and his place in the universe. One is reminded of many holy texts, secular or religious, in many different faiths. The Christian faith carries the

Revelation which Jesus brought not to any one community, but to the community of man.

We know that quite unexpectedly the vision of eternal humanity brings knowledge to the heart; that we strike upon the universal concrete in a simple experience. Religious experiences are profoundly linked with great and different cultures, but also they reach deep below the topsoil of different cultures into the ground of human reality. But I would have no theories on the matter. Through such experiences, we shall agree, humanity knows itself and its relationship with the world.

In the Islamic world I have often been aroused by the muezzin call to prayer. One could understand how scattered tribes came across the muffled sands in the early dawn before the stars had waned in the skies, how the call of the faithful became a consecration and a congregation. You feel this unitive power in the precincts of the great mosques in Iran. The almost unbelievable beauty of the blue mosques, the domes, literally melts into the glory of the morning air.

There in the shadow of the turrets, on the terrace where the people meet to pray in a mosque, people share a vision of a revelation of faith which is their religion. There is no question any more as to whether a man has dismounted from a camel or has come by car or by foot. But there under the monotheistic sky, every man is held together by the call to prayer to the One above all, the Lord of all. At that level, the Middle East can find a sustaining vision of man and of his true humanity on earth.

For many of us, these truths which spring from a root of faith and are common to man may branch out in many temples, mosques, synagogues, and churches; we may choose one or the other, and also accept some unifying element in all true visions and revelations. And, of course, for many others, the deep core of religion lies in one perfect revelation, treasured in a unique and eternal faith. We must also make room for the type of illumined vision which can take place when a man is crossing a river; we hear of saints and minstrels among the fishermen and boatmen in India. Whether it is officially religious or not, a devotional song composed by an untutored fisherman is filled with the light that we have described. We call these people bauls. These simple, pure-hearted mystics of our own day are so knowledgeable in the affairs of the inner heart, of the deepest

tides of joy and sorrow in the life of the villages, that their faces
themselves become scrolls of wisdom. You can witness in them the
forbearance, the goodness of a neighbor, the patience of a bread-
earner. All these traditions were sanctified and made into that living
reality of Indian vision which Mahatma Gandhi represented.

In his own person, looking like thousands of elderly people in
India, Mahatma Gandhi was known at once as a man of character
and as one who witnessed the power of God. In his case, as in the
case of similar persons in different religions, the consecration and
the devotion, the devotion and the service had become one.

It is to me important that a country with which we shall
surely become better acquainted as time goes on—the country of
Africa—was the proving ground of faith for two of the greatest
men of our age. I refer to Mahatma Gandhi and to Dr. Albert
Schweitzer. Their lives bear witness to a transcending vision of the
human divine. They have revealed man's power to relate himself
to the universe of man in a life of service.

His African experience gave Gandhi the knowledge and the
training for the great practice of ahimsa which actually, according
to Indian Vedic texts, is a quality of divine humanity and not at-
tributable only to the man of peace and the man of nonviolence.

This is a highly individualized version of Gandhi's Hinduism,
but to Gandhi, the value of religion lay in its power to be
"individualized," and to transform one life, and through one, many
lives. Simple in definition, such a concept gave Gandhi an in-
clusive view of religion and he saw no difficulty in belonging to
Hinduism, which he knew best, while also sharing in the deepest
and most dedicated way, as he believed, the divine truths of all
great religions. Naturally, such a vision of religion would be like
that of a sky line where separate and harmonious temples, synagogues, minarets, and church spires rose in the city of man.
This is not a synthetic or syncretistic vision but its opposite;
nor is it only beauty in the order of aesthetic experience. Somehow Gandhi believed that religions could sustain, each in its own
way, and together, the structure of man's spiritual understanding.
He believed in this approach, and worked for a large measure of
mutual respect and tolerance in the immediate future.

Thus Gandhi's vision of universal humanity made him a tireless
server of peace, not in the cause of one nation, India, but of

many nations and peoples. His criticism was leveled at discrimination practiced by his own people as well as by others. How could he speak against the violation of freedom in the colonial areas without opposing, at the same time, the lack of freedom enforced by caste or race prejudices? It was a battle not at one front but at many points. He won many victories but he had to do so at the cost of his own life; he was killed while he fought the evils committed against humanity.

The unity of religious vision and aspiration has been diversely explored. Tagore, the great Indian poet, did not formulate a philosophy, but he had a poetry of faith which has flourished and will continue to flourish in many spiritual cultures. The urge to feel and follow the religion of man, a vertical approach that establishes an immediacy of man's relationship with divine reality, and then, if needed, horizontally with institutional forms, has been with us. Tagore expressed this faith in evocative verse, through the logic of experiential reality. He saw the great community of man and the unfolding single adventure of humanity on this planet, and he looked into the horizon for a new emergence of spirit. Commemorative passages from the Vedas and the Upanishads, the mystical affirmations of great thinkers, and, basically, the voice of all great religions, made it imperative for him to declare a freedom of faith which no historical forces can impede.

Indeed, history itself is the emergence of man into a fuller knowledge of himself and the world.

Tagore's religion of man inspired him to be a messenger of humanity, to oppose fetters imposed on society or individuals under ancient and new compulsions. I remember how he once gave a talk in the U.S.S.R. in 1930, and at a banquet given in his honor warned the friendly hosts against the banishment of the free spirit. "No power on earth can mold the mind of man," he said. If any state tried to do so, the power of the human spirit will crack those molds and a new birth of mankind will take place. This was for him the affirmation of man's vision of universal humanity. He endorsed the great hopes that he saw in the educational life of the land to which he was then a visitor, and assured his friends that the power thus released could not be put back. This was well taken, coming as it did from a prophet who had brought good will and well-meaning criticism from people of an ancient but dawning power, an Asian land where spiritual realities had been treasured in culture and religion.

So we end, not with an attempt to enunciate any one religion or any particular view or vision of man, but with a submission. While we are engaged in the wonderful pursuits of our own religious commitment, let us, from time to time, look beyond our monastery walls, out of the windows of our homes, and beyond our prayer halls and fields of work, and see the great horizon of human fellowship.

Lyndon B. Johnson

Let us keep our eyes on the stars and do the possible.

Lyndon B. Johnson, born on August 27, 1908, in Stonewall, Texas, was sworn in as the thirty-sixth President of the United States on November 22, 1963, in Dallas, Texas, following the assassination of President John F. Kennedy. Less than a year later, he won election to the White House in his own right by the biggest popular majority ever posted in the United States. Since that time "L.B.J.," the prudent progressive, has secured his place in history as one of the most dynamic, driving Chief Executives ever to hold presidential office.

President Johnson, who as a young man taught school in such tiny Texas towns as Cotulla and Pearsall, was first elected to public office as U.S. representative from the Texas 10th District in 1937. He won succeeding elections to the Congress until 1948 when he moved up to the Senate as Democratic successor to Senator W. Lee O'Daniel. Following his re-election in 1954, Johnson at forty-six was named majority leader of the Senate—the youngest man to hold this position in either political party—and even under a Republican President soon became one of the most effective with his rare combination of industry, persuasion and political compromise.

Elected to the Vice Presidency in 1960, the tall, rangy Southern Senator took on genuine negotiating missions from President Kennedy, became chairman of the National Aeronautics and Space Council and the Peace Corps Advisory Council, ranged from Paris to Beirut to Manila on urgent governmental business. He also extended the scope and substance of the Vice Presidency by his work as chairman of its Equal Employment Opportunity Committee, his conferences with such heads of state as Konrad Adenauer, Chiang Kai-shek and Jawaharlal Nehru. In three years he became known as the "whirlwind" Vice President.

Now having completed his final term as America's Chief Executive, Lyndon B. Johnson continues to inspire admiration and astonishment by surpassing almost all of his predecessors in four-year accomplishments. He declared "unconditional war" against poverty, urged the nation upward toward the Great Society, signed into law the most sweeping Civil Rights Bill since Reconstruction. Persistently, yet powerfully, he sustained and inspired the nation's long dedicated war effort to preserve the independence of South Vietnam and to improve the social and economic lot of her people. With his versatile wife, Lady Bird, at his side, President Johnson demonstrated a determination to be President of all the people as well as the creator of a society of peace and plenty for all mankind.

(*The Christian credo of President Johnson was prepared by the author from the former President's pertinent speeches, statements and interviews.*)

The Great Society

In January, 1965, when I took the oath of office for my first full term of office as President of the United States, I tried to do two things to dramatize our Judaic-Christian religious heritage to the American people. First, I scheduled an open interfaith worship service at the historic National City Christian Church to mark the start of Inauguration Day ceremonies, invited fifteen hundred government leaders to attend and asked my dear friend, Dr. Billy Graham, to give the message. Second, I wanted to close my inaugural address with as moving and appropriate a biblical passage as possible. Again Dr. Graham helped me out.

The scriptural selection I used, taken from the Old Testament Book of Chronicles, read as follows: "In that night did God appear unto Solomon, and said unto him, 'Ask what I shall give thee?' And King Solomon prayed, 'Give me now wisdom and knowledge that I may go out and come in before my people.'"

In these troubled times, perhaps more than any other, public life is a lonely life. The burden of every vote, of every decision, of every act, and, yes, of every utterance is too great to be shared and much too great to be borne alone. Therefore, like many Presidents before me, I turn regularly in silent supplication to God. No man can live where I live now, nor work at the desk where I work now, without needing and seeking the strength and support of earnest and frequent prayer.

I find for myself, as I know men and women throughout this great government of ours also find, a sustaining strength from the moments of prayer, whether we assemble together or whether we pray silently alone. What has become a tradition and practice in our time is actually one of the oldest public traditions of our national life. Long ago when this country was struggling to come into being, there arose at the Constitutional Convention a discussion and a debate about holding prayers before each session at that convention. The great Benjamin Franklin spoke up to speak his views. I believe it is appropriate and timely to repeat and to endorse those words now.

Dr. Franklin told the framers of our Constitution: "Without God's concurring aid, we shall succeed in this political building no better than the builders of Babel. We shall be divided by our little partial local interests. Our projects will be confounded and we ourselves shall become a reproach and a byword down to future ages and what is worse, mankind may hereafter from this unfortunate instance despair of establishing government by human wisdom and leave it to chance and to war and to conquest."

When I was a U.S. senator, I wrote out my political philosophy for the *Texas Quarterly* and stated: "I am a free man, an American, a U. S. Senator and a Democrat, in that order." Today, I think I would stress—by putting first—that I am a Christian and that I have been a believer since I was a gangling fifteen-year-old. To this day I remember vividly the hot summer night in 1923, when attending a revival meeting put on by the Disciples of Christ in my home town of Johnson City, I felt deeply moved by their fervent preaching and singing, and yet, simple informal Christian faith. In fact, when I was baptized by immersion with other new Disciples in Pedernales River "baptismal hole," the only doctrinal question asked me was, "Do you believe that Jesus is the Christ, Son of God?"

As I grew older, I especially liked the Christian church's emphasis on independent Bible-reading as the only authority for faith and practice, its open-minded acceptance of the Protestant doctrine of the priesthood of all believers and its early ecumenical dream that all Christian churches should be one. From this homespun, frontier-flavored faith, I have drawn strength and direction for more than forty years; from its biblical inspiration, I have found clarity and courage regarding the sacredness of individuality and the place of the American people as the true philosophers of our free governmental system. For the denomination—and for its two million members—the words of St. Luke have lost none of their meaning: "For unto whomsoever much is given, of him shall much be required."

This is a time that tests the best in all of us. We of this land have so much to be grateful for. With the duties that now rest upon us, we also have much to pray for—that we as a nation be just in our strength, wise in our actions and faithful in our trust. As persons and as a nation we must never forget, "Except the Lord build the House, they labor in vain that build it."

Today I believe our national religious faith is the mortar unifying one of the world's most diverse populations. The churches have a particular responsibility in helping to maintain a sound sense of values during the great technical and social revolutions now under way. Certainly we are moving from the old values of a mostly rural past to the new experiences of a mostly urban future. We already have an abundance no other human beings have ever known. We are acquiring still another abundance of time—leisure to do with our lives as we please . . . I believe religious faith will help save the individual from a loss of identity in our urbanized culture. More importantly, I am sure our religious values will help motivate us to lives of useful service rather than lives of wasteful and self-serving idleness.

My first job after college, for example, was as a teacher in Cotulla, Texas, in a small Mexican-American school. My students were poor, and they often came to class without breakfast and hungry. And they knew even in their youth the pain of prejudice. They never seemed to know why people disliked them, but they knew it was so because I saw it in their eyes.

I often walked home late in the afternoon wishing there was more that I could do. Somehow you never forget what poverty and hatred can do when you see its scars on the hopeful face of a young child. I never thought then, in 1928, that I would be serving in the White House in the 1960s. It never occurred to me in my fondest dreams that I might have the chance to help the sons and daughters of those students, and to help people like them all over this country. But now I do have the chance. And I'll let you in on a secret—I mean to use it.

This is the richest, most powerful country which ever occupied this globe. The might of past empires is little compared to ours. But I do not want to be the President who built empires, or sought grandeur, or extended dominion. I want to be the President who educated young children to the wonders of their world.

I want to be the President who helped to feed the hungry and to prepare them to be taxpayers instead of tax eaters.

I want to be the President who helped the poor to find their own way.

I want to be the President who helped to end hatred among his fellow men and who promoted love among the people of all races, all regions and all parties.

I want to be the President who helped to end war among the brothers of this earth.

On a recent Thanksgiving Day, Mrs. Johnson and I attended a worship service in Washington. The sermon then was delivered by Rabbi Stanley Rabinowitz. The rabbi told this story, which I have remembered so vividly ever since Thanksgiving Day. He said once in the past, birds had no wings. They could not fly. They walked in the dust, earthbound. Then one day God threw wings at their feet and commanded them to carry the wings. At first this seemed very difficult. The burden was heavy. But in obedience to God's will, they held the wings closely to their sides and the wings soon grew to their bodies. At last, what they once thought were hampering weights lifted them unto the heights and enabled them to soar on to the very gates of heaven.

We cannot always do God's purpose, but we can always try to do His will. The man who does, and the nation whose people do, have the hope of reaching new heights. Our Constitution wisely separates church and state, separates religion and government. But this does not mean that men of government should divorce themselves from religion. On the contrary, a first responsibility of national leadership, as I see it, is spiritual leadership, for I deeply believe that America will prevail not because her pocketbooks are big, but because the principles of her people are strong.

In such recent world trouble spots as Vietnam, the Congo and Korea, we have met great tests and we have met them well. But I would remind you that history is not through with us. Great nations must meet many tests. We shall face many more in the days to come. It is my hope, and your prayer, that the tests of the future will find us all working in brotherhood to put down the hate of the present, to prevail over evil, to work with mercy and compassion among the afflicted, to be in all that we do worthy to be called God's children.

Richard M. Nixon

Has America the moral drive and the spiritual resources to take charge of our destiny once again, to regain the momentum and the international leadership that was ours after our victories in World War II? I believe that it has.

Climaxing one of the greatest political comebacks in American history, Richard M. Nixon of Whittier, California, and New York, New York, on November 5, 1968, won a total of 290 electoral votes in America's quadrennial national elections to become the thirty-seventh President of the United States. The national standard-bearer of the Republican party for the second time and twice Vice President under President Eisenhower in the 1950s, hard-driving, dark-haired "Dick" Nixon, fifty-six, captured more than 31,000,000 popular votes to defeat the Democratic nominee Hubert H. Humphrey by a margin of 300,000 votes. With his Vice President Spiro T. Agnew, he formally took office on January 20, 1969, upon being sworn in by Chief Justice Earl Warren in Washington, D.C.

Thus, after twenty-two years of national political life and after two heartbreak losses, in the U.S. presidential election in 1960 and the California gubernatorial race in 1962, a victorious Richard Nixon began the New Year and the new Republican Administration on a high note of hope and creative change. Born into a California Quaker family in 1913 and graduated from Whittier College and Duke University Law School in 1937, his long hard road to the presidency began with his election to the U. S. Congress in 1946. After two terms in the House, he was elected to the U. S. Senate in 1950 and in 1952 he was chosen by General Eisenhower as his running-mate in the presidential elections. At age thirty-nine, he became the youngest man in history to hold the position of Vice President.

A mature moderate, or kind of American "Mr. Middleman" in politics, the durable Republican leader consistently supported the United Nations, NATO, civil rights, Negro economic progress, foreign aid and technical and military assistance for our allies throughout his congressional career. An articulate opponent of Communism at home and abroad, Nixon nevertheless has made frequent trips to Communist-dominated countries in Europe, South America and Asia and has come to know most Red premiers personally in his world travels. Even as he moved to provide greater economic power for Negroes in the United States, President Nixon determined to keep the country from further involvement in "brush-fire" wars foreign to the national purpose. ("I will avoid future Vietnams.")

Dedicating himself to an activist, international role as President, Mr. Nixon has declared he "will articulate the nation's values, define its goals and marshal its will . . . to serve the ideals of all the people." In 1940 he married Patricia Ryan, a Whittier schoolteacher, and they have two daughters, Patricia, twenty-two, a graduate of Finch College, and Julie, twenty, a Smith College coed who in December, 1968, married David Eisenhower, grandson of the former President, in New York City.

(The Christian Credo of President Nixon was prepared by the author from the President's pertinent speeches, statements and interviews.)

America's Testing Time

More than a hundred years ago our greatest American philosopher, Ralph Waldo Emerson, wrote: "I say the real and permanent grandeur of these United States must be their Religion. Otherwise there is no real and permanent grandeur." As a lifelong Quaker and church-going Christian, I deeply believe those Emersonian sentiments are truer today than in his own time. The principal reason for this is: today is a testing time for Americans more severe even than the Civil War crisis of Emerson's era. The principal challenge for us all is: Have we the moral drive and the spiritual resources to take charge of our destiny once again, to regain the momentum and the international leadership that was ours after our victories in World War II? I believe we have.

Both as a believing Quaker and as America's thirty-seventh President, I am determined to prove that we have such God-given resources as individuals and as a people. My Quaker upbringing and my religious experience in the Society of Friends strengthen me today as they have in the past. My Christian creed includes the noble insight of Quaker founder George Fox: "There is that of God in every man," and therefore every man the world around— regardless of his race or religion or color or culture—merits my respect. The gradual abolition of slavery in the English-speaking world and the global spread of the peace movement have been concrete results of Quaker preaching and practice, and I am pledged to pursue these perfect ends with all my might. Above all, in my personal prayer life as in my public duty, I believe in God's "inner light" (as we Quakers call it), and today as President of the United States I pray for the divine guidance in my every decision, word and daily deed.

For we Americans are embarked upon a great adventure, a demanding voyage from which there can be no turning back. For better or worse, the future of mankind depends on how we as a nation manage the trusteeship of power which has been placed in our hands. From the beginning, implicit in the whole American adventure has been the sense that we were building a nation, not for ourselves alone, but as a beacon to mankind, a land that held the hope and promise of the rainbow. More than ever before the nations of the free world need such a beacon and such a hope. But they no longer look to the United States as the unquestioned champion of freedom and progress. The American right to leadership is in question, and this is a challenge we must meet.

To meet it we must take new courage: courage to grow, courage to change, courage to lead once again. There are hazards in such a course, and there are hardships. But we must embrace them. For a nation's energies do not thrive in a vacuum. Nations and individuals *need* challenge; they *need* to have their strength tested in order to discover their reach and staying power.

The world is undergoing a storm of change that affects all peoples and all societies, and we in this country are in the eye of this social hurricane. How we direct our lives and our national fortunes in the months and years just ahead will determine our country's future for the rest of this century. We have the manpower and the material resources to enter now on the greatest period of growth any nation has ever known. The question is whether we have the will and the moral drive to take charge of our destiny once again. We have lost some of our vigor and some of our confidence. Only if these are restored can we meet our moment in history; only true religion can help each one of us restore them.

For generations, America was a new nation in an old world. Suddenly we have become an old nation in a new world. We are a battle-scarred veteran, and the young countries are looking us over. They want to know if we still have those qualities that have made us great. I say we have, and this is the time to prove it. This is a testing time for Americans.

We face enormous tasks, both at home and abroad. In a sense, these are extensions of one another. Abroad, we must bring peace to a warring world; at home, we must bring peace to a warring society. Abroad, we must bridge the gulfs between the have and have-not nations; at home, we must bridge the gulfs between the have and have-not parts of our own population. Both at home and abroad we must break down the racial barriers that set man against man. These challenges, foreign and domestic, must be met at the same time. For unless we win peace abroad, whatever progress we make at home could go up in the smoke of a disaster enveloping the entire planet. Unless we win peace at home, we will lose the respect of the world and our rightful place in it.

Our message to the peoples of the world is and must be one of hope and assurance. We must declare that there is a way to cast off the shackles that have crippled mankind; we must insist that the conditions of life in most of the world today can be changed. And we must carry this message even more with deeds than with words.

Our government represents the people of the United States, but it must also speak to the people of the world—just as our whole society must. But unless we can speak confidently and proudly, unless we can speak from a platform of social order and social progress at home, we cannot expect our words to get a hearing abroad.

There are great tasks ahead—and great goals to reach. Fortunately we have the tools to work with. Man's resource of will is the greatest natural resource the world possesses. No energy source tapped by science will ever be a substitute for human will power. When driven by a sense of necessity, a sense of survival, men and nations can perform monumental tasks, and they can overcome seemingly impossible obstacles.

The challenge that faces America today is no less than one of survival. Everything we stand for as a nation, everything we have lived for, fought for and died for is being tested every day. Our ideals of democracy, our standards of fair play, our belief in human freedom and human equality are being questioned. People at home and abroad are beginning to ask, "What has happened to America?"

What *has* happened to America? Over the recent years a great deal has happened. We have become bogged down in a war that we could have won years ago. We have allowed a climate of lawlessness and violence and crime to grow to intolerable proportions. We have allowed racial tensions to increase nearly to the breaking point. We have allowed a virulent inflation to infect our economy. We have allowed many things to shift us off our proper course. As a result, there has been an erosion of pride in America and in being American, an erosion due in part to the feeling that our hopes for our country and for mankind are not being realized.

Instead of moving ahead with the American program, we seem to be floundering. There are rumbling undercurrents in our society —undercurrents which often are crosscurrents. Vast numbers of people feel that society has left them, or that they want to leave society; they feel alienated, out of tune with America's ideals, or with their conception of those ideals. Vast numbers of people are looking for inspiration, for directions, for an answer to the question, Where is America going?

A large part of this unrest stems from the fact that as the government grows in power and scope, the role of the individual grows smaller, giving rise to a general feeling of helplessness and uselessness. All of us, unquestionably, are suffering from too much government. This is nothing new in the world. It has happened to other countries before. But this is the first time it has really happened in the United States of America, and it has weakened our society; it has undermined our sense of individual responsibility.

If we are to restore our lost pride and our old vigor, if America is to resume her rightful and essential role in the world, Americans —all of us—will have to acquire new self-discipline. We will have to shoulder more responsibility. The job of being an American citizen in the 1960s and in the '70s is going to take guts, gumption and good hard work. It is going to take everything we've got, but

I know Americans, and they've got enough of what it takes to start any job that needs doing and to finish any job they start.

It is essential for each one of us to realize that whatever we as a nation achieve, whatever we produce will be done by our own energies and inspiration. Only to the extent that we can marshal these energies and encourage this inspiration can we succeed in any of the goals that we set for ourselves.

As we look across the sweep of this final third of the century, the one thing on which all else in America depends is the restoration of the place of the individual in the structure of our society. The people are the base on which our government is built, on which our society is built, on which our economy is built. The greatest glory of our nation is that the nation exists for its people, not the other way around.

And this is tomorrow's frontier: the frontier of man himself. We are approaching a golden new age potentially more glittering than any man has known or, except in his wildest dreams, imagined. Never has so much trained intelligence been concentrated in one nation. Never have such vast forces been under man's control. Never have there been available such extensions, not only of man's muscle, but of his mind—extensions that can at last make possible the full realization of man's potential. But before these potentials can come to flower, there must be a new place and a new role for the individual in American life.

If America is to be true to its destiny, true to its future, true to its promise, we must restore the sense of a driving dream. The American dream has been one of extraordinary power—precisely because it is rooted in the innermost strivings of man's spirit. It grows out of a sense of the inviolate dignity of the individual and of the immense potential of the free human spirit. Again it was Ralph Waldo Emerson who said, "I sing the infinitude of the private man." To release these energies and develop these infinite potentials is the continuing challenge of America.

To future peoples, I believe that historians will recall that 1968 marked the beginning of the American generation in world history. Just to be alive in America, just to be alive at this time is an experience unparalleled in history. Here is where the action is. Think: thirty-two years from now most Americans living today will celebrate a new year that comes once in a thousand years.

Eight years from now, in the second term of the next President, we will celebrate the two hundredth anniversary of the American Revolution. And by our decisions in this decade, we all will determine what kind of nation America will be on its two hundredth birthday; we will determine what kind of a world America will live in in the year 2000.

This is the kind of a day I see for America on that glorious Fourth of July—eight years from now. I see a day when Americans are once again proud of their flag. When once again at home and abroad it is honored as the world's greatest symbol of liberty and justice. I see a day when the President of the United States is respected and his office is honored because it is worthy of respect and worthy of honor.

I see a day when every child in this land, regardless of his background, has a chance for the best education our wisdom and schools can provide, and an equal chance to go just as high as his talents will take him. I see a day when life in rural America attracts people to the country, rather than driving them away. I see a day when we can look back on massive break-throughs in solving the problems of slums and pollution and traffic which are choking our cities to death. I see a day when our senior citizens and millions of others can plan for the future with the assurance that their government is not going to rob them of their savings by destroying the value of their dollars.

I see a day when we will again have freedom from fear in America and freedom from fear in the world. I see a day when our nation is at peace and the world is at peace and everyone on earth—those who hope, those who aspire, those who crave liberty—will look to America as the shining example of hopes realized and dreams achieved.

Today, therefore, as we make this commitment, let us look into our hearts and let us look down into the faces of our children. In their faces are our hope, our love and our courage.

Today I see the face of a child.

He lives in a great city. He is black. Or he is white. He is Mexican, Italian, Polish. None of that matters. What matters, he's an American child. That child in that great city is more important than any politician's promise. He is America. He is a poet. He is a scientist, he is a great teacher, he is a proud craftsman. He is everything we ever hoped to be and everything we dare to dream to be.

He sleeps the sleep of childhood and he dreams the dreams of a child. And yet when he awakens, he awakens to a living nightmare of poverty, neglect and despair. He fails school. He ends up on welfare. For him the American system is one that feeds his stomach and starves his soul. It breaks his heart. And in the end it may take his life on some distant battlefield. To millions of children in this rich land, this is their prospect of the future. But this is only part of what I see in America. I see another child. He hears the train go by at night and he dreams of faraway places where he'd like to go. It seems like an impossible dream. But he is helped on his journey through life. A father who had to go to work before he finished the sixth grade sacrificed everything he had so that his sons could go to college.

A gentle Quaker mother with a passionate concern for peace quietly wept when he went to war, but she understood why he had to go. A great teacher, a remarkable football coach, an inspirational minister encouraged him on his way. A courageous wife and loyal children stood by him in victory and also defeat. And in his chosen profession of politics, first there were scores, then hundreds, then thousands, and finally millions who worked for his success.

And today he stands before you, President of the United States of America. Thus you can see why I believe so deeply in the American Dream.

One hundred and eight years ago, the newly elected President of the United States, Abraham Lincoln, left Springfield, Illinois, never to return again. He spoke to his friends gathered at the railroad station. Listen to his words:

"Today I leave you. I go to assume a greater task than devolved on General Washington. The great God which helped him must help me. Without that great assistance, I will surely fail. With it, I cannot fail." Abraham Lincoln lost his life but he did not fail.

The President of the United States today faces challenges which in some ways are greater than those of Washington or Lincoln. Because for the first time in our nation's history, an American President faces not only the problem of restoring peace abroad but of restoring peace at home.

Without God's help, we will surely fail; but with God's help, we shall surely succeed. To all people everywhere, the long dark night for America is about to end. The time has come for us to leave the valley of despair and climb the mountain so that we may see the glory of the dawn—a new day for America, and a new dawn for peace and freedom in the world.